# THE COMPLETE GUIDE TO OPTION SELLING

## How Selling Options Can Lead to Stellar Returns in Bull and Bear Markets

**JAMES CORDIER**
**MICHAEL GROSS**

**McGraw-Hill**

New York   Chicago   San Francisco   Lisbon   London   Madrid   Mexico City   Milan
New Delhi   San Juan   Seoul   Singapore   Sydney   Toronto

*The McGraw·Hill Companies*

3   4   5   6   7   8   9   0        DOC/DOC        0   9   8   7   6

ISBN 0-07-144208-1

All price charts in this book courtesy of CQG, Inc., © 2004 CQG, Inc. All rights reserved worldwide. www.cqg.com.

This publication is designed to provide accurate and authoritative information in regard to the subject matter covered. It is sold with the understanding that the publisher is not engaged in rendering legal, accounting, or other professional service. If legal advice or other expert assistance is required, the services of a competent professional person should be sought.
—*From a Declaration of Principles jointly adopted by a Committee of the American Bar Association and a Committee of Publishers and Associations*

McGraw-Hill books are available at special quantity discounts to use as premiums and sales promotions, or for use in corporate training programs. For more information, please write to the Director of Special Sales, Professional Publishing, McGraw-Hill, Two Penn Plaza, New York, NY 10121-2298. Or contact your local bookstore.

This book is printed on recycled, acid-free paper containing a minimum of 50% recycled, de-inked fiber.

**Library of Congress Cataloging-in-Publication Data**

Cordier, James.
    The complete guide to option selling : how selling options can lead to stellar returns in bull and bear markets / By: James Cordier & Michael Gross.
        p. cm.
    Includes bibliographical references.
    ISBN 0-07-144208-1 (hardcover : alk. paper)
    1. Stock options.   I. Gross, Michael.   II. Title.
    HG6042.C675 2005
    332.63'2283—dc22

                                                        2004016630

# CONTENTS

# INTRODUCTION

Have you ever heard it said that the vast majority of options expire worthless? It is estimated that anywhere from 75 to 80 percent of all options held through expiration will indeed expire worthless. Furthermore, it is estimated that only 10 percent or less of all options will ever be exercised. This being the case, why aren't more investors taking advantage of this phenomenal statistic? Why is the average sit-at-home investor not analyzing endless lists of strike prices seeking the most glowing opportunities for deterioration instead of reviewing mutual fund performance tables or stock price-earnings (P/E) ratios? Why are the majority of futures traders losing money year after year, trying to pick the perfect top or bottom by buying or selling a futures contract or, worse yet, buying an out-of-the-money put or call that has a remote chance of ever showing any kind of profit, let alone a windfall?

The answer is the old trading axiom: Fear and greed–fear of risk, fear of the unknown, and most important, fear of that which is not understood. Most brokers or investment advisors, when asked about the strategy of option selling, will reply with a response such as, "You want to stay away from that. It's too risky." Yet, when asked to explain the approach in detail, few can do a thorough job of it. If the investment representatives from the industry cannot explain a particular approach to investing, how can the overall community of investors be expected to understand the approach? "Option selling has unlimited risk" is all that most investors know about the concept. The term *unlimited risk* is enough to cause most investors to cross it off their list of potential investment strategies without further exploration.

What about greed? The other knock on option selling is that it is slow. It is "boring." It has "limited" profit potential. It goes against most investor's instincts to take an "unlimited" risk for the potential for a limited profit. Most traders, especially futures traders, have been taught from their first trading lesson that in order to turn a profit, a series of small losses must be accepted to make that one big gain. It is the potential for this one big gain that keeps traders and gamblers alike coming back time after time and losing money time after time. Taking many losses in order to make one big gain is very difficult, even for the most experienced investor. Why? Because it goes against human nature. Humans are cursed with the emotion of hope when involved in an investment situation. We hope our losses will turn around for us and look for excuses to stay in our position for one more day. Yet, when faced with a winning trade, the anxiety of remaining in the position is almost unbearable.

The purpose of this book is to introduce the concept of option selling (or writing) to the average individual investor. It is our belief that the individual investor has been deprived of not only a quality resource on the subject of pure option writing but also a concrete blueprint for *how* to sell options successfully. Selling options for premium has been a favorite strategy of professional and commercial traders for years. After all, *somebody* has to be selling all those options to the general public, which seems to have an insatiable appetite for *buying* options all the time. More often than not these are the people making the real money in this business.

Many traders' first experience with futures is in buying options. This is so because their brokers told them that this was the "safe" way to trade. "Limited risk" is what they are promised. Indeed, the purchase of options does limit your risk to the amount of money that you invest in these options. Unfortunately, most of the time, the amount that you invest will be the amount that you lose if you use option buying. The odds are stacked tremendously against you. There is a very good chance that your options will expire worthless. Maybe one of your positions made money. You take what is left from that profit and reinvest in buying more options. Now there is a good chance that those options will expire worthless. Even if you manage to profit from a few, eventually the chances are that your luck will run out. When these options are all expired, you have lost your money. However, somebody made money on those options (besides your broker). Somebody took your premium and put it in his account.

If you have ever lost money buying options, imagine if you had made a premium for every option you held that expired worthless. Would you be ahead right now? You never had to pick market direction. You never had to decide when to take a profit. You never had to worry when time was going to run out for your position. You *wanted* time to run out!

This book intends to teach you how to do this for yourself. Simple concepts for selling options for premium and controlling risk will be explained not in technical jargon but in simple terms. Our intention is to demystify option selling for the individual investor. The growing popularity of selling options is undeniable. Yet it remains one of the least understood concepts in the trading world. The concept of unlimited risk will be broken down and explained. After knowing the facts, unlimited risk may not be as intimidating as it sounds.

This book avoids the same old tired trading philosophies as well as the newest fashionable technical indicators in favor of a fresh, simple approach that has as yet not commanded a book of its own. The book will avoid the dry, complex option theory and industry lingo that plagues many books about options and instead focus on bringing the mystics of option writing into a down-to-earth, commonsense investing approach that the average investor can understand in one reading. If you are looking for complex, number-crunching analysis of deltas and gammas, this book is not for you. We do not intend to show you how to design a computer program to analyze standard deviations and Gann lines and count Elliot waves. We are not writing this book based on mathematical "theory" that we have calculated from the comfortable confines of a classroom or university library.

The authors of this book are active futures brokers. Both have traded personal accounts and have more than 28 years of combined experience in the futures trading industry. We want to tell it like it is, from the trenches, in a simple straightforward manner. Who really makes money, who loses it, and why? Let us share it with you. How do we know? Because we've seen it all. We've drunk champagne with the winners and helped ease the pain of the losers.

And while the focus of this book is on futures options, almost all the strategies discussed can be applied with equal effectiveness to equity options. The differences will be discussed so that you know how to make the conversion successfully, if you choose.

It is not our intention in writing this book to put forth the proposition that selling options is the only way to make money investing in commodities, nor do we propose that option selling is appropriate for every investor. It is also not our intention to mislead readers into believing that losses cannot result from selling options. It is simply our belief that after all our years in the industry, all the fundamental and technical analysis, the backwards double-butterfly spreads, Brazilian freezes, Mississippi floods, and "mad cows," this is the only way we've found to profit consistently in the futures market.

The information in this book is divided into four parts, with each part containing four to five chapters. Part I explains why option selling is such an effective strategy and covers the basic mechanics of selling time premium, how options work, and the often-misunderstood subject of margins on short options. Part II explores our recommended core strategies for selling options, uncovers some common myths about effective option-writing techniques, points out key factors to consider when selling premium, and covers the all-too-important subject of risk control. Part III is all about analyzing and selecting the optimal markets for selling options. These are observations and techniques that we have come to realize are the most important in determining success or failure in option selling. And finally, Part IV covers how you can get started in selling options by discussing how to find the right broker, answering some common questions about selling time premium, and helping you avoid some of the common pitfalls.

Writing options may not be the Holy Grail of futures trading, but in our opinion it's the next best thing. We wrote this book to help you to make money. We will consider it a success if it achieves that end.

James Cordier
Michael Gross
June 14, 2004

PART I

# SELLING OPTIONS—WHY AND HOW IT WORKS

# 1
## CHAPTER

# Why Sell Options

Many traders are at least vaguely familiar with the lopsided percentages regarding options expiring worthless. Yet few actually know the exact percentage, why they expire worthless, and the benefits of selling options over buying options or trading futures. Fewer still are employing the strategy of selling premium. Most are deterred by the terms *limited profit* and *unlimited risk.* This is good because as an option seller, you need plenty of traders buying options to help fund your retirement!

If your goal is to make *consistent* 30, 50, or even 70 percent annual returns, option selling, especially futures option selling, may be for you. If your goal is to make 200, 300, or 1000 percent returns, like you see in all the hyped-up advertising for futures trading systems, put this book down, and go invest your money in some lottery tickets or head to Vegas. Over the long haul, your odds will be about the same.

This chapter lists the primary benefits and drawbacks to selling options. Before you learn the *how*, you must understand the *why.* The benefits are numerous and should give you all the whys you'll need to get started.

## BENEFIT 1: THE ODDS ARE IN YOUR FAVOR

The fact is that most options do expire worthless, and this has been confirmed by statistics. However, let's clarify this statistic. The actual figure is that most options *held to expiration* expire worthless. Therefore, when we refer to percentages of options expiring worthless, we are referring to the options on the board at expiration. Some studies suggest that up to 60 percent of all options are closed out prior to expiration. However, these same studies indicate that only about 10 percent of all options ever get exercised. What this means to you as a trader is that the longer you hold your short option, the better are your odds of success.

Options are a wasting asset. This means that it takes a larger move in the underlying futures contract or equity for the option to be worth more money to the option buyer. This is why such a large percentage of options are closed out prior to expiration. Buyers know that the longer they hold their options, the better is the chance that the value of those options will decay to zero. In addition, the closer an option is to expiration, the more difficult it becomes for that option to increase in price and produce or increase a profit for the buyer. Whether taking profits or cutting losses, many people will rush to the exits before expiration day comes. As a seller, you have the luxury of just waiting it out, welcoming the inevitable. Some very inventive trading techniques have been created over the years, but nobody yet has come up with a way to stop the steady march of time.

*Futures* magazine published a study in 2003 regarding percentages of options expiring worthless. The study tracked options in five major futures contracts: the Standard & Poor's (S&P) 500, the Nasdaq 100, Eurodollars, Japanese yen, and live cattle. It was conducted over a three-year period from 1997 to 1999. The research came to three major conclusions:

- On average, three of every four options held to expiration expire worthless (the exact percentage was 76.5 percent).
- The share of puts and calls that expired worthless is influenced by the primary trend of the underlying market.
- Option sellers still come out ahead even when they are going against the trend.

In terms of the first conclusion, the results of this study confirm our experience in the market. However, putting some scientifically proven data behind it is substantial. Consider that 76.5 percent of all options do expire worthless. (We contacted the Chicago Mercantile Exchange in 2001 and asked exactly what amount of options it estimated expired worthless based on its years of recorded data. After several weeks and talking to several sources inside the exchange, we finally had somebody quote in writing that the exchange's estimate was that about 74 percent of options expired worthless.) In our personal, not so scientific experience, we had the figure closer to 82 percent. Therefore, there is no exact, nondebatable figure for the number of options that expire worthless, but one has to assume that it is somewhere in the neighborhood of these figures. This means that at least three of every four and possibly four of every five options held to expiration will expire worthless. And this is shooting in the blind, throwing a dart at a board as your option picking procedure.

The second conclusion was that the amount of puts and calls expiring worthless is influenced by the primary trend of the underlying market. In some of the studies, up to

96 percent of put or calls expired worthless if they were written favoring the trend. This sounds like common sense, but you would be surprised at the number of traders who try to bet against a trend. When it comes to option writing, the old adage most definitely holds true: *The trend is your friend.* Write options that favor the trend, and you could boost your odds substantially that the options will expire worthless.

The third conclusion may be even more significant. Option sellers still come out ahead even when they are going against the trend. The findings were that even in bull markets, most calls expired worthless (although these figures were much lower than the 76.5 percent of all options that expired worthless), and most puts still expired worthless in a bear market. This means that you could be dead wrong in your analysis of the underlying market and still have a better than even chance at making money on the trade. If this is correct, you could be right in your analysis of the market only half the time and still have a little better than 75 percent of your options eventually expire worthless. If you're any good at forecasting market direction at all, you may be able to bump your averages a little to a lot higher.

David Caplan, in his excellent book, *The New Options Advantage*, states that in order to profit consistently in futures and option trading, traders must give themselves some kind of "edge" in every trade they enter. In selecting a strategy that eventually wins about 80 percent of the time *before* you even do any market research, you are giving yourself an edge.

## BENEFIT 2: TAKING PROFITS BECOMES SIMPLE

Almost every book or educational pamphlet on futures trading at one point or another refers to a central theme that has become the mantra for futures traders the world over: "Cut your losses short, and let your profits run." Traders have been drilled and instructed continuously that in order to make any money in futures trading, one must accept a large percentage of small losers while waiting for one or two large winning trades to not only recoup all the losses but also to provide an overall profit.

While we have to agree with this concept in a general sense, applying it in a real-life trading account is extremely difficult, if not impossible, for most individual investors. Stops can be placed to limit losses on futures positions, but floor traders tend to have a feel for where large concentrations of stop orders may be sitting. While we are not suggesting that these floor traders would run these stops deliberately (of course not, floor traders and professionals care about you and would *never* do that), it is very curious how a market often will crack a key point of support or resistance only to turn around and make a large move in the opposite direction.

Remember that when you are looking at a price chart, countless other traders are looking at the same chart. They all see the same points of support and resistance at which to place their stops. This is why you often will see a market touch a critical point of support or resistance and then make a rapid move through the critical level during a single trading session. All those buy or sell orders are triggered at once, causing a rapid move in the market and stopping futures traders out of their positions. There is nothing more frustrating to traders than having this happen to them and then to see the market make an immediate reversal and begin a large move in the opposite direction. Such traders were in the right market; they just couldn't stay in long enough!

This is assuming, of course, that such traders had the discipline to place stops to begin with. Cutting losses and letting profits run sounds good on paper, but the psychology of it goes against human nature. Emotions are a critical enemy of traders, and of all emotions, there is none so damaging to a portfolio as the emotion of *hope*. Hope is a wonderful emotion when applied to life outside the trading world. In the realm of trading, though, especially futures trading, it can rob you of your money and wreck an account. Traders don't want to cut a loss because they have become emotionally attached to a position. They'll watch it going against them on a daily basis and *hope* that it turns around. Books on trading answer this by telling you not to be emotional about your trading. How can you not be emotional about your trading? This is your money that we're talking about! You're going to be emotional about it no matter what you tell yourself.

What about deciding when to take profits? Letting a winner run can be even more psychologically difficult than cutting a loss short. A trader is so excited about seeing the market move in her direction that she becomes terrified that it will reverse and take back the profits it so willingly granted her. We've seen more traders go bust in not knowing where to take profits than we have seen traders who get buried with one or two large losses. The result of this fear is that most traders take profits way too soon, even when they have a nice winner going. There are no hard and fast rules as to when to take profits. Nobody knows if the market is reversing on a given day or only experiencing a short-term trend correction. This is one of the many reasons why futures trading is so difficult.

*This is one key reason why option selling can be a clear antidote to such a dilemma.*

When one sells an option, as opposed to trading the outright futures contract, the decision of when to take profits generally becomes one that you no longer have to make. The market makes it for you. As long as your option is not in the money, the value of your option eventually will deteriorate to zero at expiration. At this point, the position automatically closes out. You achieve full profit without ever having to decide if the market is correcting, going up or down tomorrow on the open, or having to decide whether to "hang in there" to wring a few more dollars out of the trade. The most you can make is the premium that you collect. In most cases, this will be your objective on the trade. In other words, you have a very clear profit objective and a very clear method of taking that profit. What is your profit-taking strategy in a winning trade? Do nothing. Simply let it expire.

This aspect of writing premium alone can be a boon to traders who have suffered losses because they are too quick to exit a winning trade or have a habit of holding the trade too long.

## BENEFIT 3: TIME IS ON YOUR SIDE

Sing it like Mick Jagger. As an option seller, you can. No matter what the market is doing, time is constantly, albeit slowly, eroding the value of the option. While the option can gain value from market movement, time will always be in your corner, working for you and against the person who bought the option. Instead of using the old ice cube melting analogy,* we have a different example that may help to illustrate the concept more clearly, especially to football fans.

As a seller of an option, you could be compared with a football team that plays defense for an entire game. How much time you start the game with is up to you. You start the game by giving yourself a predetermined point lead and giving your opponent so much time to beat you. For example, you can give yourself a 50-point lead and give your opponent two quarters to beat you (selling far-out-of-the-money options with more time value), or you can give your opponent a 7-point lead and two minutes to beat you (selling close-to-the-money options with little time value). No matter what you choose, the clock always will be running against your opponent. As time goes on, your opponent's chances of winning the game begin to decrease (and yours increase). He can't step out of bounds or call time out to stop the clock. The best part is, if you begin to feel uncomfortable at any point in the game, you can simply quit.

There are many fun comparisons to draw from this analogy. The point is that an option buyer is working against the market *and* time, just as a football offense trailing in a game has to work against the defense *and* the time left on the clock.

As an option seller, the passage of time is your greatest ally (see Figure 1.1).

## BENEFIT 4: BEING CLOSE IS GOOD ENOUGH

One of the hardest parts of trading futures is trying to decide where the market is going to go. This task can be daunting in and of itself. It can be complicated even more by the purchase of options. While buying an option does give a trader staying power to wait for a move to occur, it also places a time limit on *when the move must occur.*

One must remember that at any given time the market is reflecting the exact value of a given commodity on that particular day for that particular delivery month. Traders speculating on price moves must forecast not only current and future fundamentals but also how the trading world will react to those fundamentals. One must be able not only to study past supply/demand figures and how they affected price but also to know a little about crowd psychology. Predicting where prices will go is like trying to predict

---

*The ice cube melting analogy states that an option premium is like an ice cube sitting outside on a hot day. As time passes, a little more of the ice cube melts, until there is nothing left at all. It is a very good analogy but has become so overused that we felt that a different illustration of the same concept might shed fresh light on the subject.

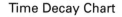

## FIGURE 1.1

Time Decay Chart

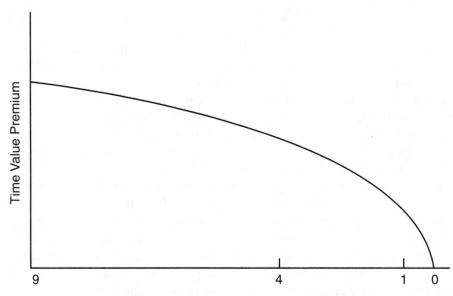

Time Remaining Until Expiration (Months)

The closer an option gets to expiration, the faster is its rate of time decay.

the direction of a hurricane. Even the experts can only make vague projections until it's almost making landfall.

Projecting where it won't go, however, can be another matter. If strong wind currents are blowing it Northeast, and these wind currents are expected to continue, one assumes that the hurricane will hit in some destination in a northeasterly direction. Therefore, the hurricane could veer off to the North or the East, maybe even way off from the direction of the wind, but it would be unlikely (although not impossible) for the storm to make a 180-degree about-face and head directly into the wind in a southwesterly direction. Knowledgeable option sellers bet that the storm will not make a 180-degree turnaround into the wind. That's all. They don't play the game of guessing where the storm will hit. That's a low-odds game. Guessing where it will not hit is much easier.

When you sell options in the way you will learn in this book, this is how you will play the market. You no longer have to try to outguess the pros as to where the market will go. All you have to determine is a price level to which you believe the market will *not* go. When you become more skilled at selling options, you will be able to identify option selling at ridiculous strike prices, in which you will be able to take advantage of traders willing to bet on the market going to these levels. A little fundamental knowledge can go a long way in this regard.

The following is an excerpt from an option seller article that we produced for publication several years back. With an ever-increasing flow of traders entering the futures and derivatives markets, the lesson is even more relevant today.

---

## OPTION SELLING 101: THINK LIKE AN OPTION SELLER

James Cordier, *President, Liberty Trading Group*

You may notice that many articles that appear in our column have a longer-term outlook for price. Unlike many analysts and traders, we do not attempt to guess what market prices will do today, tomorrow, or next week. I recommend approaching the market this way for several reasons:

1. Short-term trading is just too difficult. I'm sure there are some consistently successful day traders out there. That being said, I've never met any!

2. Markets can move very sporadically over short-term periods but over the long term will always have to adjust to reflect fundamentals.

3. As an intermediate-term option writer, short-term market gyration does not concern you. You are concerned about longer-term market direction and, more important, where prices won't go.

It is for these reasons that our articles focus on long-term fundamentals and do not generally attempt to predict what prices will do but rather what prices will not do. We believe that the most successful traders keep things very *simple*.

This is the approach that we suggest: "I do not know what price is going to do. Based on the existing fundamentals, however, and what prices have done in past years when supply and demand factors were similar to those of this year, I feel that *prices will have a very difficult time attaining a certain price level*. Therefore, I will sell calls (or puts) at that price level and not concern myself with short-term technical trading. Even if my market analysis or timing is off a bit, time value is still working for me, and I allow the market plenty of room to fluctuate in the meantime."

Remember, if you are a seller of a *call*, the market can move lower, stay the same, or even move somewhat higher. As long as the futures price is *anywhere below* your call option's *strike price* at expiration, the option expires worthless. If the option expires worthless, you, as the seller, keep all premiums collected as profit. As the seller of a *put*, you want the price to stay *above* a particular price level (strike price).

While this type of thinking can be difficult at first for the futures trader used to daily action (it was for me), I've found that this approach has improved my overall trading results tremendously.

Remember this the next time you are tempted to bite on the latest market that is about to "skyrocket." Time value and patience are your friends. Think like the option seller!

The point is that you can still have your hunches as to where the market might go; you just position yourself differently. In this way, if your price projection is right, you profit. If it is only partially right, you profit. If you are wrong, there is still a good chance that you will profit. The market can move in the direction you projected, consolidate sideways with no clear direction, or even move opposite the direction you projected. As long as you are not absolutely 100 percent wrong and the market makes a rapid and/or sustained move in the exact opposite direction that you predicted, you will profit on this position.

## BENEFIT 5: PERFECT TIMING IS NO LONGER NECESSARY

One aspect critical for success in futures trading is being able to time the market. Because of the leverage involved in trading futures, mistiming the market probably costs traders more losses than incorrectly picking the ultimate direction of prices. While some traders can gain a fairly decent insight into the long-term direction of price, it is what the price does in the *meantime* that causes them so much trouble.

A market moving in an overall trend upward owing to a long-term fundamental factor still will have moderate to severe corrections periodically. This can result for a number of reasons, including profit taking by large funds or small speculators or a sudden news story that may cause some temporary sensation in the market but in reality has little effect on the long-term fundamentals of the market.

A trader may see the trend and decide to "get in on the action" and look for a place to buy. While buying into an existing trend usually is not a bad way to go, timing will determine the odds of success or failure on this trade. If all you had to do was play the trend, futures trading would be easy, and everybody would make money. This is even more difficult in volatile markets. Traders, especially small speculators, will buy the futures and then place a stop. More often than not they will place tight stops, giving the market little room to fluctuate against them. This is what they have been taught, and this is why most of their trades will lose. They have to protect capital at all costs. Unfortunately, protecting capital does not allow much movement in a market that can and often does move sharply and rapidly in either direction for no apparent reason at all. Many, if not most, traders will be stopped out before the market begins moving in the direction of the trend again (see Figure 1.2).

Selling options avoids all this senselessness. In a bull trend, a seller simply can sell options far beneath the market, allowing wide price fluctuations within the trend that will not dramatically affect her position. In this way, she can sell options on an up or down day without the need for perfect timing. Even if she catches the market in a correction mode, the fluctuation in her option price generally will be substantially less than if she were in a futures position. Thus the trader has significant staying power in the market and is able to ride out short-term market fluctuations, unlike her futures-trading counterpart. (This generalizes futures traders as the average individual speculator. There

**F I G U R E   1.2**

July 2004 Wheat Price Chart Contrasting Buy and Sell Areas with Option Sale

Arrows show possible entry and stop points for futures traders.

are, of course, some well-capitalized traders who are willing to commit large chunks of margin capital to ride out an adverse move. In addition to a large cushion of excess margin funds, this also requires a strong conviction in the market, as well as nerves of steel.)

Even the few traders good at timing the market can get bounced out of a good trend on random news events. For instance, in early 2004, the soybean and soybean meal markets were in a strong bull trend higher. This was mainly due to the beginning of massive demand from China because the Chinese economy was in the early stages of rapid expansion. This was a substantial long-term fundamental. In late January, news stories began hitting the press about the outbreak of Asian bird flu. The media, of course, loves to sensationalize. "Millions of Poultry to Be Destroyed," headlines reported.

Media-sensitive small specs began liquidating long soybean and meal positions, their rational being that fewer chickens to feed means less demand for soybean meal (used in poultry feed), which is derived from soybeans. The number of birds destroyed, in reality, was a tiny drop in the bucket of the overall world supply of livestock. The real effect on soybean and soybean meal demand was zero. It had no effect whatsoever on the long-term demand for soybeans, which ultimately determines price direction. However, short-term direction is often controlled by factors exactly like this (see Figure 1.3).

Traders who bought soybean meal the day before the market picked up on Asian bird flu would have been right in the trend but unlucky enough to have poor timing. Many could have lost as much as $1,500 or more per contract on a price drop that appears, in retrospect, to have been fairly benign.

An option seller could have sold put premium as much as 400 points out of the money on the day before the bird flu correction and been little effected by the drop. He

## F I G U R E   1.3

December 2003 Soybean Meal Price Chart Showing Bird Flu Dip in Prices

Arrow shows the price dip.

still played the trend and the long-term fundamental. The timing of his trade, however, was insignificant.

## BENEFIT 6: DEFINABLE RISK CONTROL

Regardless of the label of unlimited risk in selling short options, option selling risk can be just as definable and controlled as any other type of futures or stock trading risk. This is mentioned here only as a benefit so that traders will know that they can control their risks. The subject of risk, however, is significant and therefore will be covered in its own full chapter (see Chapter 9).

## DRAWBACKS OF SELLING OPTIONS

Now that we have covered the many benefits of option selling, a potential option seller also must be familiar with the drawbacks of selling premium. While it is our biased opinion that these drawbacks are dwarfed by the potential benefits, we will cover them here in order to present a balanced view.

1. *Unlimited risk.* While we have already addressed the term *unlimited* and its misunderstandings, anyone considering selling option premium in a portfolio, especially a futures portfolio, should be aware that there always exists the potential for a move against one's position that could cause the investor to experience drawdowns. While spreading or writing covered positions can place maximum limits on these risks, such moves also can cut into profits received from a trade. In addition, the maximum risk on some covered positions is often still large in comparison with the premium being netted on the trade. While there are many ways to reduce this risk substantially, one always must be aware that it exists. Nonetheless, selling options on futures, even naked, entails no more risk than trading the futures contract itself, nor does selling options on stocks contain any more exposure than does trading the underlying equity.

2. *Limited profit potential.* In selling option premium, your profit potential is limited to the premium you collect when you sell the option. No matter how far the market moves in your favor (away from your strike price), your potential profit remains the same. It is for this reason that traders chasing the "big score" and trading the market for the adrenaline rush (a considerable percentage of small speculators) generally are not attracted to the concept of option writing. To use a baseball analogy, an option writer is an investor who is willing to give up his chance of hitting a home run in favor of consistently hitting singles over and over again.

3. *Potential scorn or ignorance of brokers or investment professionals.* As stated earlier, many brokers, advisors, and entire firms are either hesitant to write option premium for fear of risk, a general lack of understanding of how to employ an option selling strategy effectively, or both. This sometimes can mean higher margin or account requirements for investors wanting to sell options in their account. You may have to do a little work before finding a good broker who is qualified to assist you in selling options properly. We feel that this is so important that there is an entire chapter dedicated to this subject (see Chapter 15). In the meantime, just remember that poor advice is often worse than no advice at all.

## SELLING OPTIONS AND CATCHING CATFISH: THE LOGIC OF SELLING OPTIONS

Let's assume that a rough figure of 80 percent of options expire worthless for example purposes. What does this mean to a trader? Suppose that you and I went down to a fishing hole filled with catfish and bass. We toss a fishing line in the water. The hole is primarily a catfish haven, with 80 percent catfish and 20 percent bass. I offer to pay you $1 for every bass you pull up, whereas you must pay me $1 for every catfish you pull up. There are even a few trophy bass in the hole that, based on their weight, I will pay you $2 or $3 or even $4 for hauling in. However, these are very few and far between, and I am more than willing to take $1 for each catfish while you try and catch a trophy. Chances are that you will pull up eight catfish and two bass. You'll pay me $8, and I'll give you $2 back for your bass. I will end up netting a hefty $6 profit. You soon realize the error of your ways, and we decide to go into business with our little fishing hole.

Soon many novice anglers hear about the trophy bass in the fishing hole, paying high prizes for anglers lucky enough to catch one. They are especially interested in the highly touted "monster" bass, one of which lurks in the dark water below and pays a prize of $10 to the angler who hooks it.

The anglers line up at our hole to pay us $1 for every catfish they catch. We generally have to pay them $2 out of every $8 they pay us. Sometimes we only have to pay back $1. Sometimes, if somebody has a "hot streak," we may have to pay back $3 or $4. However, we almost always come out ahead at the end of the day.

Furthermore, we don't require them to cast 10 times. Some may come with only a few dollars and take a few casts. Some will fish all day. Most fish until they run out of money.

Occasionally, someone will catch a trophy bass. In this case, we have to pay back $3 or $4 against our $1 bet. The trophy bass causes much excitement. The newspaper comes and snaps pictures. More novice anglers and some people who have never fished before see the picture in the paper, get very excited, and stuff their pockets with dollars and come running down to our hole to pursue the elusive trophy fish. This brings us even more business and makes us happy, for alas, most of them catch catfish and put dollars in our pocket.

Pretty soon a few savvy anglers catch on to our game and decide to stop handing us dollars. They set up their own little stand on the fishing hole and begin collecting dollars for catfish. Fortunately, there are many new anglers coming to the hole now, trying to "hit it big" with a trophy bass. Many get frustrated with catching catfish and losing their money and come to the conclusion that "fishing is bad." They quit altogether. However, many new, young hopefuls appear to take their place.

Soon another group of entrepreneurs springs up. Their purpose is to take the anglers' money and give it to us and take any money we owe the anglers and give it to them. Some will even help you bait your hook and tell you where to throw your line. For this, they charge a fee. This now means that the anglers and you and I have to pay a fee on each fish that is caught, catfish or bass. Most of these "middlemen" like to talk about the big bass and get anglers excited about the "monster" bass that lurks below. "Of course, you could lose your dollars," they warn, "but think of the payoff if you catch the monster!" This gets anglers even more excited. Some take a middleman's advice and cast to the spot to which he points. This, of course, costs the angler a slightly higher fee, for the middleman must spend more time with her. The angler, of course, still catches mostly catfish.

Others anglers study the fishing hole for hours and look at depth charts at home to see where the giant fish may make its lair. Then they come to the hole with sophisticated computers and top-of-the-line fishing gear. Most fare little better than their non-sophisticated counterparts. The reason is that they are fighting a losing battle. Even though the large bass are swimming in the hole, the hole is still 80 percent catfish, and the $1 the anglers must pay for each catfish eventually is going to exhaust their money supply, even if they catch a few bass along the way.

While most of the middlemen do sincerely hope that the anglers catch a big bass and try their hardest to help them to do so, they, along with their angler clients, fail to realize that the person making all the money is the one betting on catfish. Certainly, it lacks the glamour and excitement of pursuing a "monster" bass and the big prize it brings with it. However, for making money at the end of the day, it is devastatingly effective.

A few of these middlemen become wise to the catfish betting strategy and encourage their clients to begin betting on the catfish because there are many anglers willing to take a chance on catching a big bass. However, most shudder at the thought. "Bet on the catfish?" they ask incredulously. "Why would you want to do that? It's too risky. What if somebody pulls up that monster bass? What will you do then? You bet $1 and you lost $10. That could wipe you out! You may even have to run home and get more money so that you can pay that angler the $10 you owe him. Is that what you want?"

"No, no." the ambitious angler fearfully replies. And so they go back to trying to catch the "monster" bass, and eventually the angler runs out of money.

In case you haven't guessed, this is an analogy of the strategy of option selling and how most brokers and traders (especially novice traders) view it. The anglers chasing the "monster" bass are option buyers. Lured by big gains, they throw their line in the water (enter a long option trade) with only a 20 percent chance of catching a bass (having a winning trade). Their chances of catching a bass that pays anything significant is even less. This is before they study the weather, select bait, and choose the area of the hole to which they will cast (analyze market conditions and strike prices). The fishing hole is the exchange. The middleman is, of course, the broker.

Chances are very good that the person getting paid $1 for each catfish caught (the option seller) will have most of the money before long. But most anglers will not bet on the catfish. Most don't want to bet on catfish. Most want the chance to catch the big or "monster" fish and bet $1 to make $3, $4, or even $5.

There are two caveats to betting on catfish (or selling options). One is that you have to come to the fishing hole with enough dollars in your pocket to pay up if an angler catches a big bass on her first one or two casts. The second is that from time to time you have to expect that somebody is going to catch a bass. In many cases you will already have more than enough profits in your pocket to comfortably pay the lucky winner. However, when you make your first trip to the fishing hole, bet on a catfish, and somebody pulls out a big bass on the first cast, you have to have the gumption to pay the prize and go back to your catfish bet. While the odds of this happening are low, it certainly can happen. You can see how it might be unwise for a catfish better to assume after this incident that "catfish betting is bad." Unfortunately, many option sellers make exactly this mistake and then tell all who will listen of their misfortune, especially if they had $5 in their pocket and the angler, against all odds, pulled out a $5 fish. This further perpetuates the misconception that option writing is a reckless approach to investing.

Now that you understand the basic concept, there is much you can do to increase the odds that anglers will catch fewer bass and especially keep them from catching the "monster" bass and keep reeling in those catfish. This is what this book is about.

# 2 CHAPTER

# A Crash Course on Futures

After decades of being the outcast stepchild of the investment world, futures trading finally has begun to catch the eye of mainstream investors. Perhaps it is the expanding need to diversify that is driving this trend. Or it could be that after the "Asian contagion" or the tech stock meltdown of the early 2000s, futures may not look quite as risky or intimidating as they used to, at least in relation to everything else.

New volume records are being set on many contracts at the Chicago Mercantile Exchange and the Chicago Board of Trade. New products and the continued expansion of electronic exchanges continue to point to a thriving, growing industry.

Yet, despite the popularity of futures trading, the odds remain stacked against individual investors in the futures arena.

Studies confirm that about 76 percent of all futures traders end up losing money (there is no doubt that most of these are small speculators). It is no mystery why. It is amateurs against the pros in futures. No matter how hard small investors try, the pros usually are one step ahead. If you read something on your screen, they probably knew about it yesterday. If you read something in the newspaper, they probably knew about it last week. By the time you go to trade it, it's already been priced into the market.

It is not the fact that small speculators don't have the time, nerves, resources, capital, or knowledge to compete. It is all the above. It is the fact that they are amateurs competing against professionals, and this is the real reason most futures traders lose money.

Lucky for you, you don't have to be part of this group. You don't have to go toe to toe with these heavyweights on their turf anymore. You simply can walk around the outskirts of this ongoing battle, picking up the spare change that rolls off to the side. You can sell options.

## FUTURES CONTRACTS: WHAT ARE THEY?

Before one can understand how to sell options on futures, one must understand futures themselves. Farmers originated the buying and selling of futures contracts as a way to offer a hedge against price changes in their crops.

It worked like this: A farmer has a crop of cotton growing in his field. He likes the current price that cotton is fetching at the market and would be very happy if he could sell his crop at this price. However, his crop will not be ready to sell for three months. By selling a cotton futures contract (or number of contracts) equal to the amount of cotton he has growing in his field, he can effectively "lock in" the current price of cotton.

How does this work? As an example, let's say the farmer estimates that his crop will produce 50,000 pounds of cotton this year. The futures contract for cotton is for 50,000 pounds. Therefore, the farmer can sell one futures contract of cotton at today's price for the month he expects his cotton to be ready for delivery. Now if the price of cotton falls between now and the time his cotton is ready to sell, he will make up the difference in profits on his futures contract. If the price of cotton rises, he will lose on his futures contract, but he will make up the difference on the sale of his physical cotton. It is a way for the farmer to avoid the risk of prices moving below a point at which he would be satisfied. This is called *hedging,* and it is still the primary purpose of the futures markets today.

Huge institutional farms and agricultural producers hedge their products in everything from cocoa to cattle to soybeans. Banks and government institutions hedge their exposure to currency fluctuations and interest rates. Worldwide brokerage houses hedge their exposure to the stock market with index futures contracts.

Hedgers also can be users of the actual products who want to protect against prices moving higher. A company such as Pillsbury, which uses thousands of tons of flour in a year, may want to protect against higher wheat prices and hedge by buying wheat futures. Financial institutions use futures to hedge in this manner as well.

Pure hedgers make no actual net profit from trading futures. It is only a tool to cut risk and manage price swings in a product that their business either produces or uses in some regard. Not only are these traders very well versed in their industry, but generally they also work for large organizations and have thousands or even millions of dollars in technical and human resources available to them to determine price directions and risk arrays of the commodities or financial instruments with which they are dealing. These traders are known as *commercial traders,* or *commercials* for short.

However, in order to hedge their risk, they have to have somebody assume that risk. *Speculators* fill this role. Speculators do not trade futures to manage risk or lock in prices. Usually, they are not even in the physical commodities business. They are trading the contracts purely for profit. They are willing to assume the risk of the hedgers in the hope that a price move will produce profits for them. They do not deliver the goods, nor do they take delivery. They simply buy and sell the contracts and exit before delivery comes due.

The Commodity Futures Trading Commission (CFTC) divides speculators into two groups: *large speculators* and *small speculators*. If a trader has a certain number of contracts in one commodity, usually 50 or 100, he is considered to be a large speculator in that particular commodity. While many individual investors easily can hold this many contracts at a time, large speculators generally are thought of as professional money managers or *funds*. Large investment houses or independent operators can trade commodity funds, made up of capital from many investors (similar to a mutual fund in equities). Ironically, some of these are known as *hedge funds,* supposedly because these funds can be somewhat of a hedge against adverse moves in the stock market. However, the purpose of these funds is to produce a profit.

Fund managers trade billions of dollars and trade many thousands of contracts in a day. They have the ability to move the market to a certain degree when they decide to enter or exit positions. Like commercial traders, most have huge amounts of resources available to them, industry contacts, and a wealth of personal or company experience to draw on.

There is one category left. This is the *small speculator.* Small speculators are individual investors. They are the tiny capitalists trying to enter the race between the two titans.

## CONTRACTS AND CONTRACT MONTHS

A *futures contract* is an agreement to buy or sell a specified commodity in a specified amount at a specified date. Every contract is for a specified amount of that particular commodity, currency, or financial product. Most commodities have different contract sizes depending on the unit that is used to measure it. For instance, a contract for corn is for 5,000 bushels of corn. A contract for crude oil is for 1,000 barrels of crude.

Unlike stocks, commodities trade in different contract months. Corn for delivery in July is a different contract at a different price from a contract for corn for delivery in September. As a speculator, you will want to close out your positions before these contracts come due for delivery.

Some investors new to futures express the fear that they will make some sort of mistake and that a contract for a commodity will be delivered to their door. This is simply unrealistic. There are several layers of people whose responsibility it is to make sure that this does not happen. You would be contacted by several of them (first and foremost, your broker) to inform you that it is time to exit your position, and if necessary, they probably would do so on your behalf. Even if you did intend to take delivery, there is much paperwork and arrangements to be made before this could take place.

Option traders generally do not have to worry about this.

## CONTRACT SIZES AND POINT VALUES

Another difference between futures and stocks is how price moves are calculated. In a stock, you can buy 100 shares of stock, and if the price moves up $1 a share, you make $100. Since commodity contracts vary in size and units of measurement (i.e., barrels, bushels, and pounds), each commodity has a different *point* value.

For example, the size of a crude oil contract is 1,000 barrels. The price in the crude oil contract is quoted at price per barrel. Price changes in crude oil move in 1-cent increments. Therefore, a 1-cent move in the price of crude oil equates to a gain or loss of $10 for every contract a trader holds (0.01 × 1,000 = $10). If a trader bought one contract for May crude oil at $38.00 per barrel, and the price increased to $38.50 per barrel, the trader would have made a $500 profit (50 × $10 = $500).

Contract sizes and point values for different commodities and futures contracts are listed in Figure 2.1.

## MARGINS ON FUTURES

The term *margin* has a completely different meaning in the futures world than it does in the world of equities. In stocks, one often can "borrow" money from the brokerage house to purchase stocks, at least a certain percentage of stock. This is known as *buying on margin.* The investor then has to pay interest on the money she borrowed and hope that the gain from her stock purchase is enough to pay her interest charge and commission and still show a profit. This is a way of increasing leverage.

In futures, buying or selling on margin is a built-in feature. To use the preceding example, a crude oil contract trading at $38 per barrel at a contract size of 1,000 barrels would mean that the total value of the contract is $38,000. Yet a trader can purchase (or sell) that contract for a small *margin deposit,* usually about 5 to 10 percent of the value of the contract. In the traditional way of buying stocks, to purchase $38,000 worth of stocks would require $38,000 worth of cash. However, to purchase $38,000 worth of crude oil, one only needs to put down the margin requirement, maybe $3,000. The exchange will front you the rest.

This is where the leverage comes from in futures contracts. A small move in the value of the unleveraged stock produces a small gain or loss. A small move in the value of the commodity can result in a large gain or loss. For instance, if you purchase 1,000 shares of stock at $38 a share, you plunk down $38,000. If the stock moves up to $42 per share, you make $4,000, a 10.5 percent return on your investment (4,000/38,000 = 10.5).

If you purchase a contract for crude oil at $38, put down your $3,000 margin requirement, and it moves up to $42, you make the same $4,000, yet your return on investment is 133 percent (4,000/3,000 = 133). This aspect of leverage is why futures generally are considered an aggressive investment by the mainstream investment media.

Figure 2.2 presents an example of what a margin sheet looks like. This is only a sample. Margins change all the time, and you should ask your broker for an updated margin sheet if you want to see current margins for futures contracts.

Margin requirements for individual contracts are set by the exchanges and can be changed based on the volatility of the contract. These are called *minimum exchange margins.*

Individual clearing firms can add their own additional margin on top of the exchange margins and reserve the right to increase these margins without notice. Serious traders usually look for a brokerage that offers minimum exchange margins.

## IMPROVED DIVERSITY

One reason that commodities are becoming more popular is that they offer a great amount of diversity to a portfolio. Most investors have much of their capital tied up in the stock market. If the stock market goes down, they lose money. Investors who trade individual stocks experience much frustration when they spend their time trying to pick the best-quality stocks only to lose because the market as a whole falls. They can pick the highest-quality companies on the board and still lose because of macroeconomic factors that take the whole stock market down.

Commodities, currencies, and other financial contracts are not necessarily affected by the stock market or the factors that affect its movement. In most cases they are moving completely independent of equities—sometimes perhaps even in opposite directions. For instance, talk of inflation may hurt stock prices but actually may benefit commodity prices. In addition, even if the prices of commodities are moving down, it is just as easy to go short in commodities as it is to go long.

Another reason that commodities are excellent diversifiers is that although, as a whole, prices can be moving in a long-term general direction, they are not as affected by the complex, as a whole, as much as stocks. In other words, Pfizer and Wal-Mart may move lower together because the whole stock market in general is down. However, the price of soybeans is fairly independent of the price of orange juice or natural gas. There are many more opportunities to diversify within the diversifier.

## MANAGED FUTURES

Nonetheless, trading commodity futures remains a losing game for most investors. For the reasons mentioned earlier, for most people it is simply too difficult to learn to manage the leverage and analytic skills and acquire the resources necessary to be consistently successful.

So how does the average individual investor gain exposure to these potentially lucrative markets without losing his shirt? Many investors today are adopting the

**FIGURE 2.1**

Contract Size, Hours, Tick Values

| Commodity | Exch | Hours (CT) | Delivery Mo | Contract Size | Point Value | Price Fluctuation |
|---|---|---|---|---|---|---|
| Australian Dollar | IMM | 7:20–2:00 | H,M,U,Z | 100,000 AD | 1pt=$10.00 | 1pt=$10.00 |
| British Pound | IMM | 7:20–2:00 | H,M,U,Z | 62,500 BP | 1pt=$6.25 | 2pts=$12.50 |
| British Pound | MA | 7:20–2:15 | H,M,U,Z | 12,500 BP | 1pt=$1.25 | 2pts=$2.50 |
| CRB Index | NYFE | 8:40–1:45 | F,G,J,M,Q,X | 500 × Index | 1pt=$5.00 | 5pts=$25.00 |
| Canadian Dollar | IMM | 7:20–2:00 | H,M,U,Z | 100,000 CD | 1pt=$10.00 | 1pt=$10.00 |
| Canadian Dollar | MA | 7:20–2:15 | H,M,U,Z | 50,000 CD | 1pt=$5.00 | 1pt=$5.00 |
| Cattle, Feeder | CME | 9:05–1:00 | F,H,J,K,Q,U,V,X | 50,000 lbs. | 1pt=$5.00 | 2 1/2pts=$12.50 |
| Cattle, Live | CME | 9:05–1:00 | G,J,M,Q,V,Z | 40,000 lbs. | 1pt=$4.00 | 2 1/2pts=$10.00 |
| Cattle, Live | MA | 9:05–1:15 | G,J,M,Q,V,Z | 20,000 lbs. | 1pt=$2.00 | 2 1/2pts=$5.00 |
| Cocoa | NYCSCE | 7:30–12:30 | H,K,N,U,Z | 10M ton (22,046) | 1pt=$10.00 | 1pt=$10.00 |
| Coffee | NYCSCE | 8:15–12:32 | H,K,N,U,Z | 37,500 lbs. | 1pt=$3.75 | 5pts=$18.75 |
| Copper | COMEX | 7:10–1:00 | H,K,N,U,Z | 25,000 lbs. | 1pt=$2.50 | 5pts=$12.50 |
| Corn | CBOT | 9:30–1:15 | H,K,N,U,Z | 5,000 bu | 1cent=$50.00 | 1/4 cent=$12.50 |
| Corn | MA | 9:30–1:45 | H,K,N,U,Z | 1,000 bu | 1cent=$10.00 | 1/8cent=$1.25 |
| Cotton | NYCTE | 9:30–1:40 | H,K,N,V,Z | 50,000 lbs. | 1pt=$5.00 | 1pt=$5.00 |
| Crude Oil | NYME | 8:30–2:10 | All Months | 1,000 barrels | 1pt=$10.00 | 1pt=$10.00 |
| Deutschemark | IMM | 7:20–2:00 | H,M,U,Z | 125,000 DM | 1pt=$12.50 | 1pt=$12.50 |
| Deutschemark | MA | 7:20–2:15 | H,M,U,Z | 62,500 DM | 1pt=$6.25 | 1pt=$6.25 |
| Dow Jones | CBOT | 7:20–3:15 | H,M,U,Z | $10 × Index | 1pt=$10.00 | 1pt=$10.00 |
| Dow Jones-mini | CBOT | 8:15p–4:15p | H,M,U,Z | $2 × Index | 1pt=$2.00 | 1pt=$2.00 |
| Eurodollar | IMM | 7:20–2:00 | H,M,U,Z | $1,000,000 | 1/2pt=$12.50 | 1/2pt=$12.50 |
| Eurodollar | MA | 7:20–2:15 | H,M,U,Z | $500,000 | 1pt=$12.50 | 1pt=$12.50 |
| Euroyen | IMM | 7:20–2:00 | H,M,U,Z | 100 million Yen | 1pt=2500 Yen | 1pt=2500 Yen |
| Gas, Unleaded | NYME | 8:30–2:10 | All Months | 42,000 gal | 1pt=$4.20 | 1pt=$4.20 |
| Gold | CBOT | 7:20–1:40 | G,J,M,Q,V,Z | 32.15 troy oz. | 10 cts=$3.215 | 10 cents=$3.215 |
| Gold | COMEX | 7:20–1:30 | G,J,M,Q,V,Z | 100 troy oz. | 1pt=$1.00 | 10pts=$10.00 |

| Commodity | Exchange | Hours | Months | Size | Tick | Points |
|---|---|---|---|---|---|---|
| Gold-mini | CBOT | 8:15–1:45 | F,H,J,M,N,U,V,Z | 33.2 troy oz. | 1pt=$.33 | 10pts=$3.32 |
| Heating Oil | NYME | 8:30–2:10 | All Months | 42,000 gal | 1pt=$4.20 | 1pt=$4.20 |
| Hogs,Lean | CME | 9:10–1:00 | G,J,M,N,Q,V,Z | 40,000 lbs. | 1pt=$4.00 | 2 1/2pts=$10.00 |
| Hogs | MA | 9:10–1:15 | G,J,M,N,Q,V,Z | 25,000 lbs. | 1pt=$2.50 | 2 1/2pts=$6.25 |
| Japanese Yen | IMM | 7:20–2:00 | H,M,U,Z | 12,500,000 JY | 1pt=$12.50 | 1pt=$12.50 |
| Japanese Yen | MA | 7:20–2:15 | H,M,U,Z | 6,250,000 JY | 1pt=$6.25 | 1pt=$6.25 |
| Lumber | CME | 9:00–1:05 | F,H,K,N,U,X | 80,000 bd ft | 1pt=$.80 | 10pts=$8.00 |
| Mexican Peso | IMM | 8:00–2:00 | H,M,U,Z | 500,000 NMP | 1pt=$5.00 | 2 1/2pts=$12.50 |
| Mortgage Futures | CBOT | 7:20–2:00 | All Months | $1000 × Index | 1/32=$31.25 | 1/32=$31.25 |
| Municipal Bonds | CBOT | 7:20–2:00 | H,M,U,Z | $100,000 | 1/32=$31.25 | 1/32=$31.25 |
| NASDAQ Index | IOM | 8:30–3:15 | H,M,U,Z | $100 × Index | 1pt=$1.00 | 5pts=$5.00 |
| NASDAQ E-MIni | IOM | 3:30–3:15 | H,M,U,Z | $20 × Index | 1 pt=$.20 | 50pts=$10.00 |
| Nikkei Index | IOM | 8:00–3:15 | H,M,U,Z | $5.00 × Index | 1pt=$5.00 | 5pts=$25.00 |
| NYSE Index | NYFE | 8:30–3:15 | H,M,U,Z | 500 × Index | 1pt=$5.00 | 5pts=$25.00 |
| Oats | CBOT | 9:30–1:15 | H,K,N,U,Z | 5,000 bu | 1cent=$50.00 | 1/4 cent=$12.50 |
| Oats | MA | 9:30–1:45 | H,K,N,U,Z | 1,000 bu | 1cent=$10.00 | 1/8cent=$1.25 |
| One Mo. LIBOR | IMM | 7:20–2:00 | All Months | $3,000.000 | 1/2pt=$12.50 | 1/2pt=$12.50 |
| Orange Juice | NYCTE | 9:15–1:15 | F,H,K,N,U,Z | 15,000 lbs. | 1pt=$1.50 | 5pts=$7.50 |
| Palladium | NYME | 7:10–1:20 | H,M,U,Z | 100 troy oz. | 1pt=$1.00 | 5pts=$5.00 |
| Platinum | NYME | 7:20–1:30 | F,J,N,V | 50 troy oz. | 1pt=$.50 | 10pts=$5.00 |
| Pork Bellies | CME | 9:10–1:00 | F,H,K,N,Q,U,X | 40,000 lbs | 1pt=$4.00 | 2 1/2pts=$10.00 |
| Rough Rice | CBOT | 9:15–1:30 | F,H,K,N,U,X | 200,000 lbs | 1pt=$2.00 | 5pts=$10.00 |
| Silver | COMEX | 7:25–1:25 | H,K,N,U,Z | 5,000 troy oz | 1pt=$.50 | 10pts=$5.00 |
| Silver, New | CBOT | 7:25–1:25 | G,J,M,Q,V,Z | 1,000 troy oz | 1pt=$.10 | 10pts=$1.00 |
| Silver-mini | CBOT | 8:15–1:45 | G,J,M,Q,V,Z | 1,000 oz | 1pt=$.10 | 10pts=$1.00 |
| Soybean Meal | CBOT | 9:30–1:15 | F,H,K,N,Q,U,V,Z | 100 tons | 1pt=$1.00 | 10pts=$10.00 |
| Soybean Oil | CBOT | 9:30–1:15 | F,H,K,N,Q,U,V,Z | 60,000 lbs | 1pt=$6.00 | 1pt=$6.00 |
| Soybeans | CBOT | 9:30–1:15 | F,H,K,N,Q,U,X | 5,000 bu | 1pt=$50.00 | 1/4cent=$12.50 |
| Soybeans | MA | 9:30–1:45 | F,H,K,N,Q,U,X | 1,000 bu | 1pt=$10.00 | 1/8cent=$1.25 |
| S&P 500 Index | IOM | 8:30–3:15 | H,M,U,Z | 250 × S&P | 1pt=$2.50 | 10pts=$25.00 |
| S&P 500 E-Mini | CME | 3:45p–3:15p | H,M,U,Z | $50 × S&P | 1pt=$.50 | 25pts=$12.50 |
| S&P MidCap Index | IOM | 8:15–3:15 | H,M,U,Z | 500 × MidCap | 1pt=$5.00 | 5pts=$25.00 |

*(Continued)*

# FIGURE 2.1

Contract Size, Hours, Tick Values (*Continued*)

| Commodity | Exch | Hours (CT) | Delivery Mo | Contract Size | Point Value | Price Fluctuation |
|---|---|---|---|---|---|---|
| Sugar | NYCSCE | 8:30–12:20 | H,K,N,V | 112,000 lbs | 1pt=$11.20 | 1pt=$11.20 |
| Swiss Franc | IMM | 7:20–2:00 | H,M,U,Z | 125,000 SF | 1pt=$12.50 | 1pt=$12.50 |
| Swiss Franc | MA | 7:20–2:15 | H,M,U,Z | 62,500 SF | 1pt=$6.25 | 1pt=$6.25 |
| Treasury Bills(90) | IMM | 7:20–2:00 | H,M,U,Z | $1,000,000 | 1/2pt=$12.50 | 1/2pt=$12.50 |
| Treasury Bills | MA | 7:20–2:15 | H,M,U,Z | $500,000 | 1pt=$12.50 | 1pt=$12.50 |
| Treasury Bonds | MA | 6:20p–9:05p 8:00a–3:15p | H,M,U,Z | $50,000 | 1/32=$15.62 | 1/32=$15.62 |
| Treasury Bonds-mini | MA | 8:00p–4:00p | H,M,U,Z | $50,000 | 1/32=$15.62 | 1/32=$15.62 |
| Treasury Note,10yr | CBOT | 6:20–9:05p 7:20a–2:00p | H,M,U,Z | $100,000 | 1/32=$31.25 | 1/32=$31.25 |
| Treasury Note 10yr mini | CBOT | 8:00p–4:00p | H,M,U,Z | $50,000 | 1/32=$15.625 | 1/32=$15.625 |
| Treasury Notes,5yr | CBOT | 6:20p–9:05p 7:20a–2:00p | H,M,U,Z | $100,000 | 1/64=$15.63 | 1/2 of 1/32=$15.63 |
| US Dollar Index | NYCTE | 6:00p–9:00p 2:00a–2:00p | H,M,U,Z | 1000 × Dol Index | 1pt=$10.00 | 1pt=$10.00 |
| Value Line Index | KCBT | 8:30–3:15 | H,M,U,Z | 500 × Val Line Index | 1pt=$5.00 | 5pts=$25.00 |
| Value Line, Mini | KCBT | 8:30–3:15 | H,M,U,Z | 100 × Val Line Index | 1pt=$1.00 | 5pts=$5.00 |
| Wheat | CBOT | 9:30–1:15 | H,K,N,U,Z | 5,000 bu | 1cent=$50.00 | 1/4 |
| Wheat | KCBT | 9:30–1:15 | H,K,N,U,Z | 5,000 bu | 1cent=$50.00 | 1/4 |
| Wheat | MPLS | 9:30–1:15 | H,K,N,U,Z | 5,000 bu | 1cent=$50.00 | 1/4 |
| Wheat | MA | 9:30–1:45 | H,K,N,U,Z | 1,000 bu | 1cent=$10.00 | 1/8 cents=$1.25 |

This chart shows contract sizes, dollar values, and point values.

**F I G U R E   2.2**

Sample Margin Sheet

| CBOT | INITIAL | MAIN/HEDGE | CME | INITIAL | MAIN/HEDGE |
|------|---------|------------|-----|---------|------------|
| Wheat | 1,181 | 875 | Live Cattle | 1,350 | 1,000 |
| Corn | 810 | 600 | Lean Hogs | 1,080 | 800 |
| Oats | 473 | 350 | Pork Bellies | 1,620 | 1,200 |
| Soybeans | 3,105 | 2,300* | Feeder Cattle | 1,350 | 1,000 |
| Soybean Meal | 2,160 | 1,600* | BFP Milk | 2,531 | 1,875* |
| Soybean Oil | 1,148 | 850 | Revised Lumber | 1,650 | 1,100 |
| Rough Rice | 1,283 | 950 | Goldman Sachs | 3,150 | 2,100 |
| T-Bonds | 2,700 | 2,000 | | | |
| Ten Year Notes | 1,755 | 1,300 | **IMM** | | |
| Municipal | 1,350 | 1,000 | Australian Dollar | 1,688 | 1,250 |
| Dow Jones | 5,000 | 4,000 | British Pound | 2,295 | 1,700 |
| $5 Mini DJ | 2,500 | 2,000 | Canadian Dollar | 1,350 | 1,000 |
| | | | Euro FX | 3,240 | 2,400 |
| **NYMEX** | | | E-Mini EuroFX | 1,620 | 1,200 |
| Lt Crude | 3,375 | 2,500 | Japanese Yen | 2,228 | 1,650 |
| Heating Oil | 3,375 | 2,500 | Mexican Peso | 1,875 | 1,500 |
| Unleaded Gas | 4,725 | 3,500* | Swiss Franc | 2,228 | 1,650 |
| Natural Gas | 4,725 | 3,500 | Eurodollars | 945 | 700 |
| Platinum | 2,160 | 1,600 | Euroyen (JY) | 10,125 | 7,500 |
| Palladium | 5,063 | 3,750 | S&P | 20,000 | 16,000 |
| | | | E-Mini S&P | 4,000 | 3,200 |
| **NYBOT** | | | Nasdaq | 18,750 | 15,000 |
| Coffee "C" | 1,680 | 1,200 | E-Mini Nasdaq | 3,750 | 3,000 |
| Sugar 11 | 840 | 600 | | | |
| Cocoa | 1,190 | 850 | **COMEX** | | |
| US Dollar Index | 1,729 | 1,300 | Gold | 2,025 | 1,500 |
| Orange Juice | 560 | 400* | Silver | 3,375 | 2,500 |
| Cotton | 2,240 | 1,600 | Copper-High Grade | 2,700 | 2,000 |
| CRB Index | 3,000 | 3,000 | | | |
| NYFE Index | 9,000 | 9,000 | | | |

Listing of margin requirements for futures contracts.

slogan, "If you can't beat em, join em." Growth of managed funds in futures has exploded in the last five years.

Instead of trying to compete *against* the pros, these investors are simply hiring a pro to trade *for* them. Although this does not guarantee a profit, most investors will fare much better over the long run having their funds managed professionally. Much of this will depend, of course, on the trader who is managing your money. There is more on this in the upcoming chapter on hiring brokers and money managers (see Chapter 15).

The other choice, of course, is to learn to sell options.

Some investors even may want to combine these two approaches and hire a professional money manager who *sells options* to trade their account. This, of course, is a choice you may want to consider down the road as well.

Regardless, selling options, whether done by yourself or by your money manager, automatically relieves you of many of the burdens and pitfalls that befall not only futures traders but also traders who buy options. Selling options can put you above the crowd at a point where you don't have to compete with the pros in the futures pits, at least not directly. Achieving substantial returns in the futures market, *consistently*, can become a reality without taking outrageous risks. The next two chapters will explain how option selling works and explore some key terms and features of selling options that may make it preferable to other strategies.

# 3
## CHAPTER

# Buying Options versus Selling Options

$W$hile this book is not meant to be a "how to" guide to market price forecasting or "101 option strategies you can use at home," we feel that a basic review of options and the differences between buying and selling may be helpful to novice readers exploring the subject for the first time.

We have attempted to present this information in a colorful, understandable manner instead of the dry, textbook-like descriptions found in many books about options. Our goal is to be able to have an average beginning investor be able to understand the concept of option writing well enough to use it profitably after reading this book for the first time.

For this reason, we have made a conscious effort to present the information in the format of metaphors and stories as often as possible in order for readers to be more able to comprehend what could be considered complex subject matter. Nonetheless, certain aspects of options and option selling demand some technical explanations and definitions. If you are already familiar with the basics of options and how they work, you may want to skip this chapter. However, if you are a beginner or only mildly experienced and want to brush up on the fundamentals of options, this chapter could be a helpful primer.

To that end, let's start from the beginning.

## WHAT IS AN OPTION?

The standard definition of an *option* is the right, but not the obligation, to buy or sell a particular stock or commodity at a specified price. A *call option* is the right to buy a stock

**TABLE  3.1**

Underlying Asset of One Option

| 1 Stock Option | 1 Futures Option |
|---|---|
| 100 shares of underlying stock | 1 contract of underlying commodity |

or commodity; a *put option* is the right to sell it. When buying or selling a put or a call option in stocks, one call or put is the right to buy or sell 100 shares of that particular stock. In the case of futures, one option is the right to buy or sell 1 contract for that particular commodity (see Table 3.1).

## BUYING OPTIONS

Before we can begin exploring the concept of *selling* or *writing* an option, it will be useful to discuss the subject of buying options because this is the strategy with which most option traders are more than likely familiar. The subject of *buying* an option, as well as some key definitions regarding option trading, will be illustrated in the following example.

We are using the Standard & Poor's (S&P) futures contract in both examples in this chapter because it is a market to which both stock and futures traders can relate. However, this is the general concept of how any buying or selling of options can be performed in either individual stocks or any commodities markets.

### Example: Buying a Call Option on S&P 500 Futures

What is buying an option? What does it entail? What are the potential rewards and risks? This example hopefully will answer these questions in detail.

If, in February, you buy a call option on the S&P 500 at a 1250 *strike price* for the month of June, you have the right (or *option*) to buy one contract of the June S&P 500 at the price of 1250 at any time during the life of the option. You may exercise this right at any time you choose, before expiration in June. Since this is a June option, this means that your right to buy the S&P 500 contract at this price will cease, or *expire*, in June. If this were a July option, your right to purchase a futures contract on the S&P 500 would end in July. The exact date this option expires will vary depending on the stock or commodity you are trading. Therefore, if you want to exercise this right to buy the S&P 500 at 1250, you will have to do it before your time runs out (see Figure 3.1).

The right or option to purchase an S&P 500 contract at 1250 has a value to it. In other words, the call option you are purchasing has a value in and of itself, regardless

**F I G U R E   3.1**

June 2004 S&P 500 Price Chart Showing Strike Price

SPM4 - S&P 500-Day Pit, Jun 04, Daily

of the price of the S&P 500. If June S&P 500 futures currently are trading at 1200, your right (or option) to purchase a June S&P 500 contract at 1250 would be worth more than it would be if the June S&P 500 were trading only at 1100.

But who would want to buy a June S&P 500 futures contract at 1250 if the market price were only 1100? Nobody. However, a person who thought the S&P 500 were going to move to 1300 by June very well might want to purchase the right to buy it at 1250, especially when he can purchase this right for a fraction of the cost it would run him to buy the futures contract itself. In addition, he can avoid the risk of the S&P 500 decreasing in price and losing a large amount on his futures trade. The only funds he would have at risk would be the price, or *premium,* he paid for his option. If the price of the S&P 500 does not reach 1250 by the time the option expires in June, it will expire worthless, and the trade is over.

**T A B L E   3.2**

Calculating Target Profit on a Long Option

| | |
|---|---:|
| Current price of June S&P 500 futures contract | 1,300 |
| Strike price of Mary's option | −   1,250 |
| | 50 |
| (Every 1-point move in S&P 500 futures contract is worth $250) | ×  $    250 |
| Gross profit | $12,500 |

Let's review this concept in another example. Trader Mary just read an article about the U.S. economy that was very bullish on the U.S. stock market. The fundamental outlook for equities looks very promising. There is, however, one point of concern. At the time that Mary is considering the trade, the Federal Reserve (Fed) could be getting ready to raise interest rates. This may or may not take place. However, if it does, there is a chance that the S&P 500 could fall substantially.

Mary is eager to position herself to take advantage of the situation if the S&P 500 soars, as she is expecting. However, the risk of an adverse move to the downside has her concerned enough that she does not want to purchase the futures contract outright. She instead sees that she can purchase a June 1250 call option for the small price of $2,000. Since the June S&P 500 contract currently is trading at 1150 and it is only March, Mary sees this as a good bet, considering that she feels that the price could go as high as 1300. If it does, Mary can exercise her option, buy a contract for the June S&P 500 at 1250, and then immediately sell it at 1300, netting herself a gross profit of $12,500. This is calculated in Table 3.2.

Of course, Mary will have to subtract the premium she paid for her option plus transaction costs to give her the net profit, calculated in Table 3.3.

If the June S&P 500 contract does not reach 1250 or even falls substantially, the most Mary can lose is the $2,000 she invested to purchase the call option.

**T A B L E   3.3**

Calculating Net Profit on a Long Option

| | |
|---|---:|
| Gross profit | $12,500 |
| Premium paid to purchase option | −   2,000 |
| Commission plus transaction fees | −      79 |
| Net profit | $10,421 |

Are these the only two outcomes that Mary can experience? No. They are not. Let's say that three months go by. It is now April. Mary is lying in her hammock in the backyard and decides to check her option price. She sees the June S&P 500 has traded as high as 1161 and as low as 1086 but is back to hovering close to 1150 at the present time. Mary checks her option price and sees that it is now worth only $1,000. In other words, if she bought the exact same option today, it would cost her only half of what it did three months ago (see Figure 3.2).

But how can this be? The futures contract is trading at the exact same price that it was two months ago. However, the right to buy June S&P 500 futures will now expire in two months instead of four months. Therefore, the option has less time remaining and is worth less. This is known as *time value*. All other things being the same, time

## FIGURE 3.2

June 2004 S&P 500 Price Chart Showing Price Movement

SPM4 - S&P 500-Day Pit, Jun 04, Daily

value will always be slightly eroding the value of the option each day that passes. Hence, even if Mary is correct in her market analysis, time always will be her enemy as long as she is buying options.

How is this relevant? Isn't all that Mary cares about as an option buyer is if the June S&P 500 goes above 1250? No. It is not. This is the mistake many novice option traders make. Most options never get exercised. Much of the time, the option positions, even profitable ones, are offset simply by selling them back to the market. Why?

It is at this point that we must delve into a few more definitions. If Mary bought a call option on the June S&P 500 with a strike price of 1250 and the price of June S&P 500 futures is *under* 1250, then the option is said to be *out of the money*. If the price of the contract is *at* 1250, the option is said to be *at the money*. If the price of June S&P 500 is *over* 1250, the option is said to be *in the money* (see Figure 3.3).

## F I G U R E   3.3

June 2004 S&P 500 Price Chart Showing Options In and Out of the Money

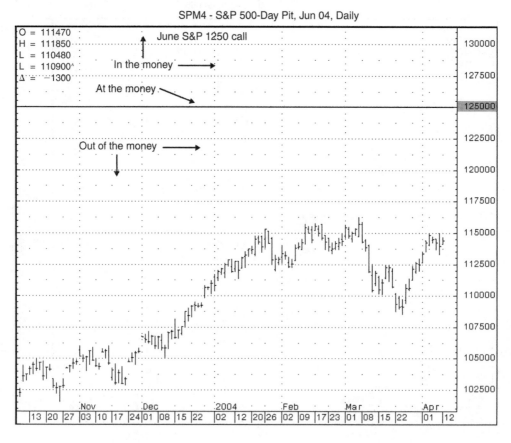

The value of an option is made up of time value, intrinsic value, and volatility. *Time value* has been discussed already. An option is said to have *intrinsic value* if it is *in the money*. In other words, if the strike price of the call is 1250, and the price of June S&P 500 is 1300, then the option is said to have 50 points of intrinsic value. If the option were exercised at this point and the futures position closed out immediately, it would yield a profit of $12,500. However, the option itself, in addition to its intrinsic value, also would have some *time value* remaining. The option itself would be worth more than $12,500. Therefore, selling the option back to the market would be worth more to the owner of the call than exercising it. The exception to this would be if the option is expiring and the owner of the call wishes to own the stock or commodity at the specified strike price.

For this reason, when somebody refers to trading options, they are generally referring to the buying and selling of the options themselves. They are actually speculating on the option prices and not on the underlying stock or commodity, although the price of the underlying stock or commodity will have a large bearing on the value of the option.

In the preceding example, since the June S&P 500 was trading at 1150 when Mary bought her 1250 call, Mary bought an out-of-the-money option with no intrinsic value. This is why Mary was able to purchase the option fairly inexpensively. Can Mary make money even if the option never goes in the money? Yes. If the price of the June S&P 500 begins to move toward 1250, the value of the option may start to increase. Although the option still has no intrinsic value, the chances of the option gaining intrinsic value begin to increase, thereby increasing the value of the option. If this value is increasing faster than time value is eroding the premium, the option may show a gain, even if it is out of the money.

In other words, if Mary bought her option for $2,000, and the June S&P 500 price moved higher immediately, but not in the money, the price of Mary's option still may increase to, say, $2,500. In this case, Mary could close the position out for a $500 profit without ever exercising her option.

Of course, to collect this gain, Mary will have to sell her option back to the market before the value drops again. If the price of the June S&P 500 has not moved above 1250 by the time the option expires, time value will have eroded all the option's value, and it will expire worthless. Mary will lose the premium she paid but nothing more.

The main drawback to Mary's position is this: Although she has absolute limited risk in that only the premium she paid can be lost, there is a high probability that she will indeed lose on the trade. The only way Mary can make money is if the futures contract makes a sharp and immediate move higher. Anything less, and time value eventually will decay the value of the option away to nothing.

In summation, the three factors that make up the value of an option are intrinsic value, time value, and volatility. If you are buying an option that is out of the money, it will have no intrinsic value. Only time and volatility will make up the price of that option.

The key advantages and disadvantages of *buying* an option are listed in Table 3.4.

## VOLATILITY: HOW IMPORTANT IS IT?

One of the three main factors affecting the value of an option, as we mentioned earlier, is volatility. Volatility measures how fast and how much the option value is moving in relation to the underlying stock or commodity. Generally, underlying markets that are making large moves to the upside or downside or are experiencing large or rapid daily price fluctuations will produce options with higher volatility and thus higher-priced options. Slowly moving or quiet markets generally will produce lower-valued options. Volatility is measured by a figure known as the option's *delta*.

Many books, seminars, and computer programs have been designed around calculating, analyzing, and capitalizing on the differences between an option's delta and volatility. Much time, effort, and money have been dedicated to designing complex mathematical formulas for trading volatility, deltas, and other Greek symbols such as gammas and

(*Continued on next page*)

**T A B L E   3.4**

Advantages and Disadvantages of Buying an Option

| Advantages | Disadvantages |
|---|---|
| Absolute limited risk | Time value always working against buyer |
| Potential for large gain | Market generally must make a large move for option buyer to profit |

## THE SELLING OF OPTIONS

Now that we are familiar with some general definitions regarding options and the strategy of buying options, we can make our first probe into the core subject of this book, which is *selling* options.

In keeping with the earlier example, let's say that trader Mary is still somewhat bullish on the June S&P 500. If she buys her 1250 call, the June S&P 500 will have to make a large move to the upside for Mary to have any hope of a profit. However, instead of buying a call, as in the preceding example, Mary decides instead to use the strategy of selling a put. But how can Mary sell this option when she doesn't own it?

The terms *buying* and *selling*, when used in relation to options, are really just terms used to describe which side of an option trade a trader is positioned. When a trader buys an option, he is buying the right to buy or sell a stock or commodity at a specified price. When a trader sells an option, he is selling the buyer that right and therefore assuming the obligation to take the other side of the market should the buyer of the option exercise the option. In other words, he "grants" the option buyer the right to buy or sell the underlying market at the specified price (strike price). This is why option selling is also known as option *granting* or option *writing*.

In options, there must be a buyer for every seller and a seller for every buyer. However, this does not mean that if you are holding an open option position, you must buy or sell your option back to the same individual who bought it from or sold it to you. You will never know who is on the other side of your trade. You simply will buy or sell the option back to the market to close your position.

Many new investors also make the mistake of believing that buying options is a bullish strategy and selling options is bearish. This is a mistake. Buying a call is for bulls. Buying a put is for bears. When selling options, the opposite is true. Selling a put is a bullish strategy. Selling a call is a bearish strategy. Table 3.5 illustrates this concept.

Let's go back to our example. Mary decides that she will use a put selling strategy to take advantage of the bullish fundamentals she sees for the S&P 500. At the time of her trade, June S&P 500 futures are trading at 1150. Rather than buy the futures contract outright, or buy the call, Mary decides that she will sell a put option. She looks at the option quotes and sees that a June 800 put option on the S&P 500 is currently at a premium of $700. She calls her broker and places an order to sell one. This is called selling the put *naked,* and it means that she is not selling it in conjunction with other options or the futures contract itself but rather is simply selling it by itself. *Covered* and *spread* strategies will be discussed later. However, we feel that it is important to understand the naked option write before exploring more complex strategies.

What happens to Mary's account when she sells the option? Her account is credited immediately with the $700 premium because somebody on the other side

**T A B L E   3.5**

Bullish and Bearish Option Strategies

| Bullish Strategy | Bearish Strategy |
| --- | --- |
| Buying a call | Buying a put |
| Selling a put | Selling a call |

vegas that take other measurements of option volatility. While it is not our intention to downplay the importance of option volatility, we believe that these studies are responsible for much of the confusion and intimidation of option trading. The study of volatility has become so complex that it is all but impractical for use by average individual investors.

Contrary to what the industry will have you believe, you do not need a complex computer program to trade options effectively. Just remember this general rule of thumb pertaining to volatility, and you should be fine: If volatility is high, conditions may favor option sellers because they can get more premium for the options they want to sell. If volatility is low, it may favor option buyers because they have to pay less to purchase their options.

This does not mean that we recommend selling options with high deltas. We generally recommend selling options with low deltas in slightly volatile markets. This allows one to sell very far out-of-the-money

(*Continued on next page*)

strikes with little chance of going in the money. Therefore, the delta is not low because the market is not moving. The delta is low because the option is so far out of the money.

How does one know if volatility is high or low? The number crunchers out there may cringe, but how about simply looking at a price chart of the underlying market? If the market has been making rapid, sporadic moves, chances are that the volatility is high in the options. If the market is moving slowly or in a fairly defined price range, chances are that volatility is low.

For those who prefer a more scientific approach, there are many Web sites and software that measure the volatility of options. Your broker should be able to give you the volatility of an option as well.

In our opinion, if you can use a little knowledge and a lot of common sense simply to pick a price level where the market will not go, volatility becomes less important. We are not, however, suggesting that you disregard option volatility

(Continued on next page)

of the market just bought the June 800 put option and paid Mary $700 for the right to sell the June S&P 500 futures at 800. This means that Mary has committed herself to buy one contract of June S&P 500 futures at 800 should the buyer of this option decide to exercise it. Most likely the only way the buyer of the option will want to exercise this option *would be* if the price of the June S&P 500 fell below 800 (see Figure 3.4).

In order to hold this position, Mary will have to put up a margin deposit. This is the same concept used to trade futures contracts, except margin requirements to hold short options generally are much less than they are to hold the outright contract. Margin is discussed in detail in Chapter 4.

If the price of the June S&P 500 is anywhere above 800 and is still there at option expiration, the option will expire worthless, and Mary will keep the $700 premium as her profit. Thus $700 is the most Mary can make. She gives up her chance to make a large gain on a big move upward in the futures market. However, she increases her chances dramatically to make a profit on the trade. At a current price of 1150, the price of the June S&P 500 can move up, remain the same, or even fall as much as 350 points, and Mary will still make the same profit on the trade.

But what is Mary's exposure? Mary's risk is that the June S&P 500 falls below 800 and remains there through option expiration. At that point, Mary would be assigned one contract of the June S&P 500, long from 800. She could choose to liquidate the position immediately and accept whatever loss it would entail, or if she liked being long the S&P 500 from 800, she simply could hold the position. Therefore, Mary's risk is that she will have to buy the June S&P 500 futures at 800. In the remote possibility that this would take place and Mary elected to remain in her position that long, she would need some additional capital to purchase the S&P 500 contract. Regardless, the $700 premium remains Mary's to keep.

While having the option exercised is not the desired outcome for this trade, one can see that selling a put option carries no more risk, and in this example, less risk, than buying the futures outright.

By selling the option, however, Mary's other risk is that the value of her option could increase during the life of the option, thus increasing her margin requirement to remain in the trade. Mary could elect to exit the trade (buy the option back) for the going market price and take a loss, or she could put up the additional margin and hold the position. This is why Mary wants to select an option with a low delta. In other words, Mary wants to sell an option that is far enough out of the money and with low enough volatility that the market can move a long way without greatly affecting the price or margin requirement of her option. Therefore, a market move that is large enough to stop out a futures trader may mean only a minor price adjustment to Mary's put option.

Nonetheless, it is this potential for increased margin requirements that often scares traders away from selling options. Yet losses in a futures position, and thus margin requirements, can both accumulate much more quickly than in a short option. Remember, you're selling options because you want to stay away from the market's up and down whipsaw moves. Done correctly, selling options should be a very slow-moving investment.

Of course, Mary does not have to hold this option through expiration if she does not want to. As in the option buying example presented previously, the value of the option can move up or down during its life depending on time value, intrinsic value, and volatility. Mary may elect to liquidate her position at any time prior to expiration simply by buying back her option at the market price for the corresponding profit or loss. Remember, since Mary is a seller of the option, *time value* is now working *for* her because it is eroding the value of the option each day. Mary wants this option to erode away to nothing and expire worthless.

There are several very effective techniques for managing risk in short options, and these will be discussed in Chapter 9. For now, the point is that most option selling trades done with the methods proposed

completely. Options with historically low volatility often can be an indicator that prices in the underlying futures contract are very calm or trading in a narrow range. However, it also can be an indicator that a market is ready to break out of trading range and make a sizable move in one direction. It therefore may not be a good idea to sell options with very low historical volatilities.

This, however, is about as detailed as we feel we need to get about volatility. While many technicians spend an inordinate amount of time studying the most minute details and comparisons between volatilities of options, we are going to go against the grain and tell you right here and now that it is probably not necessary for you to do this in order to sell options effectively. We are not encouraging you to ignore volatility. We are only stating that it does not have to be a primary focus in deciding where to trade. Just because an option has high volatility does not mean that it is a good option to sell. And just because an option has low volatility does not mean that it is a poor option to sell.

## F I G U R E   3.4

June 2004 S&P 500 Price Chart Showing 800 Put Option

in this book will, hopefully, not require you to employ one. The most important part of your risk management is selling the right options in the first place.

While there are many more intricacies to selling options that will be discussed in the following chapters, the preceding example illustrates the basic concept of the approach.

Making $700 on a trade may not sound very exciting at this point. But read on. What if you could sell groups of options, over and over, consistently having them expire in your favor while having a reliable risk management plan in place to limit your downside on the few that move against you? What if you could sell these options at very low margin requirements—sometimes as low as the premiums collected?

As we discussed in Chapter 1, it is estimated that 75 to 85 percent of all options held through expiration expire worthless. Again, consider those percentages. Option sellers make money when options expire worthless, and option buyers lose money when options expire worthless. Now, setting aside all other pros and cons of option selling for now, if your goal in a particular trade is simply to make a profit, not hit a "home run" but to make a profit, wouldn't this be a good way to go into a trade, any trade, in any market, with this statistic behind you? Before you do a lick of research or pick any entry or exit points, you know that if you stick with your trade, you'll have a 75 to 85 percent chance of profiting?

This figure gets even more exciting when you consider the extra wrinkle of leverage that applies to selling options on futures contracts.

Although there are no doubt countless financial planners and brokers reading this book who are most likely jumping up and down, screaming about risk and misleading statistics at this point, we intend to show them the error of their ways. The concept of selling time premium has been used by professional and commercial traders since the inception of derivatives. It has been only recently that the individual investment community has started catching on. Unless you love to gamble, buying options is a losing proposition.

In addition to the statistics, a seller of options generally doesn't have to pick market direction and generally doesn't have to decide where to take profits. He avoids two of the hardest decisions in investing.

We once asked a potential client why he decided on selling option premium as a means of investing. "Because I'm not a very good trader," he said, "and option selling is the only way I can make any money in the market."

Indeed.

# SPAN Margin: The Key to High Returns

While many investors who have traded commodities in the past may be familiar with the concept of margin, traders who have been limited thus far to buying equities may not. To understand selling options, it is essential that an investor have at least a basic understanding of margin and how it is used in selling option premium. Margin requirements are one of the key differences between stock and futures options.

When one purchases an option, one simply pays the premium and owns the option. When one sells an option, one collects that premium, but one now holds the open position with potential liability. For this reason, the seller of a put or call is required to put up some collateral to hold the position. This collateral is not a cost. It is simply a "deposit" made with funds from one's trading account and is known as *margin*.

For example, trader Mary from Chapter 3 sells a soybean put option and collects a premium of $400. She is now short the soybean put. However, in order to hold this position, she must put up some margin money. In this case, the margin requirement for this particular option is $820. This simply means that Mary must provide an $820 margin deposit to hold this position.

But where does this money go? Who holds the deposit? Mary does! The money never comes out of her account. Instead, it is set aside in escrow, meaning that

> It is important that one not confuse this type of margin with the concept of *buying on margin* in stocks. In the latter, an investor borrows money from the brokerage in order to purchase more shares of stock. Futures margin is a completely different application of the word *margin* and has nothing to do with borrowing any money.

**TABLE   4.1**

Calculating Margin

| | |
|---|---|
| Total margin requirement | $820 |
| Minus premium collected | − $400 |
| Total out of pocket margin | $420 |

she cannot use it to participate in other trades. However, it remains in her account. Therefore, $820 is set aside in escrow in Mary's account to hold this position. However, didn't Mary just collect $400 from selling the option?

Yes she did.

Mary can apply this $400 she collected to cover part of her margin requirement. This leaves her with only $420 that she must cover from her own funds. This is illustrated in Table 4.1.

Assuming that Mary started with a $10,000 account, Table 4.2 shows what Mary's account would look like after she sold the option.

This example does not include transaction costs, which, of course, would be subtracted from the bottom line. However, it illustrates the general idea.

The *available balance* is the amount Mary has available to invest in other positions. In futures trading, this is also known as *margin excess,* because buying and selling futures contracts also operates on the margin principle.

The amount in escrow is the margin requirement that Mary posted to hold the trade.

The *total equity* is the value of Mary's account if her option expires worthless and Mary keeps the premium collected as profit. At that time, she would have her $420 margin deposit back along with the $400 premium (profit) as part of her available balance.

**TABLE   4.2**

Mary's Account Balance

| | |
|---|---|
| Beginning balance | $10,000 |
| Add premium collected | + $     400 |
| Minus margin requirement | − $     820 |
| *Available balance* in Mary's account | $ 9,580 |
| Amount in *escrow* in Mary's account | + $     820 |
| *Total equity* in Mary's account | $10,400 |

**TABLE  4.3**

Return on Capital Invested

| | |
|---|---|
| Profit from selling option | $400 |
|     divided by | |
| Out-of-pocket funds "invested" for margin | $420 |
|     equals | 0.952 = 95.2% return |

This example of margin requirement is not unrealistic for futures options. In doing the math, one can see that selling the option can provide a very attractive return on funds invested.

If the option expires worthless, Mary's return on capital invested would be as shown in Table 4.3.

One also must consider that the life of the average option trade that we would recommend is about three to four months. Assuming that Mary were to do this successfully two more times, it would give her a 285.6 percent annual return on her original $400 investment. As long as soybeans did not crash during this time, this could be realistic. However, this example makes some assumptions and does not take into account other factors, such as risk parameters, increased volatility, early profit taking, and other considerations that will be discussed in upcoming chapters. It also does not take into account the possibility that the margin requirement could fluctuate, which it can and does do. This will be discussed later in this chapter. The point is that while some under-educated investors see option selling as "slow and boring," the preceding numbers illustrate why many enlightened investors are now flocking to option writing as their strategy of choice.

## THE EVER-FLUCTUATING MARGIN

After a trader understands the concept of margin, the next key factor that he must understand is the fact that the margin requirement for the trade is changing and being readjusted constantly, literally on a daily basis.

It is here that we must first discuss how margin requirements are calculated and who sets margin requirements. Formulas for calculating margins generally are set by the exchanges and left to brokerages to implement for their clients.

Margins for stock options and futures options are calculated very differently, and this is a key difference between the two that investors should consider. Stock option margin is calculated by a rigid formula and generally can be performed by any individual investor. If you sell a naked put or call on a stock, your margin requirement will be 20 percent of the value of the stock plus the premium collected from the option

**T A B L E   4.4**

Margin Requirement for Stock Option

|  |  |
|---|---|
| $1,000 | (20% of the value of 100 shares of XYZ stock) |
| − $ 400 | (the amount by which the option is out of the money) |
| + $ 300 | (the premium of the option) |
| $ 900 | (*total margin requirement* for selling the option) |

minus the amount by which the option is out of the money. The formula is illustrated in the following paragraph in example format.

Trader Mary is bearish on XYZ stock. However, since Mary does not want to tie up the capital necessary to short the stock, nor does she think that the stock will fall drastically, she believes that her best alternative is to sell a call. With XYZ stock currently trading at $50 a share, Mary decides to sell a March $54 call for $300. Her margin requirement is calculated in Table 4.4.

As in futures, the premium collected can be applied to meet part of the margin requirement for Mary's option (see Table 4.5).

Margins on futures options are determined quite differently. Futures margins are determined by a formula know as Standard Portfolio Analysis of Risk (SPAN). The SPAN margin is mysterious to many brokers, and we have never met anyone who could explain exactly how it is calculated. SPAN is a formula set by the exchanges and is based on the time value left on the option, the amount by which the option is in or out of the money, and the volatility of the underlying contract. Most clearing firms have advanced software that calculates SPAN margin for every option. However, attempting to explain the exact calculations for how it is determined, we feel, would be fruitless.

Suffice it to say that to find out the margin requirement for a futures option before entering the position, we would recommend calling your broker. Most brokers and brokerages that are option-selling friendly will be able to provide you with this at your request. After a few months of selling options, you should be able to estimate the approximate margin of selling options in the futures contracts with which you are

**T A B L E   4.5**

Out-of-Pocket Margin Requirement for Stock Option

|  |  |
|---|---|
| $900 | (total margin requirement) |
| − $300 | (premium collected) |
| $600 | (Mary's total out-of-pocket margin requirement) |

familiar. Of course, you will be able to see the exact figure on your statement once your position is established.

However, for those do-it-yourselfers out there, the Chicago Mercantile Exchange (CME) does provide a version of the SPAN software for individuals to use. The cost at this time is about $500, and the reviews we've heard are mixed. However, if you would like to obtain a copy of the software you can contact the CME or visit its Web site at www.cme.com.

There are still some brokerages that, for whatever reason, do not use SPAN margin and instead charge the full margin requirement for a futures contract to sell an option on that contract. These are generally non-option-selling-friendly firms, and we would suggest finding a broker who is more up to date in approach. The days of large broker-age houses treating their clients like ignorant children are over. SPAN margin has allowed individual investors to obtain a much higher return on invested capital than if they had to provide a full futures contract margin to sell an option. Don't sell option premium in futures without it!

Now that initial margin requirement has been discussed, a seller of options must be keenly aware that his margin requirement can fluctuate. In stocks, the formula remains the same throughout the life of the option. As the price of the stock fluctuates up or down, the figures in the formula obviously will change.

For instance, in the preceding example, let's assume that after Mary sold her $54 call, the price of XYZ stock increased to $52. Mary's margin requirement on the next day is illustrated in Table 4.6.

In this scenario, an additional $250 would be moved from Mary's available funds into her escrow account. This assumes, of course, that Mary wishes to remain in the position.

What if XYZ stock suddenly made a large jump and was now trading at $60 per share? Mary's margin requirement would increase substantially because her option is now in the money. Her new margin requirement would look like Table 4.7.

### T A B L E  4.6

Margin Requirement after Price Increase in Underlying Stock

|  |  |
|---|---|
| $1,040 | (20% of the value of 100 shares of XYZ) |
| − $ 200 | (amount by which the option is out of the money) |
| + $ 500 | (premium of the option, assuming that the option increased $100 in value as a result of the stock moving higher) |
| $1,340 | (Mary's new total margin requirement) |
| − $ 400 | (premium collected) |
| $ 940 | (Mary's new out-of-pocket margin requirement) |

**TABLE 4.7**

Margin Requirement after Option Moves in the Money

|  |  |
|---|---|
| $1,200 | (20% of the value of 100 shares of XYZ) |
| − $     0 | (amount by which the option is out of the money) |
| + $1,150 | (premium of the option, assuming that the option increased $850 in value as a result of the stock moving higher.) |
| $2,350 | (Mary's new total margin requirement) |
| − $  400 | (premium collected) |
| $1,950 | (Mary's new out-of-pocket margin requirement) |

This is, of course, an extreme example used to demonstrate premium fluctuations. Calculations such as this are used by non-option sellers to dissuade potential option sellers from employing the strategy. It ignores the fact that Mary could have exited this position at any time and, as an intelligent trader, would have done so long before the price moved this far.

Margin requirement for selling a futures option works differently. Your margin requirement will be based on the size and volatility of the underlying contract, the distance the option is out of the money, and the amount of time left on the option. All these factors figure into the SPAN margin requirement. The following example illustrates margin with futures options.

Trader Mary is bullish on crude oil. She knows the market can make sharp swings downward, however, and therefore decides that instead of buying the futures contract, she can sell a put several dollars below the market. Mary calls her broker and asks the SPAN margin requirement for selling a September $24 crude oil put option. Her broker calls her back a few minutes later and tells her that the total margin requirement is $1,400. With September crude oil trading at $30 a barrel, Mary sells a $24 September put for $600. Her out-of-pocket margin requirement is calculated in Table 4.8.

As in the example above in stock options, the margin on Mary's crude oil put can change as well. The same factors that affect the value of the option can affect its margin

**TABLE 4.8**

Crude Oil Margin Calculation

|  |  |
|---|---|
| $1,400 | (total initial margin requirement) |
| − $  600 | (premium collected) |
| $  800 | (Mary's out-of-pocket margin requirement to sell the put) |

requirement. For example, if after Mary sells the option September crude oil futures drop to $28, chances are that Mary's margin requirement will increase. How much cannot be calculated precisely because other factors, such as time value and volatility, will come into the SPAN calculation. The *delta* of the option comes into play here when measuring volatility. However, most individual investors do not have the time or the willingness to sit around and calculate how the delta of the option will affect their margin requirement on their option should it move one way or the other. Suffice it to say that the margin requirement will correlate loosely with the value of the option. If the value of the option increases by $100, chances are that the margin requirement will increase by an amount close to $100. It is for this reason that traders selling option premium should keep a certain amount of backup capital in their accounts to be prepared for these margin fluctuations. We generally recommend that new or conservative traders keep up to 50 percent of their account available as backup capital.

The exception to this rule would be if the exchange decides to raise minimum margin requirements for the underlying contract itself. In this case, the margin to hold the option would increase by a corresponding percentage. In other words, if the exchange raised margin requirements for crude oil futures by 10 percent, the margin requirement for Mary's option also would increase by 10 percent.

The flip side of this is that when the option deteriorates in value, as a result of either a favorable market move or time deterioration, the margin requirement for that option decreases as well. When this happens, these margin funds are released from escrow and into Mary's available funds for use in other trades. A trader's escrow and available funds balance are updated on a daily basis to reflect the daily changes in margin requirements. In other words, *if the value of the option is deteriorating, the trader does not necessarily have to wait until expiration to use the premium he collected from the option sale.* It gradually becomes available to him as the option deteriorates. This is one feature that futures option traders in particular find very attractive in increasing their leverage in accumulating positions.

## DIFFERENCES BETWEEN STOCK OPTIONS AND FUTURES OPTIONS

As you may have already deduced, there are some key differences between stock and futures options, especially when one is exploring the strategy of selling options. While stock option trading can offer excellent returns for patient investors, returns from selling futures options can dwarf their counterparts in stocks, assuming that the trader is willing to assume a bit more risk. However, if you are reading this book, it is probably safe to assume that your investment tendencies tend to lean to the aggressive side, at least for a certain portion of your portfolio.

This increased risk does not come from increased volatility in commodity prices. (Studies have shown that, historically, stock prices are actually more volatile than commodity prices.) It is the *leverage* of futures trading that provides the potential for larger profits and losses. A trader who knows how to control and take advantage of this lever-age while remaining respectful of it can reap handsome rewards. Selling futures options, if it is done correctly and not recklessly, is simply taking a very conservative approach to a very aggressive investment.

Although this book is about teaching traders how to sell futures options, it is also about showing *stock* option traders a new, potentially more potent venue for expanding their option investments. Nonetheless, the key advantages and disadvantages of both types of options are explored in the following paragraphs.

## ADVANTAGES OF SELLING FUTURES OPTIONS VERSUS STOCK OPTIONS

One advantage is that because of the differences in the ways that margin requirements are calculated for stock options and futures options, margins for selling options in futures generally are much lower than the premium collected in equity options. For instance, to sell an option worth $200 in stocks can require a margin deposit of up to $1,200 to $1,400 or more depending on the factors mentioned in our margin discussion. Assuming that this is the case, this would equate to a 14 to 17 percent return on capital invested. Not bad.

However, selling a $200 option in futures often can entail a margin requirement of only $200 to $400—a 50 to 100 percent return on capital invested. This difference can be more exaggerated in higher-valued options, which we recommend generally.

Another advantage is higher premiums for distant strikes. Because of the leverage available in futures, attractive premiums can be collected for options with far-out-of-the-money strikes. While some more distant premiums are available in certain volatile stocks, most options in equities must be sold within one to three strike prices of the actual underlying stock to receive any premium at all. In futures trading, attractive pre-miums of $400, $500, $600, or more can be collected at strike prices far, far out of the money.

In some markets with more volatile natures, options sometimes can be sold at strike prices that are double or even triple the price of the underlying contract. For instance, a stock trading at $70 may require a bearish trader to sell a call option with a strike price of $72, $74, or $76 to receive any type of premium. While a seller of calls in a market such as coffee, with coffee prices at 70 cents, may be able to sell calls with strikes of $1.40 to $2.00 or more and still receive very attractive premiums. Think about this for a moment. Coffee prices would have to increase by 100 to 200 percent within the life of that option for it to ever go in the money. This strategy can be very lucrative for traders willing to assume the risk of potential increases in margin in the meantime.*

---

*Traders should employ this approach only in markets in which they have a very bearish fundamental outlook. Although this does not guarantee profits, simply picking far-out-of-the-money options to sell because of high volatility and/or premiums is not a good strategy on which to build a portfolio.

The third advantage is liquidity. While there are many hundreds of stocks where options may be available for active trading, there are only about 50 to 60 futures contracts with an active option market. This provides a more concentrated market for options in futures. Therefore, the typical futures contract is likely to have much more liquidity in its option market than most stocks. While some futures contracts have higher option open interest than others, most of the major contracts, such as financials, sugar, grains, crude oil, etc., have substantial volume and open interest offering several hundred or even several thousand open contracts per strike price. Larger financial contracts such as the Eurodollar or S&P 500 have monstrous open interest, making it very quick and easy to trade in and out of these options and meaning that traders have to do very little in the way of "working" the order.

## ADVANTAGES TO SELLING STOCK OPTIONS VERSUS FUTURES OPTIONS

With larger profits come larger risks. Leverage is a double-edged sword, and while gains can be much higher in selling futures options, so can losses. A trader selling a 45 put on XYZ stock trading at 50 risks that he may have to buy the stock at $5 less than its current price. A trader selling a $4.50 call on wheat trading at $5 takes the same risk that he may have to buy a contract of wheat at $4.50. However, the value of his option and his margin requirement can increase substantially more in an adverse move in the underlying commodity.

In addition, if each option gets exercised and the market keeps on falling, the risk becomes more pronounced. The stock option seller is long XYZ stock from 45. If the stock falls to 40, he's out $500 (minus the premium he originally collected). The futures trader is long wheat from $4.50. If the market falls to $4.00, he is out $2,500 (minus premium). These examples really only illustrate the differences in leverage between stock and futures trading. They do make the assumption that neither trader simply decides to buy back his option when the market moves against him. In later chapters we'll show you how to all but ensure that your options are never exercised.

With roughly 80 percent of options expiring worthless, selling premium can be a profitable experience in stocks or commodities. If you have only traded stock options in the past, we would highly recommend that you consider the benefits of employing the same strategy in futures. We are not bashing equity options. Quite the contrary. Many investors have achieved substantial returns with a properly managed option selling approach in equities. Our point is to make equity traders aware that there is another vehicle with similar (in some cases, more desirable) properties that is available for diversification. Gaining substantially higher leverage can carry an increased risk in some situations but at the same time provide for substantially higher returns in an option portfolio.

# PART II

# OPTION SELLING STRATEGY AND RISK CONTROL

# 5
## CHAPTER

# Strike Price and Time Selection

Now that we know that the odds decisively favor an option seller on any given trade, we must go about the process of deciding which options to sell. While a trader theoretically could begin selling options at random and statistically still have 75 to 80 percent chance of his options expiring worthless, this figure does not take into account positions that may move steeply against the seller during the life of the trade, nor does it take into account how the other 20 percent may end up. Selling options randomly may result in about 80 percent winners, but one or two in the 20 percent of losers could end up with substantial losses. This is why a trading plan is important when selling options.

By employing the strategies discussed in this chapter, traders not only can potentially increase the percentages of their options expiring worthless, but they also can better their odds that their winners do not move sharply against them in the meantime. Proper option selection also can help traders to feel confident that their losses on non-winning trades are smaller and easier to control.

The goal of selecting the right market, the right strike price, and the right month should be to pick options that will provide a smooth, steady ride to zero at option expiration without the dramatics in the meantime. A properly managed option writing portfolio should allow its owner to sleep well at night, should be low maintenance, and should be predominantly absent of heart-pounding, gut-wrenching decisions.

Many new traders erroneously believe that this can only be accomplished through writing covered spreads. This is not true. While writing naked options may sound outrageously aggressive and even frightening to some, if it is done correctly, one should be able to sleep very well at night.

A successful option seller has no need to sit in front of a screen all day. In fact, many successful sellers of premium with whom we have worked may only check option prices once a day, once a week, or even once or twice a month. If you are trading options completely on your own, checking your positions daily is probably a good idea. If you are working with somebody you trust to monitor your positions, you may not need to check as often.

## THE INSURANCE COMPANY

It has been said often that selling options is similar to operating an insurance company. Buyers of car insurance pay insurance premiums to an insurance company to insure their vehicles. They pay these premiums month after month. In most cases, the driver never has an accident, and the insurance company keeps the premiums as profit. If a driver does happen to have an accident, the insurance company must pay up.

An insurance company tries to weed out drivers that it deems to be prone to accidents. Some of these may get insured at higher premiums (to account for the higher risk the insurance company is taking on them), and some may not get insured at all.

Your job as an option seller is to go through this exact same process. Just as most drivers do not have accidents, most of your options will never go in the money. However, as in insurance, a few bad accidents can be bad for the bottom line. An insurance company, therefore, tries to reduce the chances that one of its drivers will have an accident by checking a number of factors such as driving record, age of the driver, type of car, etc. As an option seller, you will go through this exact same process except instead of drivers, you will be studying a market's "driving record," historical tendencies, current and future fundamentals, etc. While an insurance company can in no way guarantee that the drivers it selects will not have accidents, it certainly can help its business by selecting only drivers who have what it considers a low chance of being in an accident. Thus it can lower its risk and increase its profitability. You can too.

## A SUGGESTED APPROACH

We are about to outline a strategy to follow in selling options in the futures market. In doing this, we are by no means suggesting that this is the only way to sell options successfully. There are as many option strategies around as there are traders. We are merely suggesting this approach for the fact that it is the one that has performed most consistently for us and our clients over the years based on a combined 30+ years of futures and option trading experience. In that time, we have managed, either in personal or client accounts, to employ just about every kind of option strategy you can imagine. Through it all, there was a single strategy that emerged that, although not without risk, showed over and over again that it can profit consistently in a variety of markets. Therefore, we are not going to discuss the many ways a trader can sell options. We are going to skip all the fancy delta-neutral, standard deviation, backward triple butterfly spread discussions in this chapter and concentrate on a single strategy that we believe the average individual investor can understand and begin implementing almost immediately. While we are going to review recommended option spread strategies in Chapter 7, this strategy will be all you need to get started in selling options effectively.

Based on experience and a desire for simplicity and steady and *consistent* profits, we are going to recommend a method of *naked option selling* as an initial strategy to learn. Before you jump in alarm at the thought of being "exposed" to the market holding naked short options, relax. Just because you sell it naked does not mean that you have to *hold* it naked. Although this can be a very productive approach, we also will be discussing how more conservative traders can turn their naked option sale into a covered position in Chapter 9. But we will treat a covered position as a risk-control method and discuss it at length under that heading. This chapter is about the selection and selling of the right options, regardless of whether they are naked or covered.

Again, this is not to be taken as the Holy Grail of option trading. It is not. It is simply an approach that has worked very well for both of us over the years and, if employed correctly, hopefully can work well for you. The strategy has a very high probability of success and carries no more risk than trading futures contracts. If managed correctly, many of the risks can be effectively minimized.

In a nutshell, this simple strategy is outlined as follows:

1. Select markets with very clear long-term bearish or bullish fundamentals. While it is preferable that the market also will be in a long-term trend reflecting these fundamentals, it is not absolutely necessary to be a successful option seller.
2. Sell options with two to six months of time value in favor of these fundamentals at distant strike prices.
3. Set a risk parameter on each option that you sell and sit back and wait.

It sounds very simple, and it is. This is one of the primary benefits. However, simple does not mean easy. There are a number of factors to study and consider to give yourself the greatest odds of success. These will be the basis for this chapter.

## STEP 1: FUNDAMENTALS: THE KEY TO CHOOSING THE RIGHT MARKET

In beginning your search for the best options to write for your portfolio, you must begin to familiarize yourself with the key fundamentals that affect each market or at least the markets in which you wish to trade. Technical traders may argue this point, but consider the logic. As we've already discussed, technical factors can and do move the market on a short-term basis. However, long-term and sustained price movements are caused by the underlying base fundamentals of a particular commodity. And while technical indicators may reflect these fundamentals, they do not determine the ultimate direction of the market.

Often, technical moves will occur in outright contradiction to the long-term fundamentals. This is why fundamental traders historically have had a hard time trying to trade the market, at least on a short-term basis. How many traders ultimately are right about the market and still lose money? Many. It's part of the allure of futures trading. The fictitious interview that follows reflects the frustration of many futures traders. Although this brief interview reflects no particular conversation, we've heard it hundreds of times with potential clients, and it always has the same basic theme.

*Trader John:* I knew the market was heading higher. We all knew it was going higher. There was . . . [crop damage, a supply shortage, an impending war, etc.], and I felt pretty confident that the price was going up.

*Broker:* So what did you do, John?

*Trader John:* I bought. I bought . . . [add number] contracts of . . . [soybeans, orange juice, crude oil, etc.].

*Broker:* What happened?

*Trader John:* The market went up, way up!

*Broker:* And?

*Trader John:* I lost. I lost a little money. [In reality, John probably lost a lot of money. But we'll let him off the hook here.]

*Broker:* Why?

*Trader John:* Because the market went down and stopped me out first. Then it went up.

So they got John's money and his soybeans (or whatever commodity he was trading). Who got John's money? Most likely either professional or commercial traders. They probably were watching the same fundamentals and technicals as John and were either better at timing it or had the resources to ride out the short-term move against their position. They ultimately have more resources available to them than John. They do this for a living, all day long, every day. John may be very good at what he does and may be very intelligent and very dedicated to his trading. It doesn't matter. When push comes to shove, John stands little chance trading from his computer in his spare bedroom with the few spare hours he has each week. Even if John is retired and has all the time and money in the world, unless he is willing to dedicate his entire life to trading, spend years and countless dollars and resources on becoming a professional trader, his chances of success against these heavyweights over the long term are very slim.

But what if John could level the playing field? What if, instead of beating them, John joined them? John could give up trying to duke it out with the pros in the futures pit and take a big step out of the chaos and into a favorite strategy of the very traders with whom he was competing. While we are not saying that professional traders never buy options and always sell options, it is our contention that it is the small speculator who will tend to hold simple long or short call options in order to try to profit from some future move. Pros and commercials often do hold long option positions, but this is often part of a larger combination of option and/or futures positions or some sort of hedging situation. Very few pros or commercials will try to capitalize on a move simply by buying calls or puts. The odds are too low.

We believe that markets can and do move somewhat randomly *on a short-term basis*. However, as an option seller, longer-term fundamental trading is almost custom-fit for your approach. This is why you will sell two to six months out. Selling with this much time value on your options will allow you to sell at strike prices far enough out of the money that your position may not be greatly affected by short term aberrations in a market.

If John had used this approach, he probably wouldn't have made as much money as he would have if he had captured the whole move in a futures position (Who does?). But he would have made money, probably good money, based on his initial insight. The short-term move down would not have stopped him out, nor would it have scared him out of his position if proper risk management rules were followed.

Let's look at Figures 5.1 and 5.2. Figure 5.1 shows a right market analysis and a wrong trading method. Figure 5.2 shows that John sells a put(s) and profits from being right.

John learned to stop trying to outguess what the market is going to do over the short term. Nobody can do this consistently, not even the pros. It is just too difficult. As stated earlier, markets can move at random over the short term. There are too many variables that can sway daily prices, such as media reports, fund deciding accumulation or liquidation on a given day, and just the general mood of traders on a given day or week.

The option seller is freed from these short-term concerns and can focus wholly on the bigger picture of supply, demand, and long-term price trends. In other words, such an investor can focus on the fundamentals.

But what are fundamentals, and how does one track them? *Fundamentals* are the overall factors of supply and demand that affect the price of a given commodity. If you want to learn what moves the price of soybeans will make, learn where they are grown. Learn when their growing seasons are. Learn who the largest producers are so that you can pay attention to their crops and supply situations and not be distracted by media reports from smaller producers. Learn what countries import these commodities and how much they use. Focus on key importers and overall world numbers.

Again, we do feel that technical trading has its place in option trading and do use technical indicators extensively in the *timing* of option trades. But the timing of a trade is more of an optimizing tool and not as important in option selling. The important part is selecting the right market to trade in in the first place and this often can be done through knowing the fundamentals.

Technical traders, however, can use options very effectively in their approach as well. The same selection process and risk parameters can be used just as easily, and

## FIGURE  5.1

June 2004 Crude Oil Chart Showing Buy and Stop Out Points

CLM4 - Crude Light-Pit, Jun 04, Daily

John buys futures and gets stopped out.

option sales can be substituted for futures contracts to provide a more conservative approach with a much larger margin for error. Some markets have so many different fundamentals that change so quickly that a trader may want to give longer-term technicals a bit more weight. Markets such as currencies and interest-rate futures are two examples of markets where knowing the fundamentals may be less of an advantage than in a commodity such as wheat or natural gas.

For those wishing to study the fundamentals, however, the first step is to know where to look for the right information. How does one acquire the facts and figures that combine to form the big picture of fundamental knowledge? A good place to start is the United States Department of Agriculture (USDA) Web site, which is the largest source

## FIGURE 5.2

### June 2004 Crude Oil Chart Showing Sale of $28 Puts

CLM4 - Crude Light-Pit, Jun 04, Daily

In March, John sells $28 puts for $400 each for less margin than he would have deposited for a futures contract. The market may move lower short term and then proceed higher. John remains in the market, and the options eventually expire, providing John with a good profit.

of information for agricultural commodities. Take some time to explore www.usda.gov. The Department of Energy (DOE) is another good place to mine data for energy traders, and its Web site is www.doe.gov. The exchanges also offer a wealth of fundamental information. Their Web sites can be found in the Resources section at the end of this book. News services such as Reuters, Bloomberg, and Oster Dow Jones offer subscription-based financial news that includes daily updated fundamental information.

Good brokers can be a tremendous benefit to investors in the area of providing timely and relevant market fundamentals. While it is always a good idea to have some basic understanding of the market in which you are trading, good brokers should spend their time researching these data and mining this information *for* you. Knowledgeable brokers should be able to guide you in determining which fundamental data are relevant to the market and how they could affect price and condense all the information for you in a short summary and/or a few basic charts for your review. Especially good brokers will not only save you a great deal of time but may be able to make a recommendation based on these data that actually will make you some money.

If your goal is to be a successful self-directed seller of option premium, we would recommend finding a broker with extensive knowledge in the fundamentals of the markets in which you wish to trade. This will save you countless hours of research and years of study and can make your option selling decisions much easier.

However, good brokers are not necessarily good traders, and vice versa. If you can find a broker who is both, you'd better hang on to him. He's a keeper!

While this chapter is primarily about selling options based on the fundamentals of physical commodities, this strategy can be employed with equal effectiveness in financial and index futures, although technical factors may take on a bit more importance in these markets. Since the fundamentals in futures contracts such as the S&P 500 and Japanese yen often can change very rapidly, we have found that the physical commodities lend themselves much better to a long-term fundamental approach. These include such commodity contracts as corn, soybeans, coffee, sugar, cotton, crude oil, natural gas, and copper, among others.

We have devoted Chapter 11 exclusively to the basic fundamentals of commodities and have designed it to serve as a primer for you in becoming familiar with some of the general facts you should know and follow in regard to each.

In the meantime, the lesson is: In picking options to sell, select the market in which you are going to trade first and make sure you are somewhat familiar with the long-term (bullish or bearish) fundamentals of that market. If a friend or relative asks why you are in that market, you should be able to give a two- to three-sentence summary that explains your rationale for being in the trade (not that it is any of their business).

While selling options in any market gives you favorable odds, selecting the right markets in which to sell premium can boost your odds and your returns substantially. If you can select favorable markets in which to write your premiums, you're already halfway there.

## STEP 2: GIVE SEASONAL TENDENCIES THEIR DUE

One of the more misused tools in futures trading is the seasonal chart. Seasonal tendencies, or *seasonals* for short, use historical records to graph the tendency for certain markets to move in certain directions at certain times of the year. While these tendencies are often very reliable, their exact timing and magnitude of movement are an inexact science at best. Seasonal tendencies are mostly the result of certain fundamentals that take place in a particular market during a given time of year (e.g., harvest and planting cycles, inventory accumulation periods, etc.).

Many traders who first encounter seasonals believe that they have discovered the Holy Grail of futures trading. However, trying to trade on seasonals alone can be very hazardous to your financial health. Seasonals and how to use them effectively will be explored in more detail in Chapter 12.

For now, make a note to be aware of the seasonal tendencies of a market in which you are considering selling options. Know the fundamentals behind the seasonal tendency, and analyze how they could affect prices of that commodity *this* year. While most traders do not know how to use seasonals correctly, you are going to learn how. You also will learn how option selling combined with seasonal tendencies can be a very effective strategy.

Seasonals can be powerful tools in your arsenal of option selling weapons.

## STEP 3: WRITE OUT OF THE MONEY—*FAR* OUT OF THE MONEY

Once you have formed your basic fundamental conviction in a particular market, it's time to start looking at strike prices. As we mentioned earlier, one of the main knocks on option selling is the unlimited risk factor. If you are selling at the money or close to the money options, this risk is much closer and is much more immediate than it is if your strikes are considerably farther away from where the market is trading.

Many option traders are tempted to sell only options with less than 30 days left until expiration. They do this because, all other things being equal, an option will show its maximum time deterioration within the last 30 days of its working life. While many option sellers swear by this approach, the downside is that to collect any worthwhile premium, the trader must sell at strike prices perilously close to the money. What does this mean? It means that even a small market "hiccup" can put the option in the money and either force the trader out of his position or, worse yet, subject him to ever-increasing losses.

As long-term fundamental traders who want to make money *and* sleep at night, this is *exactly* what we are trying to avoid.

Instead, the trader can sell options far out of the money and collect the same premium. The tradeoff? The trader must sell options with moderately more time value than her quick-trade counterpart. However, if she is competent in her analysis of the market, she can use this to her advantage. This allows the market plenty of room to move and allows the trader plenty of room to be wrong—and still make money. In essence, such a trader can overcome the short-term plays and technical moves against her long-term view of the market. Such a trader forces the market to make a long-term, sustained move against its core fundamentals in order to make her a loser.

In addition to employing this "distanced" view of the market, this approach has built-in benefits from a risk standpoint. Let's assume that our trader's long-term fundamental analysis of the market is wrong. She still stands a good chance of making money. Remember, the market does not have to move in the direction that most favors the trader. It can move sideways or even against the trader for a while, and the option can still expire worthless if the market does not reach her strike. The trader only has to pick where it *won't* go, not where it's going.

## STEP 4: DON'T RULE OUT MARKETS THAT HAVE ALREADY MADE BIG RUNS, HIGHER OR LOWER

Many traders will find a market with very clear fundamentals and become excited about the trade until they look at a chart. They see that the market has already had a sharp run or drop in price and think that the move is over or that prices are now "too high" or "too low." This can be a mistake, and you could be overlooking some of the best opportunities on the board.

First of all, if the market has made a large move up or down, there is probably a very good fundamental reason behind it. Find out what it is. Is it something that is permanent and cannot be changed in the near future (e.g., crop damage), or is it something that had an effect on the market but is either in the process of changing or could change quickly without notice (e.g., a temporary "halt" to imports or exports due to a trade spat).

Second, did the market make this move in a rapid, violent explosion or collapse, or did it achieve its current price level as a result of a steady, continuing trend? If it's a trend, your odds grow better already because, as we discussed earlier, options expire worthless at an even higher percentage rate when sold in favor of the trend. These can be fertile grounds for sellers of options.

If the market just made a sharp move in either direction, conditions in the market are probably very volatile. The upside to this is that the market volatility can drive option premiums outrageously high and often make them extremely overpriced. This can be a very lucrative time for option sellers. The downside is that the market will remain vulnerable to additional volatile moves in either direction, meaning that even your far out-of-the-money option could be affected to a large degree by short-term price moves. Decisions on whether to trade these markets will depend on your temperament. If you are a very conservative trader, it's probably best to stay out and leave it to the crowd with a slightly larger appetite for risk.

This is only an observation, but it has been our experience that markets that make large moves to the upside tend to correct or move back lower more decisively and over a shorter period of time than markets that crash lower trying to recover. It may have something to do with the fact that small specs prefer to be long. However, it also brings to mind an observation made by Dr. Alexander Elder in his classic work, *Trading for a Living.*

Dr. Elder compares slow and rapid market declines to a man falling down and his ability to get back up. If he simply falls down a flight of stairs, he usually can pick himself up and brush himself off and continue on with minimal effort. However, if a man falls out of a third-story window, it can take him considerably more time to recover. Dr. Elder contends that the markets behave in a similar manner. Thus bargain hunters that rush in to buy a commodity or stock after a rapid decline may be in for a disappointment, unless they are truly long-term investors. Markets fall that rapidly for a reason. Unless that reason has changed immediately, don't expect markets that have just collapsed to rebound just as rapidly.

*Conclusion*   Markets making new highs may not be the most desirable opportunities to sell call options. Markets in decline often can be better and/or safer opportunities in which to sell calls. Again, we stress the advantages of knowing the fundamentals in addition to the technical indicators that you may be seeing on a chart. A bearish technical trader who experiences a sudden rally in the market may see danger and be frightened out of his position. A bearish trader who knows the fundamentals and experiences a sudden rally in prices sees opportunity.

However, if you are somewhat familiar with your fundamentals and have done some basic historical price studies (or your broker has), you probably can tell the strikes that are more at risk and the strikes that are downright ridiculous. These "ridiculous" strike prices are the target of the astute seller of premium.

In this, we are talking about selling options against the existing fundamentals. Why? Because you may deduce that the fundamentals are bullish (or bearish) to the market but not *that* bullish (or bearish). In other words, the fundamentals are very bullish or bearish, but now those factors may be already priced into the market. When the media or the public picks up a story and runs with it, prices often get overblown. In this sole exception to trading with the fundamentals, options should be sold sparingly and only when the trader feels that the market has gotten entirely carried away.

Small specs, whipped into a frenzy by either the market's move and/or media reports will rush to buy all the calls (or puts) they can afford, regardless of strike price or premium. If you can keep your head in this chaos, you often can sit back and "pick off" these absurdly out-of-the-money premiums and profit very handsomely when conditions calm down, usually in a few days to a few weeks, with very little risk to your position.

However, these, unfortunately, are also the types of markets that give option selling a black eye. In the event that you are wrong, losses can accrue very quickly in your account. Therefore, it pays to exercise a few risk control measures that can help you to avoid a big drawdown.

1. Allocate only a small portion of your portfolio to trades such as these. While these are often the highest probability trades on the board, the consequences of being wrong can be more severe. If your regular position size is 10 option contracts, maybe only take 3 to 5 of these types of trades.

2. This is the one instance where you may use technical indicators to look for signs of tops or bottoms. In a rapid move higher or lower, look for signs that the market momentum is slowing. For instance, in a market that has been racing higher rapidly for days and then opens higher and closes substantially off the highs or even lower on the day, this can be a key signal that the market is reaching a peak or at least slowing to a more manageable pace, often a good time to sell inflated calls (or puts) far beyond the point of exhaustion.

## Selling the "Ridiculous" Option

In the summer of 2003, the media was playing up the "severe shortages" of natural gas in the marketplace. Alan Greenspan, commenting about his concerns about shortages of the commodity, added more fuel to the fire. Small specs rushed into the market and bought call options (their favorite gambling method of choice) to try to strike it rich.

Unfortunately, by the time the media had caught on to the story, the market had long since priced in the lower supplies. While long-term fundamentals still favored the bulls, the media sensation of shortages whipped fortune seekers into a frenzy. By the time Greenspan made his comments, the market had already peaked and proceeded to drift sideways to lower for the rest of the summer. Figures 5.3 and 5.4 illustrate how a trader could have taken advantage of the speculator buying frenzy by selling outrageously priced call options.

In short, know your fundamentals. A good rule of thumb to follow is to fade the media and, more important, fade public opinion. In other words, do the opposite. If you're watching a report on the evening news about shortages in coffee, don't be one of the gold chasers who calls their broker the next day to buy coffee. Chances are that it's already priced in. If your fundamental analysis brings you to the conclusion that the market could continue to move higher, sell the puts and allow for sharp corrections (when the specs get stopped out). The more conservative investor can wait for the corrections and then sell puts. If the market looks like it may be overdone and there are "ridiculous" call strikes available, sell those calls. Selling premium in volatile markets is an aggressive strategy, and you may be in for a little more "fluctuation" in your option values in the short term, especially if you're a few days early in your position entry. However, it will be a whole lot less fluctuation than if you shorted the futures and were wrong in the short term.

Remember the preceding example. If you thought that natural gas was overdone and faded the public by shorting the futures at 5 and you were early and the market went to 7, you would be smarting pretty badly and maybe even stopped out. If you're short from 15, it doesn't hurt nearly as bad.

**F I G U R E   5.3**

October 2003 Natural Gas Chart

NGV03 - Natural Gas-Pit, Oct 03, Daily

At the height of the natural gas spec buying frenzy in June of 2003, call options with strikes as high as three times the current value of natural gas were selling for premiums of $400 or more. Traders willing to sell options to this bull-happy crowd could have sold October $15 call options for premiums of $400. This is what we mean by "ridiculous" price levels.

## STEP 5: OPTION OPEN INTEREST AS A CLUE TO MARKET DIRECTION

Using open interest to gauge public sentiment can be an extremely valuable tool to option sellers looking to fade the public. The excerpt on page 67 was a weekly article written by James Cordier in May 2003 on this exact subject. In reading it again, we felt it would cover this subject exceptionally well in its unaltered form.

**F I G U R E   5.4**

October 2003 Natural Gas Chart Showing $15 Strike Price

NGV03 - Natural Gas-Pit, Oct 03, Daily

In hindsight, James's analysis proved correct as silver drifted through the summer of 2003. Checking open interest in a particular stock or commodity is another tool to use in your overall analysis of potential options to sell.

## STEP 6: SELL AHEAD OF THE "SWEET SPOT" CURVE

Almost anyone even remotely familiar with options has seen the curve in Figure 5.5 illustrating the speed at which options deteriorate.

Many option traders look at the chart in this figure and deduce that the fastest deterioration is in the final 30 days and therefore that it is best to sell options with only

# OPEN INTEREST CAN BE TIP OFF TO OPINIONS OF GENERAL PUBLIC

James Cordier, *Liberty Trading Group*
May 30, 2003

More often than not, the general public will be on the wrong side of the market, as is evidenced by the oft-sighted figure that 80 to 90 percent of futures traders lose money. Since the general public often favors buying options, one key indicator of where the public is positioned often can be determined by studying option open interest.

Begin by looking at open interest in both puts and calls of each particular market. If there is a discernible discrepancy between the number of open contracts in puts versus calls or vice versa, there is a good chance that the public is favoring one side of the market. A good rule of thumb—if given the choice—is to fade the public. For instance, if the open interest in puts in a particular commodity is 50 percent greater than the open interest in calls, and most of the traders holding long options are small speculators (the general public), then there is a good indication that the public favors the short side of the market. Funds and commercials would have sold the puts to the small traders. All other factors being equal, you may want to consider selling puts in this situation. The reverse would be true if open interest in calls was decidedly greater than puts.

A perfect example of this phenomenon is taking place in the silver market at this time. Look at the open interest in silver options, puts versus calls. Open interest in silver puts as of yesterday stood at 8,546. Open interest in calls totaled 52,677. Call open interest is over six times put open interest. One can deduce from this figure that the public likes the long side of silver. The reasons for this are open to interpretation, but I'd be willing to guess that there are more than a handful of hopeful futures traders out there willing to put up some hard-earned capital to bet on a sweeping silver rally this summer. And who might be selling these options to them? Probably professional traders and commercial silver players (and maybe a handful of sophisticated individual investors).

The caveat: These are my own personal rules, opinions, and general observations. This is not to insinuate that the public always will be on the wrong side of the market, nor is it to suggest that this can be used as a trading system in and of itself. Nothing replaces solid fundamental and technical analysis. This is one of many factors one can consider when selecting options to write. Option buyers, who often are the small speculators in the market, are trading the futures market hoping for big moves and big gains. This is why most small specs that trade are attracted to commodities—for the spectacular. The problem is that these large-scale moves that can produce profits for option buyers generally are few and far between.

It is my contention that the smart money in this business profits from the mundane. If we're lucky, 80 to 90 percent of futures traders will continue to disagree.

www.libertytradinggroup.com

**FIGURE   5.5**

Time Decay Graph

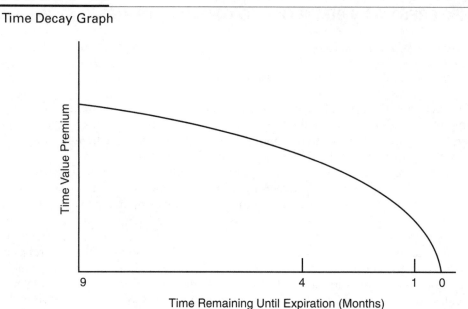

Time Remaining Until Expiration (Months)

30 days remaining until expiration. While this is one theory that works well for some traders, you'd better be pretty good at picking short-term market direction if you hope to make money consistently with this approach.

The alternative is to sell options with more than 90 days remaining. Sell ahead of the curve. Why? One reason, as we suggested earlier, is that the additional time value allows you the luxury of selling at strikes very far out of the money. The second reason is that if the market can avoid a sharp move against you in the first few weeks of your trade, you enter the last 90 days of the option's life at a much more distant strike than the seller who has waited until now to sell his option. In other words, he has to sell closer-to-the-money strikes to receive the same premiums that you received 30 to 60 days earlier. As the premiums begin to drop, your risk begins to drop as well.

A good way to gauge where your options could be in 30, 60, or 90 days is to look at option prices for several months, side by side. This is a limited tool because it does not account for market movement. But given a relatively stable market where the option seller is familiar with the fundamentals, it can be very effective in selecting proper strikes (see Figure 5.6).

If you are considering a certain strike and want to get a rough idea of what your option will be worth in 30 days (barring more than a moderate price move), simply look at the same strike price that is set to expire one month sooner. For instance, in Figure 5.6, if you are considering selling the August gold 4.00 call, look at the July gold

**F I G U R E   5.6**

Gold Option Table Showing Differences between Prices

| GC UndPr | JUN4 CALLS 3849✓ | | JUN4 PUTS 3849✓ | | JUL4 CALLS 3859✓ | | JUL4 PUTS 3859✓ | | AUG4 CALLS 3859✓ | | AUG4 PUTS 3859✓ | |
|---|---|---|---|---|---|---|---|---|---|---|---|---|
| DTE | 4 | | 4 | | 34 | | 34 | | 67 | | 67 | |
| EXP | 05/25/04 | | 05/25/04 | | 06/24/04 | | 06/24/04 | | 07/27/04 | | 07/27/04 | |
| VOL | 22.07 | | 22.08 | | 19.81 | | 19.81 | | 18.10 | | 18.10 | |
| IVS | 0.00 | | 0.00 | | 0.00 | | 0.00 | | 0.00 | | 0.00 | |
| IR | 1.45 | | 1.45 | | 1.65 | | 1.65 | | 1.80 | | 1.80 | |
| 310 | 7490✓ | +640 | 10✓ | 0 | ........ | | ........ | | 7590✓ | +640 | 10✓ | 0 |
| 315 | 6990✓ | +640 | 10✓ | 0 | | | | | ........ | | ........ | |
| 320 | 6490✓ | +640 | 10✓ | 0 | | | | | 6590✓ | +640 | 10✓ | 0 |
| 325 | 5990✓ | +640 | 10✓ | 0 | | | | | ........ | | ........ | |
| 330 | 5490✓ | +640 | 10✓ | 0 | | | | | 5640✓ | +630 | 60✓ | -10 |
| 335 | 4990✓ | +640 | 10✓ | 0 | | | | | ........ | | ........ | |
| 340 | 4490✓ | +640 | 10✓ | 0 | | | | | 4670✓ | +620 | 90✓ | -30 |
| 345 | 3990✓ | +640 | 10✓ | 0 | 4150✓ | +620 | 60✓ | -20 | 4210✓ | +600 | 130✓ | -40 |
| 350 | 3490✓ | +640 | 10✓ | 0 | 3670✓ | +610 | 80✓ | -30 | 3750✓ | +540 | 170✓ | -100 |
| 355 | 2990✓ | +640 | 10✓ | 0 | 3230✓ | +600 | 140✓ | -40 | 3310✓ | +530 | 240✓ | -90 |
| 360 | 2490✓ | +620 | 10✓ | -10 | 2770✓ | +580 | 190✓ | -60 | 2900✓ | +530 | 320✓ | -110 |
| 365 | 1990✓ | +610 | 10✓ | -20 | 2300✓ | +520 | 210✓ | -120 | 2510✓ | +530 | 430✓ | -110 |
| 370 | 1500✓ | +560 | 10✓ | -80 | 1900✓ | +440 | 320✓ | -190 | 2150✓ | +490 | 560✓ | -160 |
| 375 | 1040✓ | +470 | 50✓ | -180 | 1550✓ | +420 | 460✓ | -230 | 1780✓ | +400 | 700✓ | -230 |
| 380 | 640✓ | +330 | 160✓ | -300 | 1240✓ | +360 | 650✓ | -280 | 1490✓ | +360 | 900✓ | -280 |
| 385 | 350✓ | +200 | 360✓ | -440 | 970✓ | +280 | 880✓ | -350 | 1230✓ | +300 | 1140✓ | -340 |
| 390 | 170✓ | +100 | 680✓ | -540 | 760✓ | +230 | 1170✓ | -410 | 1020✓ | +250 | 1430✓ | -380 |
| 395 | 70✓ | +20 | 1080✓ | -620 | 560✓ | +150 | 1470✓ | -480 | 850✓ | +220 | 1750✓ | -420 |
| 400 | 30✓ | 0 | 1540✓ | -640 | (460✓) | +150 | 1870✓ | -490 | (700✓) | +160 | 2100✓ | -480 |
| 405 | 10✓ | 0 | 2020✓ | -630 | 360✓ | +120 | 2260✓ | -520 | 570✓ | +150 | 2480✓ | -480 |
| 410 | 10✓ | 0 | 2510✓ | -640 | 230✓ | +80 | 2640✓ | -560 | 470✓ | +130 | 2870✓ | -510 |
| 415 | 10✓ | 0 | 3010✓ | -640 | 210✓ | +70 | 3120✓ | -560 | 390✓ | +120 | 3280✓ | -530 |
| 420 | 10✓ | 0 | 3510✓ | -640 | 150✓ | +40 | 3560✓ | -590 | 320✓ | +100 | 3710✓ | -550 |
| 425 | 10✓ | 0 | 4010✓ | -640 | 120✓ | +40 | 4030✓ | -590 | 260✓ | +80 | 4150✓ | -570 |
| 430 | 10✓ | 0 | 4510✓ | -640 | 100✓ | +40 | 4500✓ | -610 | 210✓ | +60 | 4610✓ | -570 |
| 435 | 10✓ | 0 | 5010✓ | -640 | ........ | | ........ | | 170✓ | +50 | 5070✓ | -580 |
| 440 | 10✓ | 0 | 5510✓ | -640 | ........ | | ........ | | 140✓ | +40 | 5540✓ | -590 |
| 445 | 10✓ | 0 | 6010✓ | -640 | ........ | | ........ | | 120✓ | +40 | 6010✓ | -600 |
| 450 | 10✓ | 0 | 6510✓ | -640 | 40✓ | +10 | 6440✓ | -630 | 100✓ | +30 | 6490✓ | -610 |
| 455 | 10✓ | 0 | 7010✓ | -640 | ........ | | ........ | | 80✓ | +20 | 6970✓ | -620 |
| 460 | 10✓ | 0 | 7510✓ | -640 | ........ | | ........ | | 70✓ | +20 | 7460✓ | -620 |
| 465 | 10✓ | 0 | 8010✓ | -640 | ........ | | ........ | | 60✓ | +20 | 7950✓ | -620 |

4.00 call and see what the difference in premium is. In this example the difference is $240. Your option is likely to lose that much in *time value* over the next 30 days (although it could gain or lose more value through market movement or volatility fluctuation). If you are comfortable with that level of deterioration, you could have the right month and strike.

We do say *rough* or *approximate* because although different contract months tend to hover around the same general price levels, they will trade most often at different prices to reflect the market's expectations for the future. These differences in price can be more apparent in some agricultural commodities that are subject to planting and harvest cycles than futures contracts such as financials or currencies. If the differences in months are too great, simply adjust your comparison to a strike that is approximately the same distance out of the money.

## STEP 7: STRIKE A BALANCE BETWEEN PREMIUM AND RISK

A most popular question that many novice option writers have is what type of premiums they should seek when writing puts or calls. This is often a matter of individual preference, but we may be able to offer some suggestions.

The first factor to consider is premium collected versus margin requirement. An option selling at a $400 premium with a $600 margin requirement is a better sale than an option selling at $500 with an $800 margin requirement (as a return on capital invested). It has been our experience with SPAN margin that although margin requirements decrease as premiums decrease, return on capital invested tends to decrease as well as premium decreases. Thus an option sold for a premium of $500 may have a better return as a percentage of capital invested than an option sold for $200. Again, this is not a rule set in stone; it is more of an observation from years of option selling. However, when considering different strike prices, it may be helpful to compare premiums of different options with their respective margin requirements.

Some traders seek options that may be so far out of the money that they may only be commanding premiums of $100 to $200 each. While these options often are far enough out of the money that they probably will not be greatly affected by short-term market fluctuations, one has to weigh the premium collected versus projected risk. For starters, the commission paid to your broker will come out of this relatively small premium. Second, instead of selling 5 options for $600 each, some traders may elect to sell 15 of the $200 options, thus collecting the same premium with a perceived "lower" risk. But is it lower risk? If your risk parameter is risking to double premium collected, the $200 option easily could double in value just as fast as the $600 option. Count in slippage on your exit order, and your loss on the cheaper options could exceed your loss on the more expensive $600 options (slippage on 15 options may be greater than slippage on 5).

Third, look at what you risk in a worse-case scenario, this being that both options go deep in the money and you, for whatever reason, did not get out beforehand. Even though the $200 options were originally a few strike prices further away, you sold three times more options to collect the same amount of premium. Chances are that with a deep in-the-money move, the 15 positions at a few strikes further out are going to be a greater liability than the 5 positions a few strikes closer.

The other end of the spectrum is a trader who sells options for high premiums at closer strikes. This trader runs the risk of selling too close and being stopped on a small move or, worse yet, have her option go in the money on a small move. A balance must be struck. There is no general rule here except that you want to try to make sure that the premium collected justifies the risk you are assuming. This holds true whether you are selling 1 option or 500.

Although we promised not to get too involved with Greek figures and equations, this is a good time to bring up the concept of *delta*. Delta is the amount by which the price of an option changes for every dollar move in the underlying contract. While we aren't going to focus on delta to a great degree in this book, the delta of the option you are considering can be a great help in deciding the right strike price for you. The delta will give you a good idea of how far the option price will move in relation to the underlying market.

For instance, if you look at the delta of an option and it reads 17, this means that for every one point the futures market moves, the option price will move 0.17 of a point. This sounds simple, but one must remember that the delta is constantly changing and readjusting with every tick in the market. Thus the closer the underlying comes to your strike price, the higher will be the delta.

It is our recommendation that you seek options with low to very low deltas when you are selling. They will have the lowest chance of ever going in the money. While this sounds like common sense, some will argue that by selling options with low delta's one will have to assume the greater risk of larger position sizes than if one were to sell fewer options with higher deltas. Maybe so, but we recommend it anyway. If you know your fundamentals and you can pick strikes that will not be reached, you'll have a higher percentage of your options expiring worthless, lower stress, and more consistency. With this type of winning percentage, you should be able to withstand the occasional oddball who exceeds your strike.

Option margin, delta, and size of position all come secondary to selecting the right market in which to sell. If you pick the right market, none of these things should matter in the end. However, all your picks will not be right, and these factors *can* matter in an adverse move.

Much of this is based on the preferences of the individual investor. We've always preferred to sell options with deltas lower than 20, with premiums in the $400 to $700 range, with net margin requirements of no more than two times the premium collected.

## STEP 8: STAGGERING

The option selling plan you have been reading about in this chapter is the plan we followed for our first several years in business as a brokerage. While we've since added different trading plans using short-term option selling and option selling spreads, the original trading plan is still in place in its original form for the most part. One of the complaints we've heard about this approach is that by selling premium two to six months out, the strategy was slow and boring. Many investors who allocate a portion of their portfolio to options on futures do so not only for the opportunity for more sizable returns but also so that they can have a fun, exciting, and active portion of their portfolio that they can get in and get their hands dirty, buying and selling and calling plays. Sorry, but if you like action, the trading plan in this chapter may not be for you, except for the part about the sizable returns.

Many traders have compared the mental stimulation of this trading plan with that of "watching paint dry" or "watching a chicken sit on eggs." They do this for about the first 90 days. Then they start to get it.

You see, the final part of option selection under this plan is a concept that we call "staggering." It works like this:

*Month 1:*  Sell one to two sets of options with expirations of two to six months away.

*Month 2:*  Sell one to two sets of options with expirations of two to six months away.

*Month 3:*  Sell one to two sets of options with expirations of two to six months away.

During the first two months, there is a good chance that many, if not all, of the options sold will have shown little movement. Although the trader still believes in the program, his attention starts to wondering about possible day trades in the market he saw on the news yesterday or thinking about taking a flyer on that hot stock he saw on TV yesterday.

But then a funny thing happens. At the end of the third month, the first set of options that the trader sold 90 days ago expires. Thirty days later, another set expires, and then another. The wait paid off. The eggs hatched!

Each month you continue to sell one to two sets of options—on average—depending on when opportunities are present in the market. The first 60 to 90 days may very well seem slow and boring—until you start having options expire once or twice per month. Then it's not so boring anymore. This is what we mean by *staggering.* It is positioning your portfolio to have approximately one or more sets of options expiring every month.

This is not to imply that every set of options that you sell are going to expire worthless. But this is an ideal to which you may want to aspire with regard to structuring your option selling portfolio. It seems to have immense popularity among many of the traders whom we have advised. Perhaps it is because of the regularity for which it strives. Regardless, from a psychological standpoint, it can be desirable to be able to look at your statement and see that you have options *scheduled* to expire at regular intervals in the future. This is true whether you are an income- or growth-oriented investor.

You have now learned how to go about selecting markets and strikes for selling options effectively. These options can be sold and held naked as described in this chapter, or they can be sold as "covered" or part of a spread. Unfortunately, spreads can be tricky and even detrimental to a trader's success if she does not know what she is doing. The next two chapters explain why some types of spread trading should be avoided and suggest some select spread strategies that can be practical for today's individual investor.

# 6

## CHAPTER

# Use and Abuse of Spreads

While thus far we have only discussed selling options naked, a trader wishing to sell options like a professional may want to consider spreading as an alternative strategy. But beware: Of all the hundreds of different option strategies available, there are only a handful that we've found to be practical for individual investors.

There are some brokers and authors in the industry who are not going to like what they read in this chapter. However, our mission is to write this book in a "no bull" type of manner. We are not going to say that something outright doesn't work or that a particular strategy does not have its merits. Given the right market situation, almost any strategy will work some of the time. Our intention is to share with you the observations we have made in working with hundreds of futures option traders over many years.

The observations in this chapter mean no disrespect to the very knowledgeable authors in the field of option spreads. There are hundreds of different strategies one can employ in option spread trading, and each has its own benefits and drawbacks. We are not judging these approaches. We are only reporting on our experiences after implementing many of these strategies on a broad scale across a wide selection of market situations.

The problem with trying to learn 101 different option spread strategies is that one first must learn each detailed strategy and its benefits, drawbacks, profit potential, and risk. As if this is not difficult enough, the investor then must learn in what situations he is supposed to use each strategy. It's not enough for the market to move up or down.

The reverse triple screaming phoenix spread works best in a market that begins to move higher, then moves slightly lower, drifts sideways for two to three weeks, makes a left at the Wendy's on the corner, and then soars into expiration, making new life of contract highs the day the option closes out. In this situation, the user of the reverse triple screaming phoenix spread would net $2,500 per spread. As you can see, it is the perfect type of spread for a market in this situation.

This is a fictitious example, of course, but it serves to demonstrate our frustration with the public's seemingly insatiable appetite to "learn" complex spread strategies that they could rarely hope to use effectively. Market intellectuals love to learn these strategies and how they work. However, our experience has been that a market intellectual does not necessarily make a good trader.

Many traders new to options believe that it is necessary to learn all these spread combinations before they can trade effectively. This is not the case. Again, our point is not that these complex option spread strategies do not have merit. However, if you are looking at inverted butterfly spreads and trying to determine the proper delta balance for your triple-ratio backspread, you'd better be a professional trader who wakes up to a quote screen every morning that looks like a Greek alphabet. At the very least, you should be a very serious trader who has a lot of time to dedicate to trading and a lot of money to lose in the "educational" phase of trading. Traders who use these approaches effectively generally are people who have made trading their life, who know exactly what they are doing, and generally have paid their dues through many years of losses in learning the proper situations in which to use these approaches effectively. Our experience has been that the transaction costs alone make many of these approaches impractical for the average individual investor.

If this is you, then good luck, and have at it. However, if this is not you (and chances are that if you are reading this book, it isn't you), then read on. We wrote this book for the people who just want to make money. You don't have to be on the Pro Bass tour to go out and have a good day fishing. You don't have to be a professional to make money selling options either.

Nevertheless, there are a few things you should know about spreading before tossing your line in the water.

## OPTION SPREADS: YOUR BROKER'S FAVORITE STRATEGY

You'll find that option spreading is approved of, if not outright encouraged, by many futures brokers, brokerages, and advisory services (who are sometimes affiliated with a certain brokerage or group of brokerages). Many brokerages love option spreading and often will recommend the strategy to their clients—especially in the case where the options are covered. Why?

For two reasons. First, unlike futures trading or even options selling, the advantages of buying options or incorporating option selling into a "covered" spread (net long the options) is that the position has absolute limited risk. Thus a brokerage can calculate the client's total loss in a worst-case scenario and will make sure that this figure does not exceed the total funds in the client's account. This avoids the risk of a debit balance for the client and, more important, the brokerage. This is not necessarily a bad thing for you. It can work against you, however. With each position having an absolute maximum loss, traders (sometimes encouraged by their brokers) may position all their funds into limited-risk spreads, leaving little or none as backup. Misled by the limited-risk aspect of spreads, this type of positioning shows terrible money-management technique that has the potential to wipe out an account.

Net long spreads can be especially popular among younger, untested brokers who do not have the know-how or the experience to trade futures contracts or especially sell options with a usable risk-management agenda for their clients. Employers of these inexperienced brokers will either encourage or require these brokers to recommend either buying straight options or buying covered spread positions. Of course, if a client gives an order otherwise, they must fill it. But clients of these brokers who rely on trade recommendations often will be "steered" into covered spreads or outright long option positions. This is one reason why it is important to know the broker with whom you are working and her experience in futures and option trading.

This certainly does not represent every firm in the industry, and these brokers are not bad people. However, new brokers have to start somewhere, and many firms willing to hire and train brand new brokers want them to start out with limited liability.

In this way, when clients lose money (which they almost invariably do if they use this type of approach over time), they can lose money "safely" (with no risk of debit liability to the firm).

The second but equally important reason that brokerages love to use covered spreads is this: *They generate a boatload of commissions for the firm.* Situations that often can be played effectively with a futures contract or a single call or put also can be played with an option spread. They are pitched to the client as a way to limit risk and increase leverage, which very well may be true. The fact that the spread may have little chance of profiting (especially after hefty commissions are deducted), however, is often downplayed.

In other words, instead of buying a single option (a strategy with which it is hard enough to turn a profit), a broker may suggest a multiple-option spread in which one or more options are sold in order to pay for one or more options that are purchased. Each spread can contain two to six options or more. Thus, instead of paying one commission, the client pays two to six commissions *per spread*. For a full-service brokerage charging $90 per round turn per option, this can run into some substantial fees. It can be expensive even with a discount broker charging only $30 per round turn. The fact that the "net" out-of-pocket cost, or margin, per spread may be less than simply positioning in an outright futures or long option is irrelevant. This "net" figure often will not include fees, and even if it does, commission costs versus potential profit can make the spread impractical and generally a poor choice of investment for the trader.

To counter this hefty commission charge, some brokers may tout a large potential profit on the trade. A $500 commission for a single spread may not sound so bad if the potential profit is $5,000. But look closely. In many cases it will take an enormous move in the futures price or require prices to end up in an extremely narrow range to obtain that *potential* profit.

This is not to suggest that every broker in the business is a money-hungry con artist. Quite the contrary, most brokers are good people who do not take advantage of their clients. As in every business, though, the brokerage industry has its bad apples.

This is also not to suggest that because a broker recommends a spread to you that he is trying to con you. In many cases an option spread can be a viable alternative and a legitimate strategy to employ in a particular situation. While we feel that some of these spreads often are impractical and not the best strategy for the investor in many cases, we cannot simply state that option spreading does not have its benefits. As you will see, we have devoted an entire chapter to option spreads that we *do* recommend to investors in some situations. We are simply suggesting that investors carefully consider the costs involved versus the potential for profit.

## TIPS FOR ANALYZING SPREAD TRADES

### Tip 1: Know the Difference between *Potential Profit* and Potential *for* Profit

Potential *for* profit is hugely different from *potential profit*. A big selling point of some spreads is their *potential profit*.

Consider the following example:

*Broker:* John, if the price of heating oil increases by 30 percent in the next 30 days, this spread will make $3,500!

*Trader John:* What does it cost to get in?

*Broker:* A mere $300, John! That's over a 1,100 percent return if you're right— excluding transaction costs, of course.

*Trader John:* What is my risk?

*Broker:* John, that's the best part! Your risk is *limited* to the $300 you put in— excluding transaction costs, of course.

*Trader John:* That sounds pretty good. I sure can't afford to lose much more. It sounds pretty safe.

*Broker:* So how many do you want?

Has the broker lied or broken any compliance rules? No, she hasn't. She properly disclosed risk. She focused the client's attention on *potential profit*. If the commodity increases by 30 percent in the next 30 days, John's potential profit will be 1,100 percent, excluding transaction costs. But what is the potential *for* profit? What is the likelihood of this type of move in the market? Probably pretty slim, just like John's chances of showing any kind of profit on his trade.

   *Moral:* Focus on potential *for* profit, not *potential profit*

   While the broker's approach in this example may be legal, it certainly feels a bit unethical. But the broker sold John what he wanted—limited risk. Most brokers won't come on this strong, but some will.

   Nonetheless, many brokers will try to please their clients by offering limited-risk types of trade recommendations in an attempt to appease the client's fear of losing.

   This brings us to an important point. It is said that fear and greed drive the market. While this may be true, if you feel either of these emotions too strongly in your trading, whether selling options or otherwise, you shouldn't be trading. Your emotions will undermine you, and you will lose.

   While nobody wants to lose money, there is a difference between not wanting to lose and being afraid to lose. If you are trading scared or afraid to lose, you have already lost. Fear is common in new traders and/or undercapitalized traders. This is why many of these traders are drawn to option buying or covered spreads. "I know my risk," they tell you. "My risk is limited."

   This is why investors are willing to put their money into a strategy such as buying an option that will expire close to 80 percent of the time. "Sure I lost all my money, but I limited my risk!"

   If you walk into a pit of combat, do you want to walk in looking like Woody Allen, shivering and jumping at every twitch of the market? Or do you want to walk in like Russell Crowe in *Gladiator*? Both have no desire to get slaughtered. Both may take measures to protect themselves. But one is not afraid to lose; the other is terrified. This very concept of fear, or lack of it, is what makes one more likely to achieve victory while almost ensuring the other of an early slaughter.

   The markets work the same way. This is why we are going to strongly recommend, right now, that you highlight the words in the heading that follows.

## Tip 2: Focus on *Managing* Risk, Not *Limiting* Risk

If you use an investment vehicle that has built-in limited risk, you give up a huge likelihood of chances for profit. For success in trading, protecting your investment capital is of utmost importance. If you are afraid of what will happen if you lose it, though, you shouldn't be trading. The market smells fear like a rabid pit bull.

   The investment classic, *Market Wizards*, by Jack Schwager, seems to put forth a recurring theme in trading or investing. Many consistently successful traders and investors don't think of trading in terms of how much money they are making or losing.

They think of it as playing a game. The money is a by-product of playing the game successfully. But they do not think of every trade in terms of making or losing money. This enables them to remain unemotional, objective, and patient in their trading approach. The primary goal is still to make money. It is the way they approach it in their minds that gives them an edge.

If safety is what you seek, put your money in a certificate of deposit (CD). If you are afraid to lose, you shouldn't be trading futures or options. However, if you can give up that fear and the need for absolute limited risk and instead focus on managing your risk, you will have already placed yourself above most small-spec traders in the market.

The industry caters to the greed and fear of small speculators, which is why buying options and long option spreads is so popular with this group.

We want to clarify this concept of securing absolute limited risk versus managing risk. We don't mean to suggest that a trader approach the market like a Wild West cowboy with guns ablaze in the air. A healthy respect for the market is essential. A great firefighter may not fear the fire he is fighting, but he certainly respects it. Our point is that if you fear the market so much that you must have absolute limited risk, the high price you pay for that luxury most likely will sabotage you in the long run.

Securing absolute limited risk primarily refers to buying options. Many traders (especially new traders) become enamored of the concept of limiting risk. They are somewhat familiar with the concept of risk in the futures market, but it is a somewhat vague and disturbing notion to them. Being able to participate in these alluring markets while absolutely limiting risk is very appealing. Buying calls or puts sounds awfully good to them.

Futures traders who use stops do not have absolute limited risk. Markets can trade through stops. Most of the time, however, the stop order will fill very close to the trader's requested price. These traders are managing risk. While this book is not about trading futures contracts themselves, it is our opinion that trading the outright contract gives a trader a better *potential for profit* than buying options.

If you understand the risks, understand the market and the underlying fundamentals driving it, understand what could move the market against you, and position yourself so that the market will have to make a long-term move before your losses become significant, it becomes much easier to manage your risk. You can give yourself a remote chance of losing on a trade and still entail unlimited risk.

## Tip 3: Don't Bet on Elvis

I read in the newspaper the other day that a London gambling house took a bet that Elvis Presley would be sighted riding down London's main thoroughfare on top of a famous racehorse that disappeared in 1973 on his way to Wimbledon. On his arrival, he would proceed to qualify for the men's singles tournament and face a famous English mobster who had disappeared in the mid-1980s (who also would have to qualify for the men's singles at Wimbledon) in the first round. The bookie took the bet for 10 cents. If these events did indeed occur within a certain time frame (DNA would have to confirm that it was really Elvis), the bet would pay the gambler US $2 million. The gambling house, in essence, had unlimited risk on the bet. Do you think the gambling house's dime was safe? What if the gambling house could cut its losses as soon as somebody saw Elvis riding in on the long-lost racehorse?

The gambling house had, for all practical purposes, unlimited risk on the bet. But it managed its risk exceptionally well.

The first way the gambling house managed its risk was by picking a bet that had overwhelming odds in the house's favor. It also managed its risk by giving itself leeway to "bail out" of the bet if it appeared as though the house might sustain a substantial loss.

The bettor, however, was able to limit his risk on the bet. His risk was limited to 10 cents.

Which one do you want to be?

We are not suggesting that the odds of selling options will be *this* much weighted in your favor. We are only illustrating the differences between limiting and managing risk.

There are option buyers and spreaders out there who are willing to bet on Elvis for the chance at big gains and limited risk. This concept can be magnified with the strategy of some option spreads. We suggest that before you position in any spread, try not to get caught up in the low investment requirement and potential profit in the trade. Look at the big picture and what your odds are of profiting from the trade at all. Don't fall into the greed and fear trap. Don't bet on Elvis.

In keeping with this theme, we tend to advise against positioning in spreads that leave the trader net long options (although these spreads can be more exciting for the action-seeking trader).

The next several pages highlight some of the most popular net long option spread strategies along with some observations of which you may want to be aware.

## SPREADS NOT GENERALLY RECOMMENDED FOR INDIVIDUAL INVESTORS

### The Bull Call Spread (Bear Put Spread)

The bull call spread (or bear put spread) is a broker favorite because it limits risk and increases leverage for the investor, as well as provides a double commission for what otherwise often could have been achieved (possibly more effectively) simply by buying a call.

Bull call spreads sound good on paper, but we have rarely seen them work in practical application. In our experience, your odds are better for profiting on a straight-up long put or call. Unless the market moves to a certain point above the highest strike on the spread and remains there through expiration, both options generally will expire worthless, resulting in a loss for the spread holder.

A bull call spread is illustrated in the following example: A trader bullish on crude oil at 33 decides to employ a bull call spread strategy to take advantage of what she believes will be higher prices. In December, she buys a $36 March crude oil call for 60 points ($600). She then sells a March $37 call for 30 points ($300). The sale of the $37 call partially offsets the purchase of the $36 call, lowering the investor's out-of-pocket investment for the trade. Thus her investment in the position is cut from $600 (which it would be if she simply purchased the $36 call) to $300 ($600 − $300) (see Figure 6.1).

Also, since any losses accrued by the short $37 call are "covered" by the purchase of the $36 call; the position has *limited risk*. The risk is limited to the $300 the trader puts up for the trade.

The *potential profit* on the trade is the difference between the two strikes 37 − 36 = $1 = 100 points = $1,000. In an ideal situation, Crude oil is above $37 at expiration, in

## F I G U R E   6.1

### March 2004 Crude Oil Chart Showing $36 and $37 Strike Prices

CLH04 - Crude Light-Pit, Mar 04, Daily

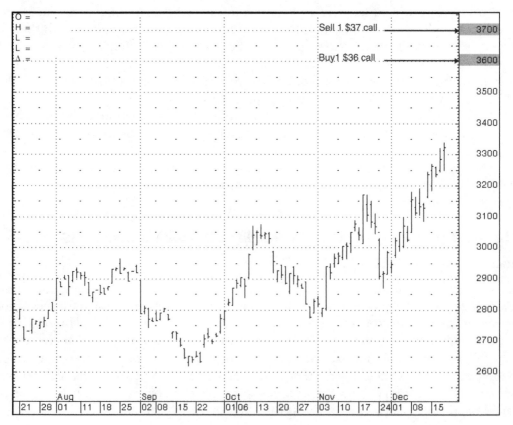

which case both options expire in the money. The $36 call is profitable up to $37, at which point its gains are offset by losses on the $37 call.

A bear put spread works the same way except on the other side of the market (with puts) when the trader is bearish on the market.

As stated earlier, on paper, the bull call spread looks great: low initial investment, potential profit of more than two times the initial investment, and *limited risk.* It sounds too good to be true!

It does, and it makes a great sales pitch to novice traders. Of course, there are situations where this strategy could work well. However, we've seen our share of bull call spreads and have only seen them work well in the trader's favor in a very few situations.

Lets examine why.

First of all, whenever you hear the terms *large potential profit* and *limited risk*, your "I will probably lose my money" antennae should go up.

## The Flip Side of the Bull Call Spread

The initial investment in the bull call spread does not include commissions and slippage on the trade. If you are dealing with a full-service broker, your commissions easily could run from $75 to $100 per option. Even trading at a discount broker for $30 per option, the cost still would be considerable. To be in the middle, we'll assume a $60 per option transaction cost ($120 total per spread). Then we have to assume slippage. Spreads often are more difficult to price than individual options, and some brokers will have to fill the options separately rather than as a spread on one ticket. We'll be generous in this example and assume slippage of only 1 point ($10) per option. Therefore, the total cost of this spread would be $300 + $20 + $120 = $440. This is still not a bad investment if the potential profit is achieved.

However, while the potential profit appears attractive, what is the *potential for profit*? For the maximum return to be achieved on this position, crude oil would have to rally over $4 per barrel in just over six weeks. (In reality, March crude oil did rally $3— the trade still lost.) Not only would this be a very large price increase in a very short period of time, but it also would take the market to new multiyear highs.

It is certainly possible for the market to make this kind of move. But is it likely? This is where knowledge of the fundamentals becomes so important. The problem with this, especially in predicting big moves, is that the market is trading at its true value every single day of the week. You have to see something coming in the future that the rest of the market does not. You have to predict almost exactly where the market will go. Then it has to make a substantial move in your favor in a very short period of time. What is the potential for profit? Probably very low.

In this case, the odds of success are even lower than the strategy of buying the $36 call outright. At least in this case, if the market moved up slightly but did not quite reach $36, you might be able to profit from short-term appreciation of the call option itself. In a bull call spread, the options often will have very similar deltas. This means that both options' values will tend to move at nearly the same rate. What you are gaining on your long $36 call, you are often losing almost as much on your short $37 call. Therefore, even if you are right and the market moves up $2, $3, or even $4, chances are that you will not be able to cash out of your trade early with a profit, especially after commissions are taken into account. The market will have to at least eclipse the $36 strike and remain there through expiration for the trader to make any profit at all. In other words, the long option has to go in the money and remain there through expiration for the buyer of the bull call spread to profit. And we already know the percentages and therefore can predict the chances of that happening.

This proved especially frustrating to me as a young broker when, as a team we put countless hours of research into a market, came up with a reasonable synopsis of the market that, surprisingly, often was correct, and then tried to position using an option spread of this nature. At the time, we felt that we were protecting clients and giving them what they wanted—low investments and limited risk. In hindsight, we were giving them little chance to profit from what was, at the time, decent research.

What would happen is we would release a bullish (bearish) outlook for a market and then recommend a bull call (bear put) spread. The investor would place the trade, and the market indeed would move higher. The investor would call in.

"You guys were right. That market did just what you said! How much did we make?" the investor would ask.

"Well John," I would reply, "we haven't made anything yet."

A long explanation of option strategy would ensue. The market had moved higher, but the neither strike had been attained. Thus, while the closer-to-the-money long option had appreciated in value, the losses from the more distant short option had almost offset all the gains. Thus, with transaction fees figured in, the position was still at a loss.

Most of the time, in the following weeks, broker and client alike would watch disappointedly as the market then topped out or went into a sideways trading range as the bull call spread slowly, deteriorated, and died on the vine.

Bull call or bear put spreads can work if the market goes exactly where you think it is going to go and stays there. But it has to be there at or near expiration to really make it worth your while. In other words, you not only have to pick where the market is going, you also have to decide when it is going to be there. And that can be very difficult to do.

As we now know, crude oil did go on to eclipse these price levels substantially in the months following the expiration of the March 2004 contract. While the options in this example would have expired worthless, a trader of a June 2004 crude bull call spread with the same strikes would have found both his options in the money at expiration. After transaction costs and slippage (assuming the same difference in premium at entry), he would have netted just over $500 per spread. Had he simply purchase the $38 call outright, his profit would have been over $3,000. Yet another reason to stay out of the bull call: It limits your profit. If you are willing to pay the heavy price to obtain limited risk, you should at least retain your right to an unlimited profit and buy the straight calls.

## Bear Call (Bull Put) Spread

The bear call spread is sort of the opposite of the bull call spread. Instead of buying the closer call and selling the more distant call, the trader is *selling* the closer call and *buying* the more distant call. Since this is a net short option spread, we tend to favor it more than a net long spread like a bull call. A trader who is neutral to bearish on the market would employ a bear call spread. Such a trader is basically selling a call to take advantage of time decay and buying a call with a higher strike for protection in case the market makes a large move higher.

The concept is illustrated in the following example (see Figure 6.2):

## F I G U R E   6.2

December 2002 Corn Chart Showing Bear Call Spread

In August, trader John thinks that corn will begin to trade lower. He decides to sell a December corn 310 call option for 10 cents ($500) because he believes that December corn will stay below 310. John wants to limit his risk, so, for protection, he buys a December corn 320 call for 5 cents ($250).

In an ideal situation, both options expire worthless, and John nets $250. Then John pays two commissions plus fees. If John pays his broker $75 per round turn, he nets $100 after paying all fees. His maximum risk is the difference between the two strikes, 10 cents ($500) minus premium collected ($250) plus commissions ($150) = $400. Therefore, John risked $400 to make $100—all for the sake of "limiting" his risk. His "absolute limited risk" was four times what he stood to make on the trade.

Although John would have been profitable in this particular example, this is not a good trade. John would have been much better off simply selling the 360 call outright. He would have cut his commission costs in half, and he would not have sacrificed half his profit to buy "protection."

But what *about* protection? John still needs to have some type of risk control. In this example he chose to "limit" his risk at all costs rather than controlling or managing his risk. An alternative approach for John could have been to keep a mental stop on his option value, setting an exit point based on the price of the futures or even entering a stop loss order on his corn option. While entering stop loss orders on options is not something that we recommend (see Chapter 9), it would have been a much better strategy than the one just illustrated. Stop loss orders are free!

While there is no guarantee that the market would not have traded beyond John's stop, there is a very high probability that John would have been able to exit his position at a loss of less than four times the premium collected had he wanted to. Yet it would not have cost him half his collected premium to do so.

John chose to limit his risk instead of managing it. While limiting risk in this manner may be comforting to the investor fearful of "unlimited" risk, over the long term, reduced profits and increased commissions almost ultimately will destroy his account. He eliminates his chances of getting caught in a big move, but chances are excellent that he would be able to exit his naked option (using almost *any* risk-control method) long before it increased to four times his premium collected. Limiting your risk to four times the premium you will collect if successful is not an efficient means of risk control. You are limiting your risk to a huge loss relative to the potential profit.

The sole time that we might consider a bear call or a bull put spread would be in a very volatile market. Most of the time, however, the spread between the strikes will be too narrow to make it a worthwhile endeavor. For instance, many traders consider this approach to trading S&P options. Yet, in most spreads, they only "limit" their loss to *10 times* the premium collected. This is not much of a limit. In almost any case, they would be better off selling naked options.

## The Butterfly Spread

A favorite of many option books (and many brokers, no doubt) is the butterfly spread. The butterfly seems to promise all things to all people. Investors who spend the time to learn how to use it must think they have discovered the Holy Grail of option trading—until they try to use it (see Figure 6.3).

The butterfly takes its name from the shape of its payoff diagram. The payoff from the butterfly is supposed to be highest at point B.

Again, we'll go back to the theme of professional traders versus individual investors. While certain strategies can be used effectively by professional and/or floor traders, they can be highly impractical for individual investors. This is one of them. You have certain advantages as an individual investor that you can use in your favor. Trying to coordinate the positioning of multiple options at different strike prices at desired premiums while taking commissions and slippage into account is not one of them.

Nonetheless, the butterfly looks great on paper. The following is an example of a typical butterfly spread and how it is supposed to work.

A trader is neutral on April crude oil. In other words, she thinks that $35 is a fair price for crude and believes that the price will be near this level on expiration day for April options. With the market trading at $35 a barrel, the trader enters the following position:

Buys 1 April crude oil $34 call at 250 points ($2,500)

Sells 2 April crude oil $35 calls at 150 points ($1,500) each for a $3,000 total credit

Buys 1 April crude oil $36 call at 75 points ($750) (see Figure 6.4)

This is not the type of book that is going to explain all the mathematical formulas and scenarios of how the butterfly spread can profit. However, the maximum profit in a butterfly spread occurs if the market expires right at $35. In this case, both short $35 calls expire worthless for a $3,000 gain. The long $34 call expires 100 points in the money for a $1,500 loss. The long $36 call expires worthless for a $750 loss.

**F I G U R E   6.3**

Butterfly Diagram

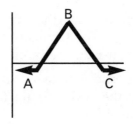

**FIGURE  6.4**

April 2004 Crude Oil Chart Illustrating a Butterfly Spread

CLJ04 - Crude Light-Pit, Apr 04, Daily

Therefore, the maximum profit on this particular example is $750. Maximum risk on the trade is $250, which would result from all options expiring worthless or all options expiring above the top strike price. In other words, the net debit on the trade is your maximum risk.

The butterfly spread and its many variations can be made to sound very good—limited risk with profit potential three times the risk.

However, while the limited risk and sophisticated nature of the butterfly spread may look appealing, it has two inherent drawbacks:

1. The trader has to pick almost exactly where the market is going and where it will be at a certain time in the future. Again, this is very difficult and exactly what we are stressing to avoid.

2. Even if the trader does happen to do this successfully, she has to cover four commissions plus fees plus cover any slippage on the fills out of her profits, which are limited by the butterfly. These hefty fees for employing the butterfly can cut any profit received substantially and make a loss on the butterfly all the more painful.

Other variations of the butterfly spread include spreads with names such as the *inverted butterfly*, the *condor*, and the *cartwheel*. Although these can qualify as credit spreads, for an individual investor, we would recommend staying away from all of them. In fact, try to avoid any spread that has the name of an insect, bird, or anything you might find in nature.

We have read commodity newsletters and brokerage "advisory" services that take option spreading to a ridiculous, almost shameless bid for multiple commissions. A recent recommendation from a newsletter we'll keep nameless was in coffee. It was selling 11 coffee calls, buying a futures contract, and then buying an at-the-money put for protection. After examining the trade, it actually made some sense. However, the market would have to move somewhat higher (although not too high) for the investor to make money—after paying 13 commissions plus covering the cost of buying an at-the-money put. It seemed to us that the same thing could have been achieved simply by buying the futures contract outright. But the writers pulled out the "limited risk" card that looked pretty good on paper. (Actually, if the coffee market had soared, risk would have been unlimited.)

Therefore, one spread—*one spread*—consisted of 12 options and one futures contract. Each spread had 13 positions. Thirteen commissions.

Following are a few rules of thumb from our experience that may indicate that a spread that you are considering is one to avoid:

1. *You can't explain the spread to your kid (wife, nephew, etc).* If the trade is too complicated for you to explain to somebody unfamiliar with commodities, you probably shouldn't be in it. My 12-year-old daughter asked me at the dinner table one night a few months ago about what I did at my job. After a brief explanation, she asked how people make money investing in things like orange juice or pigs. I went to my briefcase and pulled out a recent chart of coffee. I took out a pen and drew a line across the top of the paper from the strike price at which we had recently sold naked calls.

   "This chart tracks the price of coffee" I explained. "If the price stays below this line," I said, pointing to the horizontal line I had drawn, "we make money."

   She sat in quiet contemplation for a few seconds and then exclaimed triumphantly, "That's easy!"

   Exactly.

2. *The spread has more than three to four options involved in each position.* This is not to say that every spread with less than four options is good. It is to say that if it has more than three to four options per spread, it is probably impractical for an individual trader to use effectively. At the very least, it may not be an efficient use of your capital.

3. *The spread requires the market to move to a certain place at a certain time.* As we've discussed, picking where the market is going to go is extremely difficult. Picking when it is going to go there is nearly impossible. We advise option strategies that require you only to pick where the market is *not going to go*. Seek out simple strategies that give you a very wide profit zone. The market should be in this profit zone already when you enter the trade. In this way, you force the market to move out of the profit zone for you to lose. Avoid all trades with very narrow profit zones or zones that appear far away from the current market price.

Hopefully, this chapter has given you some real-life insight into option spreading and what to avoid. These examples by no means encompass all the impractical, low-probability spreads that are available for new traders to study, analyze, and attempt to implement. This chapter also does not cover all the classic option spread strategies that have been designed by pro traders but alas are impractical to all but the most highly skilled professional or floor trader. The guidelines presented herein, however, should give you all the insight you need to avoid the quicksand.

Now that you've learned what not to do, it is time to learn some techniques that have proved usable for real-life individual investors, at least in our experience. As we've stated, there are a few option spreads that we *do* feel can offer some substantial benefits to the typical part-time trader. These will be discussed in the next chapter.

# 7

## CHAPTER

# Recommended Spread Strategies

Now that we have covered the base strategy of selling calls and puts naked, there are some option spread strategies that we feel can offer speculators a possible advantage in the market. These strategies are the ones that have stood out over the years as actually practical for use by individual investors. They are relatively simple yet relatively effective. They offer wide profit zones and in many cases high probability for decent profits *after* commissions. They do not offer *limited* risk, yet they are relatively easy trades in which to employ standard *risk management* techniques.

Before we discuss these strategies, we feel that it is important to discuss the entry and exit of spread positions. Selling naked options by themselves is a relatively simple procedure. Decide on the premium you desire, enter the sell order at that premium, and find out if you have any takers. If it gets filled, great. If not, you can adjust your price or try again tomorrow.

Spread trading with options throws a different wrinkle into the equation. If you are selling a combination of options or a combination of options and futures contracts, the fill of one may be dependent on the fill of another. In other words, if you are trying to position in two different options to complete a spread, have limit orders on both, and one gets filled and the other doesn't, you could be left exposed to risk that you did not anticipate.

Two concepts come into play in this regard: flexibility and liquidity.

Liquidity is discussed in Chapter 8. However, in spread trading, one may wish to look for more liquid options than one would require simply to sell naked. This is so because in spreading you may not want to assume the risk of holding one-half the spread and may "need" to get a fill if you are already into one-half of the spread.

Liquidity can help to ensure faster fills. In addition, flexibility in one's expectations for pricing can be essential to get a spread established and not leave yourself exposed with only half the spread intact.

A more aggressive approach to spreading options is what is known as *legging in*. The trader who *legs* on the spread tries to establish one side of the spread at a favorable price and then waits for the market to move in the other direction, giving him a more favorable price on the other end. In other words, he is *willing* to leave himself exposed on half the spread while he waits to establish the other half at a desirable price. While we've seen some trades legged in very effectively, we've probably seen just as many result in the trader not getting the market move he had hoped for and thus having to accept a much worse fill on the second half of the spread. Worse yet, he may not get a fill at all or may have to adjust his strikes, giving him a less desirable overall position.

While there may be some situations where legging in may be worth a shot, we cannot bring ourselves to outright recommend it. Much of this will depend on your personality. If you are slightly more aggressive, you may want to attempt to leg into a spread occasionally. If you decide to go this route, you should have real-time option quotes and the ability to watch them every minute. The other alternative, of course, is to have a quality broker experienced in option spreads who has the ability to watch your spread closely and position for you.

In the following pages we will explore a few of the spreads that we do recommend as advantageous to individual investors.

## 1. THE SHORT OPTION STRANGLE

The short option strangle is simply a variation of selling naked puts and calls. As a matter of fact, it *is* selling naked puts and calls. It is simply doing both at the *same time.*

A short option strangle, or simply *strangle*, as we will refer to it, is the strategy of selling a naked out-of-the-money call and a naked out-of-the-money put on the same market. The strangle is most effective when the price of the underlying market remains in a defined range. An example of a strangle is illustrated below.

Trader John is not sure which way soybean prices are headed. In November 2003, he identified price levels on both sides of the market that he believed would be highly unlikely to be attained before the expiration of March options.

In brief, John believes that 6.00 would be far too high a price for soybeans to attain in this period, yet he also believes that the 5.20 level would substantially underprice soybeans. John places the following trade: He sells one March soybean 6.00 call for 8 cents ($400) and one March soybean 5.20 put for 7½ cents ($375). As long as March soybeans are below $6.00 and above $5.20 at option expiration, both options will expire worthless, and John will keep the premiums for a total $775 in profit, minus transaction costs. This area between $6.00 and $5.20 is what we like to call the *profit zone*. The profit zone is the price range on the chart that the underlying market can be within at option expiration for the trader to keep all premiums collected on the trade. This particular strangle has a fairly wide profit zone of about 80 cents ($6.00 − $5.20 = $0.80) (see Figure 7.1).

John enjoys several key benefits of employing an option strangle like this one:

- *Offsetting price movements*. As the market fluctuates up and down, the value of either the put or the call will increase. However, the value of the other option will decrease, at least partially offsetting the increase in the first. For instance, if the market moves higher, the value of the 6.00 call may increase, but the value of the 5.20 put will decrease, thus offsetting, at least partially, the movement in the call. Eventually, if the spread works correctly, this balancing act will

**F I G U R E   7.1**

March 2003 Soybean Chart Illustrating the Strangle Strategy

SH03 - Soybeans Day-Pit, Mar 03, Daily

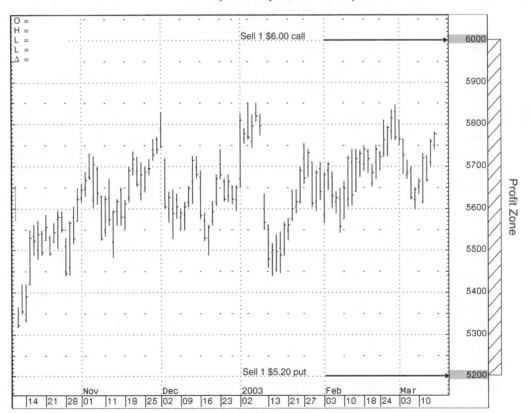

continue while time deterioration continues to erode both options. This is in contrast to selling naked on one side of the market, where the trader has no counterbalance on his position. While the decrease in one option may not offset the increase in the other exactly, owing to differing deltas, the balance is often enough to give the trader a much smoother, less volatile ride to expiration.

■ *Lower margin, higher dollar-for-dollar return.* Because of this balancing effect, the exchanges often view strangling as a more conservative position than selling outright naked short options on one side of the market. For this reason, the margin requirement for a strangle often will be less than the sum of the margin that would be required for selling either option by itself. For instance, the net margin requirement to sell the 6.00 call might be $500. The net margin requirement for selling the 5.20 puts might be $400. The sum totals $900. Yet, if both were sold together as a strangle, the margin for both could total $700. A strangle, then, often can offer a higher return on capital than selling one side of the market.

■ *The market does not have to make a large move for you to profit.* Unlike several of the spreads in Chapter 6, the market does not have to make a large move for you to profit. It simply has to stay in the profit zone. In fact, it does not have to move at all; it is already in the profit zone! You do not have to pick where the market is going or when it is going to go there. In this case, the profit zone is fairly wide, offering what appears to be a high potential *for* profit.

While the strangle is an excellent option writing strategy to use in many situations, like any other approach, it has its drawbacks:

■ *It is vulnerable to large moves in the market.* While the option sold on the other side of a strangle will offset losses of an adverse move against the other, this offsetting effect is limited. If a trader is simply selling naked puts, a large move to the upside will greatly benefit the position. This is not the case in a strangle. A large-scale, decisive move in one direction can cause a loss on one of the options that eclipses the profit on the other. A strangle still has unlimited risk on the upside or the downside and therefore must be managed like a naked option position.

■ *It has a limited profit zone.* The profit zone for selling naked options on one side of the market is unlimited. The profit zone for a strangle, no matter how wide it is, is still finite. The price must remain within a certain range. Strangling, then, is not recommended for trending markets but rather for markets that the trader feels will remain in a general trading range. Thus it would have been a much better strategy to use in March 2003 soybeans than it would have been in March 2004 soybeans.

While trending markets are not best for this approach, this does not mean that *volatile* markets should be overlooked for strangling opportunities. Volatile markets often can still trade in wide trading ranges, and the volatility can boost option premiums, meaning that a strangle often can be sold with a very wide profit zone.

For instance, the following example from one of our weekly columns illustrates how this technique can be employed in the S&P 500 futures contract with a very wide profit zone.

---

## A NEW BEAR MARKET FOR THE S&P 500 OR JUST A HEALTHY CORRECTION? OPTION SELLERS NEED NOT DECIDE

James Cordier and Michael Gross, *Liberty Trading Group*,
March 11, 2004

While day trading the S&P 500 is still a most popular pastime among many run and gun traders today, it may not be the best approach to long-term financial health. While I've run into a few traders who claim to be good at it, I haven't met one yet who has retired with all the profits he's banked.

I have worked with several short-term traders in the past and even used the approach myself on a small scale. The results were fair, and I must admit that it is an exhilarating game. However, with all the sophisticated technical tools and up-to-the-minute reporting on government financial data and news releases, it simply seems that there is still too much left to chance when short-term trading. This is especially true when trading a market such as S&P 500 futures, a market more driven by emotion than any I can think of. Emotions are an irrational animal and may not respond the way a 50-day moving average or the latest government unemployment report says it should. We never know when a train explosion in Spain or a terrorist arrest in Afghanistan will rock the market irrationally for an hour, a day, or even a week.

Unlike trading a physical commodity, where crop forecasts, demand trends, and current supply can be measured to a certain degree, the S&P 500 can be affected by so many different variables that trading on fundamentals can be much more difficult, in my opinion, than trading a commodity such as soybeans, coffee, or crude oil. This is especially true when trading futures contracts for short-term gain, where the slightest daily whim of the market can result in being stopped out or, at the very least, a disappointing loss that may cause you to question the rationale of your position. In other words, you can guess the market right, whether using fundamental judgment or good technical savvy, and be knocked out of the market by a random event. Of course, this can happen in trading commodities as well, but in my opinion, it is much more likely to happen when trading the king of the futures contracts.

The volatility of the S&P 500, coupled with the wide public interest in trading the contract, does create some outstanding opportunities in the options, however. While short-term traders are trying to decide whether to go long or short the market on today's action, sellers (or writers) of options can choose not to decide and simply take a high-probability position outside all of the market "noise."

To illustrate this strategy, look at the horizontal lines in Figure 7.2. Do you believe that the S&P 500 will remain between these two lines for the next 90 days? If you believe that the probability is high that it will, then an option strangle position may be for you.

An option selling strangle is the strategy of selling a call above the market and a put below the market—in this case far above and far below. In this example, the trader is selling a June S&P 500 1275 call for 160 points ($400) and a June 850 put for 190 points ($475). If the June S&P 500 is anywhere between 850 and 1275 at option expiration on June 17, 2004, both options expire worthless, and the trader nets the sum of both premiums, or $875 per spread, minus transaction costs.

The drawbacks to this type of approach are that if the market moves beyond these ranges, the trader is subject to the same market risk that he would be if he were outright long or short an S&P 500 futures contract. Drawback 2 is that either option could increase in value during the life of the trade, which also could potentially increase margin requirements.

The benefits of the position, however, are substantial. By selling on both sides of the market, the losses created by an adverse move in one direction are at least partially offset by gains on the opposing option. Of course, as long as the market price remains between the two strike prices, time decay eventually will erode the value of both options. This "offsetting" effect of a strangle can create a more stable, less volatile position for the investor.

The obvious benefit of the trade is that the trader leaves the market a wide range of potential movement from which he can profit. Daily news reports, breakouts, or corrections are all things he no longer needs to worry about, at least on a short-term basis.

The objective generally would be to hold the position through option expiration, thus keeping all premiums collected as profit. Remember, for the position to be profitable, the market must only remain in the described range for about the next 90 days. However, either or both options can be bought back at any time to close the position. This can be a key aspect of risk control.

An option strangle like this one is the type of opportunity that we prefer to recommend because it provides a wide profit zone for the investor. It is one that I'll advise any day over trying to guess what tomorrow's newspaper will bring.

## Risk Management and the Strangle

Managing risk on a strangle sometimes can be easier than managing risk on a naked position on one side of the market. If you use the 200 percent rule (exit a position when an option doubles), then if the put and the call were sold at approximately the same premium, you could exit either the put or the call when it doubled in value. The odds of the market making a complete reversal and moving far enough to cause the other option to double would be unlikely, although not impossible. Therefore, if the 200 percent rule

**F I G U R E   7.2**

June 2004 S&P Price Chart Illustrating a Strangle

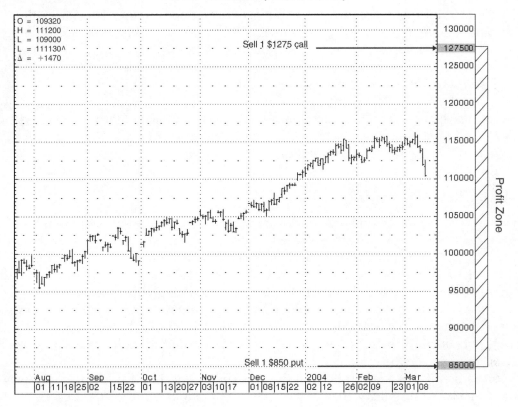

SPM4 - S&P 500 Day-Pit, Jul 04, Daily

is used in a strangle position, there is a good chance that one could come close to break-ing even, even when losing on one side of the trade.

In other words, one option would be covered at 200 percent, whereas the other would expire, leaving the trader net even for the trade. Assuming each option was sold for $500, the equation would work like this:

| | | |
|---|---|---|
| Call option exited at double premium | ($500) | (loss) |
| Put option expires worthless | + $500 | (profit) |
| Net | 0 | |

Of course, slippage and transaction costs must be figured into the equation, so a trader would not truly break even. In addition, for demonstration purposes, this illustration assumes that each option was sold for exactly the same price when, in reality, this is rarely the case. Regardless, losses would still be minimal in this example, which makes the strangle a bit more attractive to risk-adverse investors.

More aggressive investors can choose to give the losing side of the equation a larger cushion for movement, risking it to triple original value or more. They are willing to withstand temporary increases in the values of the options (to a certain extent) as long as the underlying market price remains within the *profit zone*. The strangle gives them this luxury because they know that the other side of the strangle is at least partially offsetting their loss. As we discussed earlier, however, this offsetting effect is limited.

In conclusion, traders generally should use the same risk-management techniques for a strangle that are used for selling naked options on one side of the market (discussed in detail in Chapter 5). The offsetting effect of the strangle simply gives the trader more flexibility in deploying these techniques.

## 2. THE RATIO CREDIT SPREAD

The ratio credit spread is the only option spread that we will recommend that involves the buying of an option. We struggled when deciding how we would justify the use of the ratio credit spread in this book because it seems to exhibit some of the same characteristics as the spreads we advised against in Chapter 6. Suffice it to say that in the case of the ratio spread, we feel that the benefits simply outweigh the costs.

If the ratio credit spread is employed correctly, a trader can profit from it even if the market moves in exactly the opposite direction the trader had hoped. Only if the market substantially exceeds the trader's price target can the trader lose on a properly constructed ratio credit spread.

Ratio credit spreads can be slightly complex to select and implement. However, what they lack in simplicity, they make up for in potential and probabilities.

### Benefits of the Ratio Credit Spread

The ratio credit spread can offer an investor an array of advantages:

1. It has a wide profit zone.
2. The price of the market is already within the profit zone when the trade is entered.
3. It does not require the trader to pick where or when the market is going to move to be profitable.
4. It can offer a significant *potential profit* in addition to a very high potential *for* profit.
5. It can withstand considerable market moves against it without incurring the degree of margin increases that may be incurred in a naked position. This

gives it additional staying power in the market. For this reason, ratio spreads also can be deployed as a risk-management tactic for traders skittish about selling options naked.

In addition to its risk-management benefits, a ratio spread offers the investor a key feature very popular with futures traders: *It offers the trader the possibility of a substantial payoff* should the market end up in a certain smaller profit zone within the overall profit zone. Therefore, although the trader does not have to select where and when the market is going to move to be profitable, if she *is* able to do that, her profit potential could increase significantly.

## Drawbacks of the Ratio Credit Spread

While the ratio credit spread may seem to offer the best of both worlds, it has some drawbacks of which traders should be aware:

1. It employs at least three or more options in each spread, making it a more expensive spread from a commission standpoint.
2. It can be slightly more difficult to calculate profit zones and breakeven points.
3. It can be cumbersome to position at the desired premiums on both sides.
4. Ratio spreads share the same basic drawbacks of selling naked, theoretically unlimited risk and potential for margin increases in adverse market conditions. However, as opposed to selling naked, both these potential liabilities can be lessened substantially with the proper use of a ratio spread.

A good broker can go far in alleviating drawbacks 2 and 3. Concerns over drawback 1 will have to be weighed by the individual trader against potential for profit, as well as potential profit.

## Diagram of a Ratio Credit Spread

A ratio credit call spread generally is considered a bullish strategy, whereas a ratio credit put spread generally is considered a bearish strategy. An attractive selling point is that even if you're wrong, you still make money. Only if you are very, very right, one might say "too right," would you lose money on the trade.

In a ratio credit call spread, a trader would buy an at-the-money or slightly out-of-the-money call while simultaneously selling two or three (or more) far-out-of-the-money calls on the same market. The sum of the premiums collected will be more than the premium paid out to purchase the near-to-the-money call. Thus it produces a "credit" to the trader, making it a net short option spread (the kind we like). If the trader is entirely wrong and the market does a complete nosedive, all the options in the spread will expire worthless. However, this still leaves the trader with her net credit as her profit.

The catch is that the credit also must be enough to cover all the transaction costs and still produce enough profit to make the trade worthwhile.

In an optimal scenario, the trader will profit not only from her short calls expiring worthless but also from her long call expiring in the money. The following is an example of a ratio credit spread:

In March 2004, Trader John is bullish on the soybean market. With July soybeans currently trading at 10.25 and option volatility high, John sees that out-of-the-money calls are offering great premiums. While John is bullish on soybeans, he does not think that they have what it takes to reach the $13 price level. However, since he feels that the market will still move higher, he decides to employ a ratio credit call spread.

John executes the following trades:

Buys one July $11.00 soybean call for 34 cents ($1,700)

Sells three July $12.50 soybean calls for 16 cents ($800) each (see Figure 7.3)

### F I G U R E   7.3

July 2004 Soybean Chart Illustrating the Ratio Spread Strategy

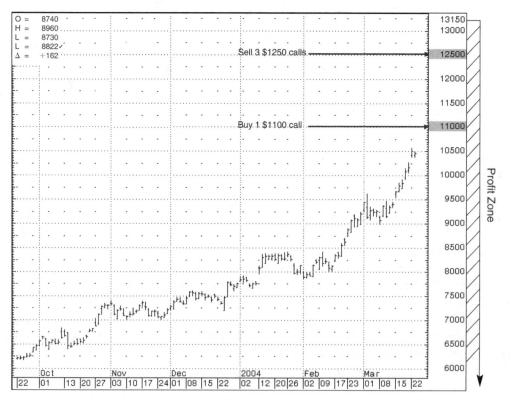

SN4 - Soybeans Day-Pit, Jul 04, Daily

John collects a total of $2,400 ($800 × 3) in premiums and pays back $1,700 of it to buy a closer-to-the-money call. Therefore, John nets a $700 *credit*. The *ratio* of the spread is 3 to 1; that is, he sold three options and bought one option. Thus the term *ratio credit spread*.

What does this accomplish? Two things:

1. It will make John profitable as long as July soybeans are below 13.15 (the *breakeven point*) at expiration.
2. If John is wrong and soybeans go straight down and end up at some pathetically low price at expiration, John will still make a profit.

If soybeans go straight down or even move higher but do not reach the $11 price level, all the options in the spread will expire worthless, meaning that John will keep the $700 credit as his profit. Of course, he must subtract his transaction fees from this figure, but even after doing so in this example, he still pockets a tidy profit.

The only way that John can lose on this trade (at expiration) is if July soybean options expire with the futures contract trading above 13.15. In this case, if John had not yet exited the position, he would incur a loss of $100 for every 1 cent the market was above 13.15. This is a scenario of which John does not want to be a part. Therefore, the same vigilant risk control that one would employ in selling naked options would apply to selling ratio spreads.

A fair question many traders ask is, Why doesn't John just sell the 13.00 or 13.20 puts naked? This is why: As the market moves higher, the three short 12.50 calls are increasing in value, thus working against the trader. Yet the 11.00 call is increasing as well, at least partially offsetting any temporary losses on the 12.50 calls. If the 11.00 call goes in the money, this rate of appreciation will increase. In an optimal scenario, the 11.00 call expires in the money, and the 12.50 calls expire out of the money. Therefore, the trader reaps the benefits of selling options (he keeps all premium collected on the 12.50 calls while taking another profit, possibly a substantial profit, on his long 11.00 call).

The potential for profit on this trade is high—the profit zone is anywhere below 13.15. Since this has been addressed, this is one trade where we can let ourselves indulge and think about the *potential profit*. The maximum profit on this spread is $8,200. Before you go getting too excited about ratio spreads, remember that in order to get this type of profit, you have to pick where the market is going to be and when it is going to be there. This is very difficult, as we've already discussed. The difference with being wrong in this case is that the market can nosedive, the trader can be completely wrong, and he still will make money. Theoretically, the maximum profit can be attained if the options expire and July futures close at 12.50 on expiration day. This assumes, of course, that the options do not get exercised. Futures options rarely get exercised unless they expire in the money. The profit will be less than $8,200 the further away the market is from 12.50.

How do we get $8,200? At a futures price of 12.50, the 11.00 call would be worth $1.50 in the money. In soybeans, this would amount to $50 × 150 = $7,500. To this we add the credit John received when he sold the spread ($700), for a total of $8,200.

This is the formula for calculating the potential profit on a ratio spread:

Credit received when entering the spread plus the total dollar value difference between the two strike prices in the spread

By dollar-value difference, we mean the monetary value, in dollars, of a move from the bottom strike to the top strike. In this example, it would be from $11.00 to $12.50. Therefore, the total dollar value would be $1.50 × $50 (every 1 cent move in a soybean contract is worth $50) = $7,500.

## Breakeven and Risk on the Ratio Spread

The profit on the 11.00 calls increases gradually until it reaches the peak profit level of 12.50, at which point the short calls go in the money and begin to erode the profits on the long call. While the long call will continue to offset one of the short calls one for one, the other two short calls will begin to eat away at the $7,500 profit accrued between 11.00 and 12.50. Therefore, profits begin to decline above 12.50 and keep declining until the futures price reaches 13.15, at which point John begins accruing losses. Since two of these calls are uncovered, John will accrue losses as though he were short two contracts of July soybeans from 13.15.

A ratio spread can be more conservative than selling naked in that balancing the long call versus the short call helps to smooth out short-term moves in the market and helps to avoid the larger drawdowns that can happen as a result of simply selling short. The tradeoff for this is the reduced profit if all the options expire worthless (profit would be greater if one just sold the three 12.50 calls naked.

This approach is more aggressive in that it seeks the higher gains generally associated with option buying or futures trading while avoiding some of the risks. However, transaction costs can be high for a ratio spread, and it still carries with it a brand of "unlimited risk" should a substantial breakout occur to the upside (or downside if it is a ratio put spread).

## Delta-Neutral Trading

Many traders may have heard the term *delta neutral* in regard to option spread trading. As we mentioned earlier, the delta is a figure that measures the volatility of an option. A delta of 33 would mean that for every 1 cent the futures contract moved in price, the option price would fluctuate 0.33, or about a third, of a cent. Many traders try to have the deltas of the options on either side of the trade balance each other out. This can further assist in "smoothing out the equity curve." In other words, the options will tend to appreciate or depreciate at approximately the same rate, thus providing a lower-volatility trade to the investor.

In this example, if the delta of the 12.50 call was 10 and the delta of the 11.00 call was 30, the trade would be considered delta-neutral (3 × 10 = 30).

The problem with staying delta neutral is that the deltas are constantly in flux. They can change by the minute. Traders who really get into delta-neutral trading will keep adding positions on either side to keep "rebalancing" the position. Not only can this get expensive commission-wise, but it also creates a large, cumbersome position.

Our advice is to be aware of deltas in spread trading but do not feel as though they dictate the terms of your trade. If the trade is good, simply be sure that there is some adequate backup capital to cover fluctuations in your position, and enter the trade. Do not become obsessed with deltas or delta-neutral trading.

While deltas may play a significant role in the analyses of institutional traders, individual investors whom we have met who are hung up on delta-neutral strategy generally are traders who are undercapitalized and do not understand the concept of having backup money for a trade. They want every penny working in a trade right now because they need to make money right now—and lots of it!

We do not want to get too down on delta-neutral trading because it is a very popular concept right now. Simply be aware that you should have backup capital available for any option selling trade whether you are selling naked or spread trading.

We generally recommend that our investors have no more than 50 percent of their account margined at any given time.

## 3. SELLING COVERED CALLS

Selling covered calls is very popular strategy among equity option traders for good reason. Selling covered calls in equities can be done with virtually no additional risk to the investor if she is already assuming the risk of holding the underlying stock. Selling covered positions takes on a slightly different twist in trading futures. This is so because the leverage involved in selling calls on futures positions can make it a less practical strategy when employed in this arena.

### Covered Calls in Equities

Selling covered calls in equities is illustrated in the following example:

Mary is long 100 shares of Exxon stock from $40 a share. Mary intends to hold her stock for some time. If the stock gets to $44, however, she would like to sell it and take a profit. Rather than put a limit order on her stock, Mary can sell a $44 call and collect a premium.

Let's say that it is March and Mary decides to sell a June $44 call for $200 (2.00 × 100 shares = $200). If Exxon stock is anywhere below $44 on expiration day, Mary will keep the $200 as profit, and she will still have her Exxon stock. Therefore, Mary has generated $200 in income without assuming any additional risk. The only risk that

Mary has is the risk that Exxon stock will decrease, which she already had before she sold the option. Therefore, the risk of selling the option is nil. The option is *covered* because Mary owns the underlying stock.

But what if the Exxon stock is at $46 at expiration? Mary's option would expire in the money and be assigned or exercised at $44 per share. This means that 100 shares of Exxon would be sold for Mary's account at $44 per share, effectively closing Mary's Exxon position at the price she wanted. Mary still keeps the premium as hers. Therefore, Mary profited on the appreciation of the Exxon stock and from the premium of the call option.

To some, selling covered calls on equities is a "can't lose" proposition. To a certain extent, this is actually true. You can't lose on the call itself. However, to sell a covered call, you also have to own the underlying security. Therefore, you must be ready to accept the risk that the stock will decrease in value. But many equity traders already hold shares of the stock, and therefore, selling calls on those stocks presents no additional risk at all and is used as a good way to generate income if the investor plans to hold the stock over the long term.

The only drawback to selling covered calls in equities is that it limits the upside potential on the stock itself. If you own the stock from $40 and you sell a call at $44, you are capping your potential capital gain on the stock at $4. However, to some investors this is perfectly acceptable. The question you must ask yourself in employing this technique is, "Is the premium I am collecting worth capping my upside gain in the stock? If so, then selling covered calls can be an excellent way to generate income on your current stock portfolio.

## Selling Covered Calls in Futures

Selling covered calls in futures is quite a different animal than selling covered calls in stocks. In fact, it is as different as buying 100 shares of a stock or buying a contract for a commodity. The difference is in leverage.

If you buy 100 shares of stock at $20 a share, you pay $2,000 and own the stock. If you buy a contract on a commodity, you may put a $2,000 margin deposit down to control a contract for $30,000 worth of that commodity. In the stock, small changes in price usually mean small gains or losses. In commodities, this is a different story.

If you bought the stock at $20 and it fell to $19, you would have a loss of $100. If you bought a contract for crude oil at $20 and it fell to $19, you would be out $1,000. Of course, this works the other way too, and profits from a correct futures guess in the market can be substantial.

If you want to sell covered calls in futures, it can work exactly the way it works in stocks. If you are already holding the underlying contract, there is no additional risk to selling the short call. The problem is, with the way futures contracts work with leverage, most futures traders are not looking to hold the contract for the long term. If the futures price starts moving lower, chances are the trader will want to get out, or he will have a stop in place and get stopped out before the market takes too much of his capital. In other words, where the stock trader may be able simply to ride it out and stay in for the long haul, the futures trader cannot afford to do this.

If the trader does exit his futures position, he will be left with a naked call above the market, which may or may not be a good thing. However, it was not the original position he intended, and he runs the risk of the market rallying higher again and having the short call work against him as well. In other words, at this point he would be back to trying to outguess the market again, which is entirely what he was trying to avoid in the first place.

The other drawback to selling a covered call in futures is that calls often can be sold so far above the market that it leaves plenty of room for the underlying price to rise without ever going in the money. The trader then may be looking at substantial profits on his futures position and want to take profit on the position. However, should he exit his futures position, he then would have to deal with what could be a substantially appreciated short call that may or may not expire worthless. If he elects to simply close the call out at the same time that he exits his futures position, it would cost him a little or a lot of the profit he received from the underlying contract.

Our point is that if you want to make money with options in futures, selling covered calls is probably not the best strategy in which to do so. If you are a futures trader first and are looking for a way to add some extra spice to your trading, selling covered calls (or covered puts if you are short) can provide some limited benefits. However, because of the complexity of writing a covered call or put on a futures contract and figuring out the potential scenarios and risk dimensions, we question if it is worth the small amount of excess profit or decreased losses it may provide.

Needless to say, selling covered calls is recommended for the equity traders reading this chapter. However, we don't consider it to carry as many benefits in the futures arena.

Selling covered calls generally requires no additional margin, whereas selling both ratio credit spreads and strangles does have margin requirements based on SPAN, just like a naked option. However, since the positions in these spreads at least partially offset each other to a certain degree, margin requirements often are less than those for selling naked.

## KEY POINTS TO REMEMBER ABOUT RECOMMENDED SPREADS
### Short Option Strangle
*Benefits*

- Double premiums
- Reduced margin (increased return on equity)

- Short call and short put partially offset adverse moves against either

### Drawbacks
- Vulnerable to breakouts in either direction

## Ratio Credit Spread

### Benefits
- Prices of long and short options tend to move together, reducing volatility to investor
- Potential for large gains
- Large profit zone (trader profits even if long option expires worthless)

### Drawbacks
- Potentially higher transaction costs
- Tedious to calculate profit and loss zones
- Cumbersome to position at desired premiums

## Covered Call Writing

### Benefits
- No additional risk to holders of equities (or futures)

### Drawbacks
- Somewhat impractical for futures option traders

Now that we've covered selling naked options and some of the spread strategies that can benefit you as a trader, it's time to explore how to actually position in these trades. Chapter 8 will explain some key factors in entering and holding option positions such as liquidity, order placement, and how not to get assigned.

# 8

## CHAPTER

# Liquidity, Order Placement, Assignment, and Limit Moves

## LIQUIDITY

The subject of option liquidity is one that produces many varying opinions on what is right and what is wrong and what is safe and what is risky. Given the choice, any investor would prefer high liquidity. But one of your advantages as an individual investor is that there will be option premium for you to sell that may not be practical for a large institutional investor to trade. Whereas the large fund manager may need to trade several hundred or even thousands of options at a single strike price and therefore need very high liquidity, you may only need a few hundred contracts of open interest to sell enough options to satisfy your desired position. This may give you access to options that may have better odds of expiring worthless (i.e., further out of the money strikes) than would be available to the institutional trader.

We've seen many investors trade for years in options with as few as 500 to 700 contracts and have rarely seen a trader run into problems with exiting a position due to liquidity. It may take a bit longer to get a fill, and one may need to be a bit more flexible on pricing (on entering or exiting the position), but we cannot remember a time when the floor broker said, "We have no buyers at any price."

Obviously, we would suggest looking for options with higher liquidity. But do not pass up what you feel is an excellent option trade simply because the option has only a few hundred contracts outstanding. We would draw the line and say that most investors probably should not trade options at strikes with less than 500 contracts outstanding. The optimal open interest to look for is option contracts with 1,000 or more contracts open interest. Obviously, the more contracts you intend to sell, the higher open interest you should seek.

You also will want to consider the open interest in the surrounding strikes. If all the options tend to be in the same range of open interest, then your strike is probably okay. If your strike has 500 contracts open interest and the next higher strike has 5,000 contracts open interest, there could be a reason. It is probably best to go with the higher-volume strike in this case (see Figure 8.1).

## TIMING

In trading futures, stocks, or any number of other types of vehicles, timing of the entry is an essential element of a successful trade. In selling options, it becomes somewhat

### FIGURE 8.1

Gold Option Prices Showing Open Interest

| GC<br>UndPr<br>DTE<br>EXP<br>VOL<br>IVS<br>IR | AUG4 CALLS<br>3867✓<br>64<br>07/27/04<br>18.20<br>0.00<br>1.82 | | AUG4 PUTS<br>3867✓<br>64<br>07/27/04<br>18.20<br>0.00<br>1.82 | | OCT4 CALLS<br>3879✓<br>126<br>09/27/04<br>18.34<br>0.00<br>2.12 | | OCT4 PUTS<br>3879✓<br>126<br>09/27/04<br>18.34<br>0.00<br>2.12 | | DEC4 CALLS<br>3892✓<br>183<br>11/23/04<br>17.73<br>0.00<br>2.50 | | DEC4 PUTS<br>3892✓<br>183<br>11/23/04<br>17.73<br>0.00<br>2.50 | |
|---|---|---|---|---|---|---|---|---|---|---|---|---|
| 320 | 6670✓ | 0 | 10✓ | 8 | 6820✓ | 0 | 60✓ | 10 | 6950✓ | 1 | 70✓ | 375 |
| 325 | 6170✓ | 180 | 10✓ | 0 | .......... | | .......... | | 6470✓ | 0 | 100✓ | 300 |
| 330 | 5720✓ | 18 | 60✓ | 737 | 5860✓ | 8 | 100✓ | 383 | 6100✓ | 14 | 190✓ | 4513 |
| 340 | 4740✓ | 67 | 90✓ | 321 | 4940✓ | 0 | 180✓ | 1448 | 5170✓ | 1798 | 290✓ | 1759 |
| 345 | 4280✓ | 0 | 120✓ | 377 | 4500✓ | 0 | 230✓ | 0 | .......... | | .......... | |
| 350 | 3810✓ | 735 | 150✓ | 2718 | 4150✓ | 60 | 380✓ | 1231 | 4360✓ | 8247 | 470✓ | 10305 |
| 355 | 3370✓ | 0 | 210✓ | 52 | 3670✓ | 0 | 400✓ | 25 | 3900✓ | 0 | 510✓ | 0 |
| 360 | 2950✓ | 1036 | 290✓ | 2832 | 3340✓ | 33 | 570✓ | 807 | 3600✓ | 458 | 710✓ | 1654 |
| 365 | 2550✓ | 0 | 390✓ | 200 | 2940✓ | 0 | 660✓ | 418 | 3210✓ | 1 | 810✓ | 508 |
| 370 | 2180✓ | 1595 | 520✓ | 5401 | 2610✓ | 27 | 830✓ | 4740 | 2900✓ | 706 | 1000✓ | 4991 |
| 375 | 1810✓ | 199 | 650✓ | 781 | 2300✓ | 1 | 1020✓ | 706 | 2610✓ | 101 | 1210✓ | 542 |
| 380 | 1510✓ | 2929 | 850✓ | 1424 | 2070✓ | 912 | 1290✓ | 1153 | 2350✓ | 1415 | 1440✓ | 8353 |
| 385 | 1250✓ | 211 | 1080✓ | 253 | 1820✓ | 10 | 1530✓ | 1654 | 2110✓ | 350 | 1690✓ | 11 |
| 390 | 1030✓ | 1941 | 1360✓ | 582 | 1540✓ | 217 | 1750✓ | 525 | 1890✓ | 3346 | 1970✓ | 370 |
| 395 | 850✓ | 232 | 1680✓ | 64 | 1350✓ | 5 | 2050✓ | 15 | 1690✓ | 58 | 2270✓ | 14 |
| 400 | 700✓ | 9177 | 2020✓ | 3538 | 1220✓ | 3613 | 2420✓ | 1576 | 1520✓ | 13738 | 2590✓ | 7029 |
| 405 | 570✓ | 561 | 2390✓ | 318 | 1030✓ | 1299 | 2720✓ | 10 | 1360✓ | 134 | 2920✓ | 1 |
| 410 | 460✓ | 2702 | 2790✓ | 228 | 890✓ | 3992 | 3090✓ | 1106 | 1220✓ | 4372 | 3280✓ | 1963 |
| 415 | 380✓ | 3044 | 3200✓ | 4 | 780✓ | 326 | 3470✓ | 1 | 1090✓ | 599 | 3650✓ | 2 |
| 420 | 310✓ | 12230 | 3630✓ | 449 | 730✓ | 4351 | 3910✓ | 52 | 980✓ | 5822 | 4030✓ | 1758 |
| 425 | 250✓ | 1425 | 4070✓ | 5 | 590✓ | 388 | 4270✓ | 0 | 880✓ | 1501 | 4420✓ | 180 |
| 430 | 200✓ | 9859 | 4520✓ | 173 | 510✓ | 3493 | 4690✓ | 229 | 750✓ | 6303 | 4790✓ | 362 |
| 435 | 170✓ | 233 | 4980✓ | 0 | 440✓ | 646 | 5120✓ | 0 | 710✓ | 422 | 5240✓ | 0 |
| 440 | 140✓ | 7920 | 5450✓ | 1 | 390✓ | 168 | 5560✓ | 0 | 630✓ | 3055 | 5670✓ | 8 |
| 445 | 110✓ | 154 | 5920✓ | 0 | 340✓ | 42 | 6010✓ | 0 | 560✓ | 36 | 6090✓ | 0 |
| 450 | 90✓ | 7535 | 6400✓ | 601 | 240✓ | 16422 | 6420✓ | 0 | 460✓ | 16089 | 6490✓ | 4361 |
| 455 | 70✓ | 49 | 6890✓ | 0 | 230✓ | 0 | 6900✓ | 0 | 440✓ | 21 | 6970✓ | 0 |
| 460 | 60✓ | 1340 | 7370✓ | 0 | 220✓ | 3175 | 7390✓ | 0 | 360✓ | 5692 | 7390✓ | 0 |
| 465 | 50✓ | 251 | 7860✓ | 0 | 200✓ | 12 | 7860✓ | 0 | .......... | | .......... | |
| 470 | 40✓ | 281 | 8350✓ | 0 | 170✓ | 3072 | 8340✓ | 0 | 310✓ | 1709 | 8330✓ | 0 |

less important. One of the reasons that you sell options in the first place is to avoid the "where do I get in?" dilemma. Therefore, the timing of your trade is not as important as your conviction about the long-term fundamentals. The flexibility of selling distant options can make up for a lot of oversights or outright mistakes in timing. Timing becomes even less important when it comes to spread trading because the spread or total credit received often can remain the same, even though the value of individual options may be fluctuating.

Nonetheless, although not as important as in futures trading, the right timing can be the difference between collecting a large premium or a small premium on your option sale and therefore must be something to consider when placing a trade. Since this is not a book on technical trading, we are not going to delve into all the technical indicators and chart patterns that may or may not help you to predict a market rally, correction, or reversal. Suffice to say that technical indicators can be used in the timing of your trades to optimize premiums on entry and possibly exits.

There are two schools of thought regarding momentum and the entry into a short option trade. For example purposes, we will use selling calls to illustrate these two approaches. However, the methods can be reversed just as easily and used for selling puts.

While these methods may seem painfully obvious, deciding which method to subscribe to will help you save time and make decision making easier for you.

*Method 1 (more aggressive).* Sell the call when the market is moving higher. Traders in this school of thought sell their calls when the market is moving against the calls, thus driving their values higher and producing more premium for the sellers.

*Method 2 (more conservative).* Sell the calls when the market is moving lower. When the price of the underlying contract is moving away from your strike, the premium for the option should be falling. However, the market's momentum is already carrying it in the direction that you, the call seller, want it to move. This can mean a lower premium for you but also can give your option a "head start" on deterioration.

In the end, whichever method is used generally comes down to personal style.

## PLACING OPTION ORDERS

Once you have determined that your option has enough open interest for your intended purposes and have decided that the timing is right to sell the premium, it is time to place your order. While several types of orders can be entered when selling options, for our purposes here, we will review the two most common:

*Market order.* A market order is an order to sell your option(s) at whatever price the market is currently willing to pay for them.

*Limit order.* With a limit order, you specify the price at which you are willing to sell your option(s). It is then up to the market to determine whether it wants to pay your price or not.

*We strongly advise against placing market orders when selling option premium.* You will want to place *limit orders* when selling your options. This ensures that if filled, you will get your desired premium for the option that you are selling. Do not be too eager to enter the trade. Pick the price you want to get for the option, place the order, and let the market come to you. The order always can be adjusted. A market order in an option is simply inviting huge slippage and a poor fill for yourself.

## HOW TO PRICE YOUR OPTION

There are two prices you'll want to look at before placing your order—the bid and the ask. At the risk of becoming too elementary, the bid and the ask are defined below.

*Bid*—what the highest-priced buyer is currently willing to pay to buy the option.

*Ask*—what the lowest-priced seller is currently willing to pay to sell the option.

When these two come together, an option trade takes place.

In slowly trading options, the bid and ask will have to be considered before placing your order. If there is a bid that has been sitting all day at 6 cents and an ask that has been sitting all day at 8 cents, you may start with an ask such as 7½ cents and work down if you are willing to accept these prices.

In an actively traded option, generally the last price traded is as good of a place as any to price your limit order if your objective is simply to get a fill. You can always adjust it slightly lower if your order is not getting filled. However, if you want to enter an order at a higher asking price, you always can do so and wait to see if the market moves enough to push the option value higher and bring a buyer at your price. Some traders favor the approach of placing "wish" orders at the beginning of the trading day at premiums well above the current listed price. Occasionally (as a result of market movement or a desperate buyer), these get filled.

Working a limit order can be time-consuming if you are determined to get a fill. A good option broker can be very helpful in this regard. If you have a good relationship with your broker, you can give her "limited discretion" to fill your order in your best interest. This can give the broker the leeway to work your order and make necessary changes in the order without contacting you every five minutes. Of course, you should only give this type of freedom to a broker in which you have established a great degree of trust.

The other alternative, of course, is to set your price and wait for the market to come to you. This can be an excellent strategy. The only risk is that the market moves away without filling you first, resulting in you not selling the strike price that you wanted.

## NO LOCK LIMIT IN OPTIONS

One fear that many futures traders have is getting caught in an adverse limit move. In other words, the trader is long the futures, and the market "locks" limit down. This means that there are far more sellers than buyers—so many, in fact, that the market has moved its exchange set limit for the day and is locked at that price for the day. If there are no willing buyers at that price level, the market will remain at that price until the following morning. In very volatile market conditions, the market can *lock limit down* or *lock limit up* for several days in a row because all the orders are on one side of the market.

As a futures trader, if you are on the right side of a lock-limit move, it can be a windfall of profits. If you are caught on the wrong side, quite the opposite could be true.

To put it bluntly, if you're caught on the wrong side of the market, and the market is locked limit, this means that prices are moving rapidly against you and you cannot get out. Your losses are multiplying daily, and there is nothing you can do about it.

To the fear mongers of "unlimited risk" in option selling, the following fact may be of interest: Options do not lock limit. Options do not have a daily limit move. Therefore, you almost always can get out. Granted, it may not be at a price that you like, but you can get out. This fact alone can provide peace of mind for traders who fear getting "stuck" in a position.

Futures traders often look at option values when the futures contracts are locked limit up or down. It is thought that the option values will reflect the "true" value of the market.

It generally will take a major fundamental development to cause the market to lock limit up or down, especially for several days in a row. A good example is the cattle market in December of 2003 when the first case of mad cow disease ever was discovered in the United States.

## WORST-CASE SCENARIO

On December 22, 2003, the U.S. Department of Agriculture (USDA) announced that a cow in the state of Washington had tested positive for mad cow disease. This was as shocking as it was unprecedented.

On that day, almost anybody long the cattle market probably had the same basic thought: "Get out, get out, GET OUT!"

Unfortunately, if you were long futures contracts, this was not possible. The market was locked limit down the morning of December 23 and remained so through the Christmas holiday and into the following week. With everybody selling and nobody buying, the long futures traders were stuck in their positions with nothing to do but watch the market open limit down for several days straight and wait until it started trading again at a much lower price (see Figure 8.2).

**F I G U R E   8.2**

February 2004 Live Cattle Price Chart

LCG04 - Live Cattle, Feb 04, Daily

Often in the case of jolting market news, the market not only will price in a worst-case scenario but also likely will overreact. While the limit move in cattle futures prices was 150 points (1.5 cents) at the time, the options were already pricing in a move of 18 cents lower. Put option values reached their peak the first two days after the move as traders clamored to either cover short put positions or tried to hedge long futures positions by buying puts.

Exiting long positions was the only objective of many speculators. Although this may not have been the best course of action at the time, it was indeed possible for option traders. The same cannot be said for futures traders.

By the beginning of the following week, cooler heads began to prevail. Market limits on futures were expanded to allow the market to start trading again. And while the futures market price was still moving lower, a very peculiar thing began to happen to the put option values. They began to decrease! Nobody really knew how much a single case of mad cow disease would affect beef demand or prices in the long term. However, in the first few days after the announcement, all that anybody wanted to do was exit longs, whatever way they could. The option values priced in the overreaction.

This is another testament to selling far-out-of-the money options. Although volatility had driven the option values and margins to a much higher level, losses for a cattle trader would have been much less if he was short puts rather than long futures. The size of his losses would have depended on how far out of the money he had sold puts. The further out of the money he had sold premium, the less his losses were likely to be.

By Monday, when the trade began to look at things in perspective, the option values began pricing the futures market somewhat higher. Option traders who waited out the market's initial reaction would have been wise to wait until this point to exit. They still would have taken losses, but they would have been less severe than they were the previous week, and positions could have been closed out in an orderly, rational fashion rather than in panic.

We use this example because it illustrates several key points about option selling and risk:

1. Options do not *lock limit* up or down, and you almost always can get out if you want out, as long as you are willing to accept the price the market is offering. Yet, in moves made based on big, breaking news where panic buying or selling is evident solely from the news story, it is often better to wait until the "dust settles" after the market's initial surge to exit short option positions. The futures market may lock limit up or down, but the option market often will price in a worst-case scenario in the first day or two after such a news event, only to back off once rational thought returns to the market. This means that out-of-the-money option volatility and therefore premiums can be at their highest in the first few days after such an event. If your short options already have priced a worst-case scenario, the situation therefore can only get better, right? Losses often can be pared by waiting a few days after such a news event to exit.

2. The mad cow illustration is indeed a "worst case" type of scenario for an option seller or a futures trader. Yet it illustrates the differences between futures trading risk and option selling risk. Put sellers as a whole would have fared substantially better than futures traders in this type of move. This would have been especially true for traders following our approach of selling far-out-of-the-money strikes. Futures traders would have suffered the full brunt of the move, and they would have been locked in their positions until the market decided to let them out, probably at losses as high as 18 to 20 cents per contract. Option traders, even ones who sold naked puts, could have exited at almost

any time, most likely at a fraction of the losses incurred by their futures-trading counterparts. Traders who used a risk strategy of buying some close-to-the-money options to help "cover" their naked positions (see Chapter 9) would have fared substantially better.

3. It illustrates the importance of diversification. If cattle puts were only a small part of your portfolio, this incident, although unpleasant, probably would only be a minor setback in your account.

4. It illustrates the importance of selling out-of-the-money options. This is fairly self-evident. The further out of the money, the lower the likely loss is in such a move.

This is the type of example that option-selling naysayers point to when they try to convince you that option selling is no good, dangerous, etc. However, as you read in the preceding above, if you were positioned far enough out of the money, had properly diversified, deployed a proper risk-management technique, and kept your head rather than panicked, you could have exited your position calmly, absorbed the loss, and moved on. The impact may have been even less if you were in a partially covered or spread position.

However, the most notable feature about this example is its rarity. A fundamental change in a market with this speed and magnitude could be a once-in-a-decade occurrence. We are not talking something like the soybean market going through a weather rally. In that case, you know that you're in the growing season, and you've probably seen the weekly weather reports growing increasingly hot and dry (or wet, cold, etc.). This mad cow example is a completely unexpected turn of events that could not have been predicted through any type of analysis (think 9/11). You may sell options for many years and never run into a case such as this. However, it is important to know because, again, this is the type of example the unenlightened "experts" love to use to scare you away from selling options. You can replace that fear with knowledge.

You can never completely eliminate the risk of something like this taking place. But you can plan for it, be prepared for it, and if you've managed your portfolio properly, learn from it and move on.

## OPTION ASSIGNMENT: WHEN YOUR OPTION EXPIRES IN THE MONEY

Another fear that many new option sellers may experience is the fear of getting assigned. We've heard the fear in many a new trader's voice at the mere utterance of the ominous word *assignment*. To these potential option sellers, we have one word of advice: *Relax*.

In almost every case, if you are selling options as we are suggesting in this book, you will not be assigned unless you want to be assigned. In fact, being assigned does not necessarily mean that you are even taking a loss. Although the idea of *assignment* or having your option *executed* may sound frightening, it is really only the process of having your investment shifted from one vehicle to another.

Theoretically, options sold on American exchanges can be executed or assigned at any time during the life of the option. This process is initiated by the option buyer. However, in almost every case, this is not beneficial to the option buyer unless the option is actually in the money and is at or near expiration. As we stated earlier, in most cases, if the buyer of the option wants to exit the position, it is more profitable simply to sell it back to the market.

In other words, *for all practical purposes, you do not need to worry about being assigned unless your option is expiring in the money.* Therefore, if you don't want to be assigned, it is best to buy your option back before this situation occurs. If you are using any of the

**F I G U R E   8.3**

March 2004 Silver Price Chart

SIH04 - Silver-Pit, Mar 04, Daily

risk-management techniques described in this book, chances are that you will be out of your options long before you were even in a situation where your options might be exercised.

If you do happen to get assigned, it is no big deal. There is nothing that you have to do. It is all handled by your broker. Instead of holding a short option, you are now long or short a futures contract from your strike price. If you do not want to be in this position, you can simply close it out immediately. It will cost you an extra commission, but it is just as easy as buying or selling an option. This is another area where a good broker can be extremely helpful.

## EXAMPLE: JOHN GETS ASSIGNED ON SILVER CALLS

Trader John was short March silver 700 calls when the options expired on March 15 (see Figure 8.3). When the options expired, they were 16 cents in the money. John's option was assigned the next day, meaning that John was now short one contract of March silver from 700. He could choose simply to hold the contract and play the futures market, or he could immediately close the position for a 16-cent loss. However, the loss would be no greater than it would have been had he simply bought his option back with the March contract at the same price.

Even if the option is assigned, John still gets to keep the original premium he collected from the sale of the option.

It is in the subjects covered in this chapter that much of the misunderstanding and fear relating to option selling is contained. However, knowledge replaces fear. You now have an argument for futures traders that tells you that option selling is risky. You know something about the right orders to place when entering a position and what type of liquidity with which you may be comfortable. And although nobody wants a limit move against her position, you know the reasons why it is better to be short options on such a rare occasion than it is to be caught in the futures contract.

With this knowledge in hand, it is now time to explore the most important subject in option selling—the subject of risk management.

# 9
## CHAPTER

# Risk Control in Option Selling

The fact that 75 to 80 percent of all options held through expiration expire worthless always produces an initial question in the new option trader's mind: *"What about the other 20 percent?"*

Having most of options that you sell expire worthless is the easy part. What to do with the other 20 percent then becomes the whole ballgame. Risk management in option selling is probably the most important aspect of your entire portfolio strategy.

While we have pointed out several times that the risks of option selling often are much fewer than most of the trading world makes them out to be, one cannot ignore the fact that option selling nonetheless carries some inherent risks. A good quarter or even a good year of option selling profits can be negated or even turned into a sizable loss if only one or two losing trades are left to go astray.

The focus of this chapter, then, is not on picking winners but on how to manage the losers. "How do I manage my risk?" is almost always one of the primary questions a new or even experienced option seller asks. Our hope is that after reading this chapter, you will be able to enter into an option writing approach to your portfolio confident that you can handle or at least be familiar with appropriate strategies of risk management.

## RISK MANAGEMENT BEGINS BEFORE YOU ENTER A POSITION

We will begin with the old words of wisdom: *"An ounce of prevention is worth a pound of cure."*

Risk management of your portfolio begins not after you enter your position but *before* you enter any position. Risk management will be one of the primary factors you use to decide on an appropriate strike price(s) at which to sell premium.

## Risk-Management Checkpoint 1: Sell Far-Out-of-the-Money Options with Low Deltas

Many option sellers point out that options experience their greatest time decay in the last 30 days of their trading life. The logic goes that these would be the ideal options to sell because they will show the fastest deterioration and thus show a profit sooner. While this is true, generally it also means that in order to collect any worthwhile premium, the trader will have to sell very close-to-the-money strike prices. While this often can produce fairly quick profits for the option seller, the problem is that even a brief market hiccup can put the option in the money, possibly producing quick and sizable losses.

Trying to sell short-term options puts you back in the game of picking short-term market direction, the exact thing we are trying to avoid by selling options in the first place.

We had a new client this year who was very excited about starting his option selling portfolio. For the purpose of the story, we will call him Ted. Based on long-term fundamental data and historical volatility, we recommended to Ted that he sell far-out-of-the-money coffee calls for his account. Ted liked the idea of the trade, but the fact that the options did not expire for almost four months troubled him. It was not the fact that he didn't think the options would be profitable—he did. But four months seemed like an awful long time to wait, even though the trade would have approximately doubled his capital invested had the options expired worthless. Ted wanted *action*.

"If ya'll think the price is going down, why don't we sell the 76 calls that expire next month?" he reasoned.

The calls we were recommending to Ted were more than 70 cents out of the money, and coffee was trading at about 70 cents per pound at the time. Coffee prices would have had to more than *double* for the options to go in the money. Ted wanted to sell options that were only 6 cents out of the money that expired in less than 30 days. While the options may have had close to the same deltas at the time, Ted's options stood a much higher chance of going in the money.

We tried to explain to Ted that while the fundamentals painted a relatively bearish picture for at least the next six months, it did not mean that prices could not stage a temporary rally in the meantime and put his options in the money. The 140 calls we were recommending would remain well out of the money, even if the coffee market rallied 10 or 20 cents.

Ted was unswayed. He made the mistake of thinking that because the fundamentals were bearish, it meant that the market would go down, period. Unfortunately for Ted, that is not always how it works. Ted went ahead and sold the near-month 76 calls.

Of course, the following week the market experienced a fund-led rally that saw it gain over 10 cents in just two weeks. Ted eventually bought back his positions at more than three times the price at which he had sold them, losing about $1,200 per option.

Sellers of the 140 calls barely felt a pinch. The market rally was short-lived, and the coffee market again settled back down into its previous trading range. The 140 calls expired worthless a few months later, doubling the invested capital of the traders who had sold them at the time Ted sold his.

The moral of the story is not that selling close to the money is bad. Mathematicians who argue that options with matching deltas carry the same risk are wrong. Once an option goes in the money, its delta increases very quickly. Selling options close to the money can work, but it is a much more aggressive strategy than selling further away with more time.

Therefore, the first building block in your risk-control strategy should be to select far-out-of-the-money options with low deltas. In limiting yourself to these types of options, you give yourself a wide margin of error for the market to make short-term fluctuations without affecting your position drastically. While these options can still lose money, you force the market to make a large-scale, sustained move (against your position) before your options will reach your risk parameters. In addition, since the deltas are much lower, if the market is moving against you, the option values generally are moving against you much slower than they would be if they were in the money or close to being in the money. This gives you plenty of time to make decisions and, should it be necessary, to exit your position in an orderly fashion *on your terms* rather than being forced out or panicking and making a rushed, emotional decision.

### Risk-Management Checkpoint 2: Diversify Your Option Portfolio

While diversification often is heralded as a necessity in almost any type of investment, nowhere is it more crucial than in option selling. By diversifying your option sales across different markets, you reduce your exposure in any given contract to a limited portion of your portfolio. Therefore, if a worst-case scenario does unfold, it should not have a large-scale impact on your account.

By diversifying, however, we do not mean that you should diversify your futures option selling portfolio over 25 different markets. Remember that option selection may start with identifying markets that offer very favorable fundamentals for selling puts or calls. Most markets will have mixed or cloudy fundamentals much of the time. Do not diversify for the sake of diversifying, but strive to find other markets with clear fundamentals in which to expand your portfolio. Most of our option portfolios are diversified over four to six different futures sectors at any given time.

Diversifying across many markets not only will increase your chances of having close to 80 percent of your options expiring worthless, but it also will *decrease* your chances of having losers take sizable chunks out of your account. By diversifying only into markets with fundamentals that you believe are favorable to your position, you can increase these odds further in your favor.

### Risk-Management Checkpoint 3: Set Your Risk Parameters When You Enter the Trade

This is a standard rule of futures trading regardless of whether you are selling options, trading spreads, or trading outright futures positions.

When Michael was learning to scuba dive several years ago in the Florida Keys, one of the key safety points constantly drilled into divers heads was this: *Plan the dive; dive the plan.* In other words, before the diver ever jumps in the water, he has worked out a detailed plan as to what he wants to accomplish, how much time it will take, how much air he will need, and when he will be back to the boat.

The same type of plan should be implemented in your option selling portfolio. *Plan the trade; trade the plan.* When you sell an option, you should know *before* entering the position what your risk-management plan will be. What technique will you be using? When will it be enacted? What is your breakeven? What would be your loss on the trade if the technique were implemented properly? Improperly? Who will be putting your risk plan into action—you, your broker, or somebody else?

Knowing this and having a plan in case the market throws you a curveball is the number 1 key to avoiding *emotional decision making,* which, as we know, is a primary enemy of a successful trader. Countless numbers of traders experience hefty losses that could have been cut to insignificant amounts if a proper risk-management plan were followed.

"Lets watch it for a day and see what it does" is not a risk-management plan.

What are these risk management techniques? We will now explore them along with the benefits and drawbacks of each.

### RISK-MANAGEMENT TECHNIQUES FOR OPTION SELLERS

Many traders will call and ask us about a complex technique they read about that virtually ensures they "can't lose" if they work it property. "I sell a call, and if it goes in the money, I buy a futures contract, and if the futures moves against me, I buy a put and . . . , " and they continue on and on discussing offsetting and then offsetting the offset.

Rather than delving into all these techniques and picking apart piece by piece what can happen to your account, let's sum it up in two short sentences: *Don't do this. It probably won't work.*

Not only will it probably not work, but you also probably will end up losing more money than you would have by just getting out. You will pay more commissions, adding to your losses. You will spend more time trying to untangle and watch and counteroffset your growing position, all in an effort to get back your growing loss. This is time spent that could be used to find new and profitable trades.

Trying to offset a losing short option position with futures contracts is like trying to get rid of the rats in your garage by releasing rattlesnakes. You may get rid of the rats, but then what?

If you start using futures as a risk-management tool for your option selling, you're back in the game of trying to time the market and decide what it is going to do on a short-term basis. As we've indicated, if you are trying to trade short term, you could be leaving the fate of your funds in the hands of Lady Luck more than anything else.

Therefore, we strongly recommend the KISS (keep it simple, stupid) approach to risk management in your option selling. Over the years, we have found that the simplest approaches are almost always the best approaches. The following are the three techniques that we have found to be most effective in our years of option selling.

### Technique 1: Buy Close-to-the-Money Options to Offset Your Far-Out-of-the-Money Short Options

This is a variation on ratio spreading, but it can be adapted to work very well for the marginally conservative investor. It involves using a certain portion of proceeds from your short option sales to buy a small amount of near-the-money options. If the market moves toward the options you have sold, the options that you bought closer to the money will increase in value faster, thus offsetting, at least partially, losses or increased margins on the short options. This effect is magnified further if the long options go in the money.

For example, if you sold 10 far-out-of-the-money wheat calls, you would take a certain percentage of the premium collected from the sale of these options and buy a small number of *near-the-money* or *at-the-money* wheat calls for the same month or a closer month.

What percentage of your collected premium you use will depend on how conservative you want to be. Less conservative traders may only use 10 to 20 percent of the premiums they collected to buy this "protection." Other, more conservative traders can use up to 50 percent of their collected premiums to buy more of a protective position. How many you buy also will depend on your risk temperament. You do not have to buy a lot. One in-the-money long call working for you can offset several far-out-of-the-money calls that you are short.

If all the calls expire worthless, you keep the premiums you collected minus what you paid for the protection. If you are wrong, and the market and prices move higher, the at-the-money calls gain value much faster than your out-of-the-money calls, at least partially offsetting losses on your short calls. In addition, this can keep you in a trade much longer without being "squeezed out."

Protecting your short options in this way also has the added benefit of potentially larger profits. If the long calls you bought for protection expire in the money and your short calls expire out of the money, not only will you profit from your short calls expiring, but you also could make a substantial bonus from the profits of your long calls. This strategy works equally well with puts. We highly recommend this approach, especially to investors new to selling options. The only downside is that it reduces profits from your short options. The section on *ratio credit spreads* in Chapter 7 contains more details on how one long option can offset several short options. Although this risk-control method may not be considered an actual ratio spread, the overall concept is the same. We consider it an excellent, albeit slightly sophisticated, risk-management strategy. A good option broker can help you to make the right choice in selecting your "coverage" so that profits can be maximized (see Table 9.1).

## Technique 2: Set an Exit Point Based on the Value of the Option Itself

More aggressive traders who do not want to sacrifice a portion of their premiums simply can place an exit point on the value of the option itself. This is the simplest way to manage your risk in option selling. It involves little calculation, is easy to implement, and has the least number of variables as far as knowing what your anticipated loss would be. If you sell an option for 50 points, you exit the position if the option reaches 100 points (or 90 or 120—whatever your risk tolerance is).

In our experience, we've found a good place to set this "stop loss" in many circumstances is at double the premium received. If you sold an option for $400, exit the position if the option value reaches $800. This amount seems to give the market plenty of room to move while at the same time holding losses to a manageable level if things do not go as planned. We will refer to this as the *200 percent rule,* for if the option increases in value to 200 percent of the value for which you sold it, you exit the position. However, this level is not set in stone and can be adjusted depending on the individual market as long as this is done before the trade is entered. We do recommend the 200 percent rule to some beginners not only for its simplicity but also for its overall effectiveness.

**T A B L E   9.1**

Buying Options to "Cover" Short Options

| Benefits | Drawbacks |
|---|---|
| Counterbalances adverse moves against short option positions | Slightly more sophisticated approach |
| Trader can withstand large moves against the position while incurring only minimal (if any) loss. This allows the trader to remain in the trade long enough for the options to expire. | Increased transactions costs |
| Potential for large gain if long option expires in the money | Cuts into profits on short in-the-money options if all options expire worthless |

Many traders will assume that this means placing a stop loss order like they would if they had a futures or even a stock position. *We do not recommend actually placing a stop-loss order for your option.*

The reason is this: Let's say that you place a stop-loss order to buy your option back at 100 points. This means that if your option is bought or sold for 100 points at any time, your ticket is to be filled at the next available price. A single fill for that option at that price is enough to trigger your stop. If somebody places a market order, it could easily fill at your stop price, triggering your stop, even though it may be a bit "out of line" with the rest of the market. (Surely, a floor trader would never do this deliberately!) Your stop order then becomes a *market order,* and in options, market orders can suffer tremendous slippage.

This can be especially true if you are not trading in the most liquid option markets. You end up with a terrible fill, and somebody ends up selling your options back to you and getting a heck of a deal (surely not the floor trader who would never trigger your stop).

If a trader sold an option for 50 points and enters a stop-loss order at 100 points, there is nothing more frustrating than seeing the option trade at 75 to 80 points all day and then jump suddenly up to 100 points, see the options fill at 105, only to settle back to 75 to 80 points for the day. For this reason, some traders like to add the variation that the option value actually must *settle* above the stop point at day's end before they will enter their exit order (for the following day's open). While we think that this can be a good technique, it does expose the trader to potentially larger losses if the underlying is moving rapidly against the trader's position.

While it can open the door to second guessing yourself, we advise using only *mental stops* in implementing this technique for the reasons stated above. While, in using mental stops, it can be tempting to "hold" your order even as the option value exceeds your risk parameter, doing so is not advised. Trade the plan. In the long term, it will save you much financial pain.

There is, of course, no guarantee that you will be filled at your desired exit point, even when using a stop order. However, if you are trading far-out-of-the-money options, you should be able to close out the position within a few points of your desired exit level in most market conditions. A good broker can be very effective in helping you to exit at the right time.

The drawback to this technique, of course, is that some or even many of the options that you exit eventually will expire worthless. Granted, we have seen many well-capitalized investors choose to "ride it out," especially if the option is still far out of the money when the premium hits their risk parameter. However, we also have seen account performance hurt by riding it out for too long.

Look at it this way: Our offices are on the western coast of Florida. In Florida, we have our share of tropical storms and hurricanes. Every summer and early fall we have to keep one eye on the weather forecasts to see if there are any "areas of activity" in the

Gulf of Mexico, Caribbean Sea, and Atlantic Ocean. Almost every summer there will be at least a few storms that threaten to come our way. The newscasts will issue warnings of the storm. Having Tampa Bay in our backyards, we tend to listen to these newscasts. Often if a storm is approaching, the county will issue a *voluntary* or *mandatory* evacuation order. Many people do not like to evacuate (because of the time, trouble, and money involved) and commit themselves to "riding it out." Most of these people have been very fortunate over the years because our area has not experienced a major storm in a long time. However, what will happen to these people if and when the big storm finally does come? They and their families could experience severe trauma, injury, or worse.

If you are troubled by the fact that you exited an option and it eventually expired worthless, you should consider the preceding example. You evacuated, and the storm missed your house. It cost you a small expense. This may happen many times to you. When the big storm comes someday, however, you will be long gone before it arrives (see Table 9.2).

## Technique 3: Rolling Options

The concept of *rolling* options is not necessarily a risk-control technique in and of itself. It is more of an expansion on Technique 1. Rolling options can be done if the trader has stopped out of a short option sale using Technique 1 yet still feels that the fundamentals favor the position and wants to be in the trade. In this circumstance, the trader closes out the short options at double premium (or whatever her risk parameter was) and "rolls up" to a higher strike price (or down to a lower strike price if she sold puts). In other words, the trader closes the original position (short calls) and sells more calls at a higher strike price.

This accomplishes three things. First, it removes the trader from options that have either increased in delta and/or have become closer to the money and puts her back in options that are far out of the money with lower deltas and have a much lower chance of going in the money. Second, it allows the trader to stay in a market that she feels

### T A B L E   9.2

Premium-Based Exit Strategy

| Benefits | Drawbacks |
| --- | --- |
| Simple and easy to implement and understand | Psychological temptation to override stop |
| Effective in limiting losses | Many of the exited options eventually will expire worthless |
| Probable loss can be estimated before entry | Fast-moving markets can cause option values to exceed stop level (vulnerable to large adverse moves) |

eventually will be profitable. Third, from a psychological standpoint, it allows the trader to avoid or at least reduce a loss in that particular market, even though in reality it is actually an entirely separate trade.

The concept of rolling options can be illustrated in the following example.

In April, trader John is long-term bearish on the coffee market. Although John is not quite sure prices will go down right away, he feels relatively confident that coffee will not be trading at substantially higher prices later in the year. John decides to sell five September coffee 1.00 calls for 200 points ($750) each (see Figure 9.1).

Over the course of the next 30 days, September coffee rallies more than 9 cents per pound, a fairly large move for futures traders but of relatively less significance to John because at its highs, September coffee was trading at just over 72 cents (see Figure 9.2).

**F I G U R E   9.1**

September 2003 Coffee Chart Showing 110 Calls

CFU03 - Coffee, Sep 03, Daily

John sells September coffee 1.00 calls.

**F I G U R E   9.2**

September 2003 Coffee Chart Showing 9-Cent Rally

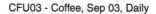

CFU03 - Coffee, Sep 03, Daily

Nine cents is a fairly large move for futures traders but not as significant to John.

Nonetheless, John's options increase in value from 200 points to 400 points during the course of the move. John had decided on risking the trade to double premium and therefore exits his position at 400 points—a $3,750 loss (5 × $750) plus transaction costs.

John, however, is convinced that the fundamentals do not support coffee prices over $1.00. He sees that the September coffee 130 calls are now trading for 200 points each, with much lower deltas than the 1.00 calls. John sells 11 of the 130 calls for 200 points each.

Why does John sell 11 calls? He sells 5 to collect the original premium he intended to keep as profit. He sells 5 more to recover the loss he accrued in his 1.00 calls. And he sells 1 additional option to cover the transaction costs for rolling the position.

Therefore, if September coffee stays below 130 without the calls reaching John's risk parameter, John will erase his loss and make his originally intended profit on the $1.00 calls. In John's mind, the loss "never happened" (see Figure 9.3).

**F I G U R E   9.3**

September 2003 Coffee Chart Showing John "Roll" His Options

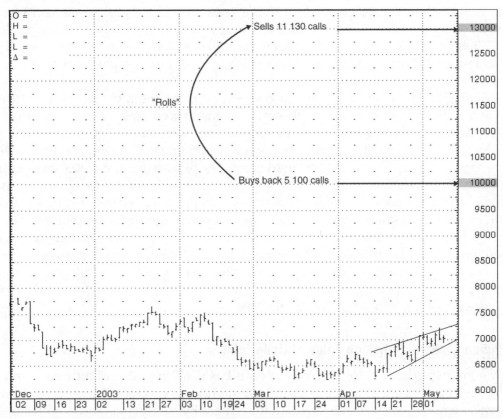

CFU03 - Coffee, Sep 03, Daily

John "rolls out" of 1.00 calls and into 130 calls.

In this example, John indeed would have been successful. However, rolling options is not necessarily best for every trade in which you stop yourself out. If a market has moved against your position to the point at which you are forced out, there must be a reason for it. It is best to know what it is before deciding to reposition in the same market. In addition, this is a time where you should be reexamining the original fundamentals that caused you to enter the trade initially. Does the long-term (two- to five-month) picture remain unchanged? If it remains the same and you still like the market and the position, this may be a candidate for rolling.

A good question to ask yourself is this: If I had never been in the position and now were looking at this market anew, is this a trade I would enter, or do I see better opportunities elsewhere? Do not make the mistake of simply rolling in order to "not take a loss" or for "revenge" on the market that took your money. John might make his money back in soybeans, silver, or crude oil. He reentered the coffee trade because he thought it was the best opportunity for making a profit. This is the only reason you should do so as well.

The major risk of rolling, of course, is that the market can continue to move against your new positions, potentially magnifying your losses to a painful degree. For this reason, rolling options can be considered a more aggressive strategy for some traders.

There is no rule, however, that states that the position must be doubled up. If you are simply considering selling the higher-priced strikes as a completely new trade, any number of options can be sold.

Rolling as illustrated in John's case generally is for the highly capitalized trader who is not intimidated by losses. In theory, if a trader has enough money, and if the market continues to move against him, he simply can continue to roll his positions into higher strikes, doubling down each time. It is an option play on the futures trading technique of *scale trading*. Eventually, the market is going to reach a point where it stops moving against the trader, and the last set of options that he sold will expire worthless, giving him all his money back. However, this strategy can require hoards of capital and can result in substantial losses if you run out of money before the options expire. For this reason, it is not recommended for the average investor. Still, it can be a valid approach, and if you have the capital to keep doubling up your investment, it is almost guaranteed.

For most investors, however, one roll will be enough. If you roll your positions and stop out again, you probably have misread the market somewhere and are best moving on to a different trade (see Table 9.3).

## Technique 4: Basing Risk on Value of Underlying

The alternative approach to setting exit points based on the value of the option is to set exit points on the actual price of the underlying futures contract. This is considered to be a more aggressive approach to risk management by some. It can mean withstanding large increases in the value of your option and/or margin requirements over the short

**T A B L E   9.3**

Rolling Options

| Benefits | Drawbacks |
|---|---|
| Allows a trader to remain in a market in which she feels that her position is fundamentally sound | Can result in magnified losses if the trader has fundamentally "misdiagnosed" the market |
| Allows a trader to recoup losses from her original position in which she was stopped out | |
| Psychological confidence gained from "being right" | |

term. It also can be slightly more difficult to gauge what your probable losses would be. Exiting the position with little time left on the options may only result in nominal losses or none at all. Exiting the position with much time left on the option could mean a larger loss. However, this technique can also increase the chances that your position ultimately will be profitable.

Let's first examine why an investor would want to consider such a strategy. The figure of 75 to 80 percent of all options expiring worthless would not take into account options that you sold and then had them double in value, at which point you exited them. As discussed earlier, many of these would still expire worthless and therefore would have to be considered part of the large percentage just listed, yet for you they would have been losing trades.

Traders who can't stand the thought of exiting an option that they still feel eventually will expire may want to consider this method. However, if this method is used regularly, chances are that eventually one could experience a more sizable loss. Nonetheless, it can be a very effective method of risk control, especially if it is used only in certain market situations, such as options with little time value remaining.

There are two ways one can employ such a strategy. One is to hold the position unless a certain technical condition is violated (e.g., support, resistance broken, trendline violated, etc.).

A second way to implement this method is to risk the option until it goes in the money. In other words, if you sell a call or a put at a particular strike, risk the trade until the futures reach that price. This works better with options sold closer to the money. It can be used with options sold at distant strike prices and eventually should produce profits most of the time. However, in the event that the strike would be attained, losses could be substantial. Yet, with strikes sold relatively close to the money, it can be an excellent method of risk control. Technical traders often prefer this method because options can be sold just beyond points of key support or resistance. In this regard, we favor it as well.

The following example illustrates this concept:

In January of 2002, trader John is long-term fundamentally bullish on T-bonds. When he senses that there may be an uptrend developing in late January, he takes it as his cue to position in the trade. However, John is afraid of trading the T-bond futures because short-term moves easily could stop him out of his position. Instead, he elects to sell the June 96 put because he believes that prices will at least remain above that level through expiration in May.

John knows that a quick correction in the market could occur at any time that easily could cause his option to double or more in value without actually reaching the 96 price level. Therefore, John decides that he will stay in his options unless the 96 price level is violated. He accepts the fact that his options could increase substantially in value during the course of the trade. He has backup capital available should this occur (see Figure 9.4).

**F I G U R E   9.4**

## June 2002 T-Bond Price Chart Showing Risk to 96

USM02 - 30 Yr US Treasury Bonds - Pit, Jun 02, Daily

John sells June 96 T-bond puts and risks a price move to 96.

John enters the trade with June T-bonds trading at near 102. T-bonds experience several small dips lower and back higher over the next few weeks, any of which may have stopped him out of a futures position. In March, T-bonds experience a severe downturn, causing John's options to gain significantly in value. However, the price of T-bonds has not yet reached his strike price. Instead of closing or rolling, John sticks it out, as per his original risk plan. He has much confidence in his fundamental conviction and is not going to be swayed by short-term market swings.

Eventually, prices begin to ascend again and go on to prove John right. The option values come back to where they were, then begin to decay, and ultimately expire worthless.

Traders closing positions at 200 percent of premium were losers. John was a winner.

What if, however, John had been wrong? What if prices had continued to fall all the way down to 96? John would then have bought his options back at whatever price the market demanded at that time. While it is difficult to determine what the value of John's options may be in this situation without including several pages of hypothetical forecasting models, John most likely would have experienced a loss greater than the trader who exited at the 200 percent premium level—more if the market moved quickly and reached his strike with much time left until expiration and less if it moved slowly and reached the strike with only little time remaining.

This strategy, while very effective in many situations, carries a higher degree of risk. Experience with fundamental analysis of a particular market is really what determines if this is an appropriate approach for you. It is not recommended for the beginner (see Table 9.4).

## SOME FINAL WORDS ON RISK CONTROL

While some may disagree, we do not recommend the practice of adding "offsetting" futures positions to a losing short option position. Adding more of any kind of position to a loser is, in our opinion, simply digging a deeper, more complex hole. It may work in some situations, but in our experience, most cases lead only to quagmire.

The simple methods just offered have been the most effective in our years of option selling.

If we could stress one point about risk control in option selling, however, it would be this: Your risk-control strategy begins when you are looking for options to sell. Your objective is not to pick winners. Your objective is to stay out of losers. Do this, and your winners and your profits will take care of themselves.

Not to beat a dead horse, but once again, this all comes back to fundamental knowledge of the market in which to trade. Know the factors or scenarios that could occur to produce a price move to your strike (regardless of what risk method you are using). Analyze the chances of any of these things taking place. You can never account for everything, but you can account for what is currently known.

If you have done this and are comfortable with the market and the strike price, using some traditional technical indicators to help you time your entry (such as

**T A B L E   9.4**

Basing Risk on Value of Underlying Contract

| Benefits | Drawbacks |
|---|---|
| Allows trader to profit from more trades than would a premium-based risk approach<br>Allows very wide range of market movement while permitting the trader to remain in the trade | Losses on the few trades that are losers could be substantial |

stochastics or simple moving averages) can be beneficial. If your research is good, chances are that you'll do just fine. Remember, this is option selling. You have a great deal of room to be wrong! However, a good risk-management plan will be in place to take care of those times when you are too wrong.

While the technical ups and downs of a daily chart should not greatly concern a longer-term option trader, continue to watch longer-term weekly and monthly charts for possible trend changes and/or breakouts. If these correspond with your fundamental analysis, you could have a great opportunity to sell calls or puts for many months. If it is in contrast to your fundamental analysis, you may want to reconsider your position or adjust your risk parameter.

One final caveat in risk control: You should continue to track long-term fundamental developments over the course of your trade. Just because these fundamentals tend to change slowly does not mean that they do not change, and it does not mean that occasionally they cannot change quickly. Most news items are not fundamental changes; they are simply what they are, news items. However, look for new themes starting to develop in your market.

Talk of a new type of beetle eating the leaves of the crop in which you are invested may be just a news item. Continued talk of it over the course of several weeks, along with talk of "crop damage" or potential "yield adjustments," could be another matter. If there is a fundamental change in the market in which you are positioned, and it seems to be affecting price, it can be a good idea to get out first and ask questions later. Just remember that generally it takes a major development to change the long-term fundamentals of a commodity, and most news stories that you hear or read about the market are, at least as far as you are concerned, "noise."

Experience is probably the only way to learn the difference.

# PART III

# MARKET ANALYSIS AND OPTION SELLING

# 10 CHAPTER

# Fundamentals versus Technicals

The debate between fundamental and technical analysts has raged for decades. For novice readers, it may be important to clarify the difference before proceeding any further. *Fundamentals,* by definition, consist of the economic factors behind a commodity or financial instrument, such as supply and demand and the factors that affect or could affect supply and demand. For example, the fundamentals of cotton would include the size of last year's crop, the amount of cotton left from that harvest that is still available for export or domestic use, the pace of exports this year, the progress of the upcoming crop, and projected weather that could affect its growth. These are all fundamentals, and if it looks like a lot of information to monitor, it is.

Assuming that one is able to monitor all these factors, the next task is to form a "big picture" of the market and then try to determine how these factors could affect price over the next three to six months. Doing this is a key task in selecting markets where option selling may be a favorable strategy and in determining strike prices that may be profitable.

*Technical analysis,* on the other hand, is the study of charts, chart formations, and an array of technical indicators that affect volume, price momentum, strength of buying or selling, and so on. Because technical trading is more concrete and tangible (e.g., buy when prices hit this line), it attracts both the mathematical and the statistical crowds along with novice traders. Pure technicians believe that all the current fundamentals are always priced into a futures contract at any given time and therefore that there is no use in studying the fundamentals—it's all in the price patterns.

This may be true to a certain extent. All the current fundamentals probably are already figured into price. What the pure technicians overlook is that studying fundamentals is not done to determine how they are affecting price *today*, but rather it is done to project how these factors could affect price in the *future*.

Our opinion is that both should play a role in option trading. This book, however, focuses more on fundamental analysis for two reasons:

1. Because we believe that the fundamentals should be the determinant of which market to trade. Fundamentals will help you to determine the markets where conditions are appropriate for selling out-of-the-money strikes on one side (or both) of the market. We see technicals as more of a timing or optimization tool to be used in entering the trade after the market in which to trade has been decided.
2. Because most books focus on technical trading. Therefore, there is already a wealth of information available to traders who want to learn to trade technically. Fundamentals are discussed much less in trading books and magazines, and we feel that it is time to give them their due.

The following story, told by James Cordier, is about one of his early experiences in learning the differences between technical and fundamental analyses and illustrates the importance of following both.

During the first few of my 20 years trading the commodity markets, one of the most commonly asked questions that I received from potential clients was "Are you a technical or fundamental trader?"

My answer was always the same, "Technical, of course."

At any given moment, I could pick up the phone and be asked my opinion of cocoa prices, pork bellies, or even Treasury bonds and have the answer shortly after punching up the chart.

"Well, Mr. Duke, I can tell you right now that I would cover any short positions you might be holding in cocoa. I show a Relative Strength Index reading of only 12, and it looks like the slow stochastic could cross at anytime."

"Interesting," says Mr. Duke, "What about pork bellies? How do you see bacon prices faring?"

"As for bellies, stick a fork in um, they're done! That's a head and shoulders top for sure."

"And Mr. Cordier, what about interest rates and the Federal Reserve? What do you see there?"

"Well, Mr. Duke, that one is a little tougher." I would coolly reply, "But looking at the June bonds, I can't remember ever seeing a market this oversold. I think I'll give bonds a strong buy. Besides, Mr. Volker would not put us in a recession. Would he?"

It was at the first commodity seminar I had ever attended that the technical seed was sown. The home office in Chicago had decided that it would send the brass to help give our branch office 90 miles to the north a jump-start. The office had just opened and consisted of the owner, two managers, and four hungry kids who had just passed their Series 3 (commodity broker license) exams. This would be my first formal training in a business I had been dreaming about for many years.

One nice suit after another would approach the podium and, using the latest technology in overhead projecting, would point out the highs and lows of various price charts where a savvy investor could have made a small killing.

After listening to one analyst explain how easy it was to go long on the *buy* signals and take profits on the *sell* signals, it was time to hear about *formations*—bull flags and bear flags, double tops and double bottoms. Everyone there, including me, thought, "Okay, these could be the secrets to our future success!"

Turning to a fresh page, I drew the chart that was illustrated on the fuzzy screen above.

"Here is an example showing a sharp rise in price that is followed by a period of consolidation, otherwise known as a *bull flag*," the speaker continued. "The sharp rise in price is the *pole*, and the consolidation is the *flag*. Later, a break above the consolidation will project an equal increase in price as the pole itself.

"Wow, that seems easy enough." I thought.

The next morning I went into the office armed with what could be the tools I needed to become a successful broker. The first thing was to back test what I had learned the previous night. Sure enough, after looking at just two or three charts, I found that there *were* pennants and flags and heads and shoulders everywhere! Shortly thereafter, out came the straight-edge ruler, and lines were drawn above and below support and resistance levels. Sprinkle in a few key indicators, and *voilà!*

"I will be technical trader, thank you."

A few weeks later I was spending all my time studying the current issues of *Commodity Perspective* morning, noon, and night. For several hours each day I carefully paged through one commodity at a time, looking at each chart like a surgeon examining a patient until I finally found it. There it was right in front of me—December wheat, *bull flag!*

This chart had a flag formation so clear, so discernible, so absolutely perfect, that the only thing it was missing were the stars and stripes themselves. That weekend I started saying to myself, "Blue Horseshoe loves December wheat."

Monday morning was here, and it was time to start on my road to riches. The grain markets were called to open steady, so I expected that I should be able to enter the trade I had studied all weekend long at the price I had hoped for. The flag formation consisted of a "pole" that measured 11 cents, followed by four days of consolidation. Buy here, and wait for the breakout to the upside, which should net us about a dime ($500 per contract). It was just like it said in my lessons. Now it was go time!

The opening bell rang at 9:30, and wheat started trading at $2.44, up ½ cent from Friday's close. I placed the order using a large red telephone that had no buttons, only a receiver. About ten minutes later, the floor was calling back with the fill, $2.44½, up 1 cent on the day. After a couple of hours had passed, trading had slowed considerably, this after what seemed like quite an active open. Corn and soybeans were both sporting modest gains, whereas wheat prices generally were steady to a shade higher. As the end of the trading day was fast approaching, grain prices started moving higher. With each new high, the sound of the clacker board seemed to get louder. At the close, December wheat settled at $2.46½, up 3 cents on the day and 2 cents above my entry price. What a great business!

After the dust had settled, I pulled out my charts and a pen to add a 3-cent bar to the December wheat. The breakout to the upside had started, and we should look forward to a payday in the next couple of sessions. "This technical trading really does work!" I thought.

As I was getting ready to leave for the day, I noticed my manager and another broker huddled in front of a screen.

"What do you see there, Jerry?" I couldn't help but inquire.

"Well it looks like wheat will be heading higher. It crossed the wire that Egypt is rumored to be in the market for over 200,000 metric tons of wheat, and the sale could come as early as tomorrow"

Cha Ching! What a great business!

Driving home that night I kept telling myself, "Don't be greedy. If the market is up 7 more cents in the morning, take the money and run. Stick to the program. Do your homework, and find the next trade."

I decided after a long celebratory dinner that I would do just that.

Pulling out my charts, I started paging through the different commodities for hours that night. I was at it again. However, nothing looked as good as wheat did from a couple days earlier, and it was getting late, so I wrapped it up for the night. Besides, I had a big day ahead of me. My trading career was about to take off, courtesy of my new best friend, the chart book.

At 8:00 A.M. Tuesday, walking through the large double doors at the office, I could not wait to get the opening call. My manager was staring at his screen, so I poked my head into the often-opened door and asked, "Did the Egypt tender go through? Did they buy all two hundred?"

Jerry looked up at me with an unfamiliar smile and said, "Yeah, they bought their wheat."

"Yes!" I thought. "But what is with him? Oh well, maybe he should study his charts a little closer." I proceeded to my desk and pulled out my books and the phone numbers of my clients long the wheat. Soon, I would have good news to report.

It was almost 9:30. I was about to reap the fruits of my labor. Would the wheat market move up the additional 7 cents today, or might I have to wait a while longer?

Finally, the clacker board started clicking, first corn, and then soybeans. For some reason, wheat was taking longer. Then wheat opened. What? Down 4! Down 5! What was going on? What about the bull flag? It was perfect! What about Egypt?

The broker in the cubicle next to me stood up and asked in his usual calm voice, "Cordier, what is going on?"

"Wheat—the wheat is down almost 6 cents!" I said.

Steve replied, "Well, you know that Egypt bought wheat last night and . . . "

"I know they did, so why is it falling?" I demanded.

"It was French. Egypt bought 210,000 metric tons of wheat from France."

"French! Schmench! What difference does that make!" I blurted, incredulous.

Steve, who got his start in commodities at a grain elevator, then said to me in what was almost a whisper, "You . . . have a lot to learn."

As it turned out, December wheat had rallied days before, when rumors surfaced that Egypt could be in the market with a large purchase. Consolidation then followed as traders waited for the announcement.

In this case, the market move of December wheat was predicated totally by the origin of the wheat that Egypt was about to purchase. An Egyptian purchase of U.S. wheat may have been positive for Chicago Board of Trade (CBOT) wheat prices. A purchase from France was benign. It was a disappointment for U.S. wheat traders, and therefore, prices fell. It was my first lesson in the world of fundamental trading, and things have never been the same since.

It was a huge eye-opener to me to discover that there was a whole other world of trading information beyond my charts, measurements, and indicators. The technical charts reflected what was going on with prices and how they were moving. The fundamentals were the reasons *why* they were moving.

As I discovered, relying on my charts alone to try to predict market movement was like trying to put together a puzzle with only half the pieces.

Throughout this book, we have repeated a central theme of how important it is to know the fundamentals of a particular market before positioning in that market. However, we also have pointed out that this knowledge should not be used as a substitute for technical analysis. Rather, it should be used in conjunction with technical indicators to optimize one's overall option-selection process. For pure fundamentalists, using technical indicators can greatly enhance your performance by helping to determine optimal entry and exit points. For pure technicians, knowing the fundamentals can help to boost returns by giving you a better feel for which breakouts, reversals, and buy and sell signals are more likely to be the real deal and which are false signals.

For instance, let's assume that two markets, orange juice and live cattle, are trading in a narrow trading range. The U.S. Department of Agriculture (USDA) has just released a report showing that the most recent Florida orange harvest yielded the largest crop in five years. Frozen orange juice supplies in storage are at a 12-year high. The market is awash in juice. Cattle, on the other hand, have been projected for months to soon be experiencing a drawdown in supply based on last year's 50-year low in the calf crop.

Both markets break out to the upside. Both markets indicate buy signals on key technical indicators. Which market is more likely to start a sustained uptrend, and which is likely to fall back into the range or lower?

The simple answer is that the cattle market is more likely to experience a sustained move higher, whereas the orange juice market is more likely to fall back down. However, this may not be the case, at least in this particular example. For unknown reasons, the opposite could be true. Additionally, both markets could rally, or both could fall back down. Over the long term, however, taking the fundamentals into account should help you to select more winners and cull more losers.

The pure technical trader would buy both on the breakout and give little regard to the fundamentals. However, given the exact same situation over different markets 10 times in a row, the technician who only takes the buy signals in markets with favorable fundamentals almost surely will outperform the pure technician. It simply adds another, very potent tool to the screening process.

We suggest selecting potential markets in which to sell premium by studying the fundamentals first. Once a select group of markets has been placed on a "watch list" consisting of markets with very bullish or very bearish long-term fundamentals, these markets then can be monitored for technical buy and sell signals.

The point is that fundamental traders can benefit by incorporating technical analysis into their trading, and technicians can benefit greatly by incorporating fundamentals into their selection process.

Novice traders often will favor technicals because they are much quicker and more tangible to learn. There are formulas and measurements and rules. Although the realm of technical trading is immense, a trader can learn one simple indicator, and Bingo, he has an instant trading system. He's ready to go at it.

Studying the fundamentals and how they are likely to affect price is more abstract. It requires independent thinking. It takes time, education, judgment, and experience. The argument that fundamentals are already "priced in" may be something that pure technicians tell themselves in order to free their minds from the burden of having to study the economics of a particular market.

On the other hand, fundamental traders who would attempt to trade the market without some sort of technical guidance almost surely would be shooting in the dark. Markets can make large moves against the fundamentals and at times may even move up and down randomly as technical factors sway it back and forth. Large fund traders are mostly technicians and can move markets for short periods on technical buy or sell signals. These moves sometimes can fly in the face of the existing fundamentals. A trader would be foolish to ignore technical trading completely.

Over the long term, however, a market's price ultimately will be determined by its fundamentals. For this reason, you should gain at least a basic understanding of what the key fundamentals are for the markets you are trading. It is one of the key advantages that you have over the large fund traders. They are slaves to their systems. You can use technical indicators while retaining the ability to think for yourself.

## FUNDAMENTAL DATA: THE LESS THE BETTER

You will find that the fewer key factors that go into price makeup of a particular commodity or futures contract, the more benefit fundamental analysis can be. You will find that most physical commodities, such as soybeans, unleaded gasoline, and coffee, will have three to five key fundamental factors that affect most of their price moves. Financial contracts, on the other hand, can have many factors that can or could affect price, many that cannot be forecasted with any degree of accuracy (e.g., government decisions or votes). It may be true then that fundamental analysis is more of a benefit to traders of physical commodities. When trading financial contracts such as bonds, currencies, or even gold (considered a financial), you may have to rely more on technical savvy because fundamentals often appear very cloudy or mixed at any given time.

## THE KEY REASON FUNDAMENTALS ARE SO IMPORTANT IN OPTION SELLING

There is one final, albeit key, reason why we feel that incorporating fundamentals is so important in selling options. Technical trading is all about forecasting and measuring where and when prices might move. It promises nothing in forecasting where prices will *not* go. As an option seller, this is your *primary* concern.

Granted, it would be nice if prices moved immediately away from your strike as soon as you sell your options, providing fast deterioration and profits. However, most of the time, this probably won't be the case. In the end, it doesn't matter if your strike is $3 out of the money or 3 cents—your option will still expire worthless, yielding the same profit. Therefore, you are mainly concerned with selecting a price level that the current market will *not* reach. Fundamentals can be tremendously helpful in this regard.

It is our opinion that using fundamentals to determine where prices will *not* go is not only more effective but also ultimately easier. This is a key concept of this book and one that we hope you will remember. We are not going to take a side in the ongoing fundamentalist versus technician debate. The debate is always about which is a more effective price *forecasting* model. Which one is more effective in determining where prices will go? There is, of course, no correct answer. Either way, it is very difficult to determine where prices will go.

However, in determining where prices *won't* go, if forced to choose one over the other, we'd have to take fundamentals. Why?

Let's use an example to answer this question. Suppose that you have been following the development of this year's U.S. soybean crop. At midsummer, the market has already priced a certain sized crop into the market (as most technicians argue it should). During the course of a week, rumors begin to surface of a strange disease eating away at leaves in certain growing regions. Traders are unsure to what magnitude it has spread or what effect it will have on yields. The following week, the talk continues to swirl. More outbreaks are reported, and some people start to suggest that the fungus on the plant is stunting the growth of the new soybeans.

At this point, the market has already started to move higher on the uncertainty. Nobody knows how this could affect yield or, ultimately, price. However, it is probably safe to assume that yield at least will be slightly affected. It could turn out to be the blockbuster story of the summer, causing major crop damage and a sweeping price rally. Or it could fade into obscurity, gaining only occasional mention as a factor causing a minor reduction in yield. It is uncertain what will happen or how high prices will move to factor in the reduced yield. Trying to buy a futures contract here or purchase a call option to take advantage of higher prices could be very tricky.

However, how likely is it that prices would move *below* the level at which they were trading before this disease was announced, when normal yields were being assumed? If prices a few weeks ago were reflecting a certain amount of anticipated supply and now that supply has been reduced (to what degree, we do not know), does it not follow logically that prices would have to be trading somewhere higher than they were a few weeks ago to account for this shortfall?

In other words, you may not be able to determine fundamentally how high prices could go, but it seems like a pretty good bet that prices are not going to fall back to where they were a few weeks ago because it appears that supply is smaller now than it was then. All the option seller has to do is sell puts below where the price was a few weeks ago and wait.

This example is simplified of course, but it demonstrates how a key fundamental development can be exploited by an option seller where it may be more difficult for a futures trader or option buyer to profit.

## USING TECHNICAL ANALYSIS FOR TIMING

One of our basic convictions in this book is that an option writer should select the market in which she would prefer to sell puts or calls based on a fundamental scenario that she feels will make the market biased toward moving higher or moving lower over the intermediate to long term. The trader then would look for favorable technical setups as opportunities in which to enter positions in these markets. Again, while this is not a book on technical trading, we will use a few simple indicators in the following examples to help illustrate our points.

### Example 1: Technical Entry on Live Cattle Short Puts

In researching the fundamentals for live cattle in early 2004, trader John has determined that the fundamentals will favor the upside in cattle prices in the coming months. The U.S. border is still closed to imports of Canadian cattle, the U.S. calf crop is near 50-year lows, U.S. beef demand remains near all-time highs, and John feels that the market may be significantly underpriced after the mad cow scare back in December. John considers this a very friendly fundamental setup. He begins to watch the charts for possible favorable points of entry.

In this case, one of John's favorite technical indicators is a slow stochastic (shown in Figure 10.1), which is a measure of moving averages. The wavy lines on the bottom of the chart are what this popular technical indicator looks like. One line represents a moving average of prices for the last 30 days; the other represents a moving average for the last 10 days. When the 10-day moving average crosses the 30-day moving average at or

**F I G U R E    10.1**

April 2004 Live Cattle Chart with Stochastic Illustrating "Buy" Signals

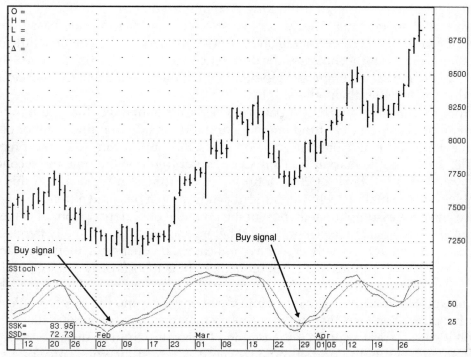

John sells puts below the market on technical buy signals in a fundamentally bullish market.

near the bottom dotted line (this is known as *oversold* territory), technicians take it as a buy signal. When this same crossover happens at or near the upper dotted line, technicians take it as a sell signal.

Traders can set these moving averages to reflect whatever price periods they desire.

Since John's fundamental bias is bullish (he believes that the existing fundamentals will pull prices higher), John will look for technical buy signals as opportunities to sell puts far beneath the market. He will not sell calls on the sell signals because his fundamental bias is to the upside. Therefore, he takes only the buy signals in this market and ignores the sell signals.

The problem with technical indicators is that they rarely look this simple when you are using them in a real trade. Technical analysis books always make it look very simple and easy because they use examples in which the indicator worked very well.

We used one here as well, but only to demonstrate how a trader can combine his fundamental judgment with his favorite technical indicator.

In most cases, the technical buy and sell signals may not be very clear, at least not until well after the move has already taken place. This is yet another reason why incorporating fundamentals into your thinking is so important.

We would suggest that after you have selected a market to trade based on what you feel are very clear long-term bullish or bearish fundamentals, you do a little historical testing with a few technical indicators (such as the stochastic, relative strength index, 100-day moving average, etc.) to determine if there is one that the market seems to be adhering to better than others.

Probably the easiest technical pattern to look for is markets that are trending. If you have a market with clear fundamentals, and it is already trending in favor of those fundamentals, you could have a great option selling opportunity. In the preceding example, the live cattle market was already in an uptrend by the time the second buy signal was issued in March of 2004. John had three things in his favor on this trade: favorable fundamentals, a technical indicator indicating a buy, and a trend.

We make the assumption that most of the potential or current option sellers reading this book have most likely seen a price chart before and are at least initially familiar with basic chart patterns and possibly one or two indicators. If you are not, there are many free online tutorials from futures and stock brokerages (it is their favorite subject) and other sources that can teach you the basics. There are also many excellent books available for those that feel that it necessary to delve into the finer details and theory of technical trading (although we don't feel that this is necessary to be a successful option seller).

We want to stress again that the timing of your option sales does not have to be perfect. Remember that in option selling, even if you mistime your entry or are even outright wrong on market direction, in many cases you can still end up making money on the trade.

Using technical indicators and/or chart patterns certainly can help you in the timing of your option sales. Using fundamental research can help you in selecting markets favorable to option selling. Combining the two can be a potent approach that produces winning option selling trades.

We feel so strongly about combining the two that, in our business, we continually research the fundamentals of the futures markets and screen out the ones that we feel offer the best option selling opportunities for our clients. Since many investors do not have the time to perform this research on their own, we also provide a technical analysis and opinion of the market to assist them with the timing of their positions.

Nonetheless, even if you are working with a broker who is well versed in fundamental analysis, it may help you to know some of the basic economics and key figures of individual markets that help to determine price direction (or nondirection). For those who may wish to learn the key fundamentals of some of these markets for self-study, Chapter 11 is for you.

# 11

## CHAPTER

# Key Fundamentals of Select Markets

Every stock, every commodity, and every futures market has fundamental factors that determine its value. Fundamentals for a stock may include factors such as financial position of the company, profitability, price-earnings (P/E) ratio, and so on. Fundamentals for a commodity may include current supply on hand, projected new crop growth, and consumer trends in preferences. Fundamentals in a financial contract may include government policies, interest-rate adjustments, and economic growth rates. For our purposes, we will define a *fundamental* as the current or future supply and demand or any factor that can have an effect on either the supply or the demand for that particular commodity or financial product.

Not to review economics 101, but the balance between supply and demand ultimately will be what determines the price of a commodity or financial product. If supply is high and demand is low, prices probably will be low or move lower. If supply is low and demand is high, prices probably will be high or move higher. If interest rates rise, fewer people want to buy bonds, and bond prices fall. If part of the soybean crop is damaged by a lack of rain in the summer, there are fewer supplies to go around in the fall, and prices rise.

We have already discussed how trading fundamentally can be a much more feasible approach in option selling than in futures trading. If a market is fundamentally bullish, chances are that it has already priced in those fundamentals to a certain extent. Thus, if you buy a futures contract, you may be buying right before the market goes into a corrective mode. However, if the fundamentals remain bullish, chances are that the correction will be mild and/or short-lived (by long-term standards) before prices either stabilize or continue to press higher. As a futures trader, these inevitable corrections can force you out of your position and cause losses that sometimes can be severe, even if your fundamental analysis is correct.

By selling options, you can increase your chances of profiting from a correct fundamental diagnosis. If you are bullish and sell puts, you can sell at strike prices far below the market. Your position can withstand a certain degree of movement against it. However, if your fundamental analysis is correct, the market will not go into an all-out sell mode as long as these fundamentals continue to hold up. Thus, even if the market has already priced the existing fundamentals, it probably won't fall substantially, meaning that if you sold options far enough away, they should be safe and ultimately profitable.

This is the ideal scenario anyway.

To form a fundamental bias toward the markets, however, you first must know the key fundamentals that you should be following. This is the purpose of this chapter. There are some markets that lend themselves more favorably to fundamental analysis than others. These are generally markets with three to five key long-term fundamentals to watch. Markets with many fundamentals (such as the stock market or gold) are more difficult to trade fundamentally and must be given more technical consideration. Having some fundamental knowledge, however, can help you to trade any market.

The following are some key fundamentals to watch in a group of select markets that we have chosen to review in this book. This is certainly not a complete list of markets or fundamentals. Nonetheless, after reading this chapter, hopefully you will have a starting point for beginning your fundamental selection process.

## GRAINS AND OILSEEDS

### Soybeans

While China and a handful of other nations grow nominal amounts of soybeans to feed their own populations, the United States and Brazil are the world's primary suppliers. For this reason, it is a good idea to focus on the U.S. and Brazilian crops when analyzing soybean supply.

The U.S. soybean crop is planted primarily in April and May and harvested primarily in September and October. The Brazilian crop is planted primarily in October and November and harvested in March, April, and May. Weather disruptions during the growing seasons often can cause price moves.

Key figures to watch are U.S. and world *ending stocks*, current and projected. Ending stocks are a comprehensive figure and consist of the amount of the commodity left over at the end of the crop year. In the United States, the new crop year begins on September 1. Ending stocks are the total amount of supply left over after total annual usage has been subtracted from annual supply. Therefore, ending stocks are a way of measuring total supply and demand. A rudimentary form of fundamental analysis is looking at past years' ending stocks and then looking at the average price level of the commodity during that year or the following year. There often will be a correlation between prices and ending stock levels. You then can compare this year's projected ending stocks with those of previous years where figures were similar to get a rough idea of a price range where the market should gravitate toward this year. Although this may not tell you where prices are going, it can be a big help in projecting where prices won't go.

It goes without saying, then, that any factor that may change the projected supply or projected demand could change ending stocks, which, in turn, could move prices. Weather, pests, shipping disruptions, and political unrest are just a few of the things that can affect supply. Increased or decreased consumption, trade spats, and competition from substitute products are a few of the factors that can affect demand.

A key fundamental shift in the soybean and grain markets in the first decade of the 2000s has been the emergence of the Chinese as a major importer of corn and soybeans. The corn and soybean bull markets of 2003–2004 were driven primarily by unprecedented demand from China.

Most of the information you will need to get a basic fundamental picture of the grain or any agricultural market can be obtained for free from the U.S. Department of Agriculture (USDA) at www.usda.gov. The key report to watch is the *monthly supply/ demand report* (which measures U.S. and world supply and demand and updates projected ending stocks). Other key reports to watch are the *quarterly grain stocks report* and *planting intentions* (released in the spring).

## Corn

Corn and soybeans are grown in similar locations during similar growing seasons and often can be interchanged for one another when farmers are deciding on how many acres of each to plant. Frequently, this is decided based on which crop they feel may be more profitable in a given year.

Unlike with soybeans, the United States has no major competitors when it comes to exporting corn and is by far the world's largest producer and exporter. While China was known to export a considerable amount of corn in the past, the Chinese liquidated a vast amount of surplus stocks in the early 2000s, and the Chinese now consume domestically most of the corn they produce. Argentina, however, has been steadily increasing corn production and could one day become a key source of corn on the world export market.

For now, U.S. supply and export demand are the key figures to focus on when researching corn. Most corn information is released in the same reports listed for soybeans and can be found at the same place, the USDA. The news services listed in the resources section of this book also can do a good job of keeping a trader updated on factors that could affect supply and demand. However, we strongly recommend focusing on the monthly figures released by the USDA and not getting caught up in daily news releases. The exception to this would be when you notice a supply or demand trend developing.

## Wheat

Unlike corn or soybeans, wheat is grown almost globally. While Russia, China, and India are larger producers, the United States remains the world's largest exporter. Competing with the United States for export business are Australia, Canada, Argentina, and the European Union.

Supply, demand, and ending stock figures for wheat can be found in the same reports as those for corn and soybeans. However, when analyzing wheat, one should pay more attention to world figures as opposed to only U.S. figures. Since wheat is a global commodity, events in other major producing nations can have a strong effect on wheat prices (see Figure 11.1).

### FIGURE  11.1

USDA Report Showing Wheat Ending Stocks

| | 2000/01 | 2001/02 | 2002/03 | 2003/04 8-Apr | 2003/04 12-May | 2004/05 8-Apr | 2004/05 12-May |
|---|---|---|---|---|---|---|---|
| **All Grain Summary** Production, Consumption, Stocks and Trade Total Foreign Countries, USA, and Total World (Million Metric Tons) | | | | | | | |
| **Wheat** | | | | | | | |
| All Foreign Countries | | | | | | | |
| Production | 520.7 | 527.8 | 523.2 | 485.8 | 486.0 | 0.0 | 532.0 |
| Consumption | 547.7 | 552.9 | 571.3 | 556.5 | 555.1 | 0.0 | 561.6 |
| Ending Stocks | 182.6 | 180.7 | 153.7 | 113.0 | 114.4 | 0.0 | 109.7 |
| USA | | | | | | | |
| Production | 60.6 | 53.0 | 43.7 | 63.6 | 63.6 | 0.0 | 56.6 |
| Imports | 2.4 | 3.0 | 2.0 | 2.0 | 2.0 | 0.0 | 1.8 |
| Consumption | 36.2 | 32.4 | 30.3 | 32.8 | 32.8 | 0.0 | 32.6 |
| Exports | 28.0 | 26.2 | 23.0 | 32.5 | 32.5 | 0.0 | 26.0 |
| Ending Stocks | 23.8 | 21.2 | 13.4 | 14.5 | 14.3 | 0.0 | 13.6 |
| World Total, Trade | 104.0 | 110.8 | 110.0 | 101.9 | 103.6 | 0.0 | 101.6 |

Source: USDA

For instance, in 2002, global wheat production dropped considerably when adverse weather hampered growing conditions in Australia, Canada, and the United States. Drought conditions developed, oddly enough, in all three locations simultaneously. While this is not an abnormally rare event, it certainly was not positive for building world wheat stocks. Prices rallied sharply in the summer of 2002; however, as you can see, this did not happen overnight. Traders following wheat fundamentals would have read the reports of dry weather and heard talk of reduced yields. And although there was no way to predict the sharp rally that continued through September, such traders could have positioned themselves in such a way as to profit if prices did not fall sharply, a scenario that would seem unlikely with the crop problems (see Figure 11.2).

## FIGURE 11.2

September 2002 Wheat Chart

Simultaneous droughts in three major exporting countries triggered a sharp rally in wheat prices in 2002.

## REGIONAL COMMODITIES AND THE PLIGHT OF ORANGE JUICE

While some commodities have an equal global value, such as gold, crude oil, and wheat, others may involve regional dynamics that can require a different level of study.

While global commodities are produced in several different countries, there are other commodities that may be produced in only one or two specific countries or regions. Since there are fewer supply figures to follow with such commodities, they sometimes can lend themselves better to fundamental analysis than globally produced commodities. These are known as *regional commodities*.

Regional commodities include products such as orange juice, live cattle, and lumber.

For instance, Brazil is the major supplier of orange juice to the United States. The United States produces the balance of its orange juice needs domestically. And while oranges are grown in both California and Florida, only the Florida oranges are used to make juice.

Therefore, following Brazilian and Florida orange production can be a good place to start when studying orange juice fundamentals. The Frozen Concentrate Orange Juice (FCOJ) contract at the New York Board of Trade is strongly affected by rises or drops in Florida or Brazilian orange production. Again, the USDA is your source of information. The monthly supply/demand reports will list projected production figures along with U.S. and Brazilian ending stocks during the growing seasons.

While U.S. demand for orange juice has remained relatively stable historically, there is a key fundamental change taking place that could affect juice prices for years to come.

By 2004, many commodities had enjoyed price increases on the back of a stronger global economy and a small amount of inflation. Frozen orange juice was not one of them. Why?

At the time of this writing, a dietary change is currently taking place in the United States that has an estimated 15 to 20 million Americans increasing their protein intake and lowering their carbohydrate intake. Liberty Trading Group recently calculated a 3 to 4 percent decrease in orange juice consumption versus the five-year average—a *substantial* shift in demand. At the same time, Brazil, the world's largest producer of oranges, broke its output record for the third time in a row in 2003. Florida growers harvested bumper crops in two of the three years preceding Brazil's record.

With consumption down, you would think that growers would have cut back production. Think again. Once the investment has been made and young orange trees are in place, you are looking at a 6- to 10-year span of production driving on autopilot. While some commodities such as corn or soybeans enjoy the old adage, "*Low prices cure low prices,*" other commodities, such as cocoa, coffee, and orange juice, grow on trees, which means much longer life cycles where overproduction cannot be cut back overnight. This often means that producers of these commodities endure long-term pain and suffering before low prices can be cured.

Added to the burdensome supply of orange juice is the change in its growing region. After devastating frosts hit northern Florida groves several times in the 1980s and 1990s, orange production began to migrate south. Currently, almost all major production is located south of the Orlando area, where the chances of temperatures reaching below 28°F become very remote. This migration south has helped to deliver one record crop after the other. Thus prices in the early to middle 2000s are now less than half of what they were just a few years earlier in the 1990s (see Figure 11.3).

This is a key example of why knowing fundamentals can be important for a trader in analyzing potential option sales. Would you have wanted to take the technical buy or technical sell signals in orange juice during this time period?

**F I G U R E   11.3**

Orange Juice Weekly Chart, 2002–2004

OJ - Orange Juice A (FCOJ-A), Weekly

## CATTLE

Live cattle for delivery against the Chicago Merchantile Exchange contract are produced almost exclusively in the United States. Therefore, monitoring U.S. beef supply and U.S. beef demand is a key approach to making long-term price projections.

The USDA cattle on feed report is released once a month and breaks down how many young animals are on feed and how many animals have been marketed during the preceding month. Thus it is a gauge of both supply and demand and is the key report to watch in the industry.

Traders in cattle futures often watch what is known as the *cash market*. These are the actual auctions of cattle ranchers selling their cattle to packing houses. The prices paid for these cattle often constitute a good measure of demand for beef and also can have a broad effect on futures prices, although the reverse also can be true. Cash cattle usually trades during the last two or three days of the business week. Often packers and producers will hold at their bid or asking prices until later in the week when one relents, resulting in the cattle being sold.

Cattle traders also watch daily *box beef prices*, which are a measure of what supermarkets and other retail outlets are willing to pay for certain cuts of beef. These can be obtained through a good news service.

Cattle traders are often a different breed because the cattle market has a very small set of fundamentals to watch, yet their complexity is enormous.

## ENERGY

Most people, even nontraders, are somewhat familiar with energy fundamentals. Oil is produced in the Middle East (OPEC), Russia, Venezuela, Nigeria, Norway, and the United States. Of these regions, the Middle East is the largest exporter of crude oil. The United States is by far the largest consumer of crude oil, followed by China and Japan. China's emergence as an economic force since its entry into the World Trade Organization (WTO) in 2001 has produced a massive increase in crude oil demand from that country and added tremendously to the global daily crude oil draw.

Key reports to watch for energy and petroleum are the weekly American Petroleum Institute (API) report, which measures energy storage levels and draws, and periodic reports from the U.S. Department of Energy (DOE).

Energy markets are swayed heavily by seasonal factors as well, and we are not going to cover them heavily in this chapter. The fundamental and seasonal tendencies of crude, heating oil, unleaded gas, and natural gas will be covered extensively in Chapter 12 on seasonal analysis.

## PRECIOUS METALS

We have all heard of gold prices quoted in such terms as the "Hong Kong A.M. gold fix" or the "London P.M. gold fix." Gold prices are sometimes hot, sometimes not, but gold is gold no matter where it is being traded. Often thought of as a safe haven, gold always has been a staple benchmark of financial security. Understanding the many nuances that cause the yellow metal to fluctuate in price, however, is quite thorny. On one occasion, a report showing an overheating economy will be quite bullish for precious metals because gold is considered a hedge against inflation. Then another report will suggest a robust economy, and gold prices sink with thoughts of higher interest rates.

News of intensifying conflicts in the Middle East can whip gold traders into a buying frenzy, yet gold prices fell for days following the terrorist attacks of September 11. If this sounds baffling to you, you are not alone. The value of gold seems to tread on a narrow emotional landscape.

Not all hard assets, however, contain such elusive reasoning for their price fluctuations. Metals such as copper, silver, and platinum have more discernible price-driving forces that make them slightly easier to analyze fundamentally. Knowing what these forces are can prove to be quite helpful. Not so long ago, all the metals seemed quite interchangeable; if one went up, they all went up, and vice versa. Now the dynamics have changed, especially for silver.

At the end of 2003 and the beginning of 2004, the metals all were enjoying what would be considered by most a pretty impressive bull move. The leader of this market was clearly copper. Insatiable Chinese demand for all industrial metals during these expansive growth years catapulted copper prices to a level not seen in almost two decades. With copper changing hands at over $1.35 a pound, a production boom was ignited in countries such as Chile, the world's largest producer, and Indonesia, the world's third largest producer. These mines started producing at full capacity in order to cash in at very profitable price levels.

Other metals followed in step as gold rallied above $430 for the first time in six years. Also enjoying a high percentage gain was silver, starting at around $5; the once precious metal traded as high as $8.35 an ounce. It was a rally sponsored by huge fund and speculative buying. But could silver move even higher? Could the market once made famous by Bunker Hunt at least hold its gains? It never had a chance.

Oddly enough, silver's biggest enemy is high-priced copper. The once-mighty metal has been reduced to a copper-mining by-product. It is estimated that almost half of all silver production is found in leftover ore mined for copper.

As if the production figures were not bad enough, silver demand has just taken a huge hit. Twenty-eight percent of silver's usage has evaporated with the development of digital photography. Silver's days in the spotlight are numbered.

Therefore, the exploding demand for copper, coupled with a decreased demand for silver, meant a glut in silver. This is what we mean when we talk about a *key fundamental*.

Financial news services updated information about the copper boom regularly during this period. Unfortunately, with a massive increase in copper production came a massive increase in silver production. For silver, the demand just wasn't there.

With China's new economy apparently here to stay, it will be interesting to see how continued demand for copper will affect the price structure between these two commodities.


## COFFEE

You may have noticed over the last few years that coffee shops have been springing up nearly everywhere. Has coffee become a fashion statement, or does it just taste that good?

Maybe both, from Seattle to Miami and all points in between, coffee seems to be a mainstream, absolute must for just about everyone. Coffee retailers seem to have it nailed down. Drinks now contain flavors never imagined by our parents—Amaretto, hazelnut, cinnamon, and French vanilla, just to name a few.

The United States is the largest consumer of coffee, followed by Germany and then Japan. This begs the obvious question: With all the seemingly new demand for coffee, why is the price so low?

First of all, if you are a coffee drinker, be very thankful that beans are produced worldwide. Fifty-seven different countries grow coffee, making it truly a global commodity. Second, while consumption is up in many parts of the world, in others it has slacked. There is currently heated debate as to the exact figures, but most industry resources claim that global demand is quite flat. World consumption increased about 1 to 2 percent from 1999 to 2003, barely a noticeable amount when considering supply.

There are two basic types of coffee, arabica and robusta. Arabica coffee tends to have a milder flavor and usually is grown at higher attitudes. Robusta coffee has a heavier flavor and tends to be produced on low lands. Arabica is the preferred coffee in the Western Hemisphere and trades at a premium price. Like many fine foods, these two coffees often are blended to create yet another distinctive taste.

Arabica coffee is the contract traded at the New York Board of Trade. Robusta coffee is traded on the London International Futures Exchange (LIFFE). Arabica coffee is the primary product of many Central American countries and Colombia. Robusta is grown in many countries, including India and Vietnam. Brazil is by far the worlds largest producer and exporter of both arabica and robusta coffees. Therefore, Brazilian production can have a large impact on coffee prices.

Throughout the early and middle 1990s, global coffee production and consumption had found a comfortable balance, at approximately 95 million bags. (1 bag = 60 kilograms or 132 pounds). While there was always supply to meet demand, there was rarely any surplus, and thus production often was watched with a keen eye. Any disruption to this equal balance often sent prices skyward. On more than one occasion weather played a major factor, because cold air descending on Brazil's once coffee-rich southern region could cause panic. In 1994, Brazil experienced a crop-damaging freeze, which cut production to just 17 million bags, down from 28 million bags produced in each of the two previous years. This was not the first time southern Brazil lost a large percentage of its precious coffee beans, but it may have been the last.

Beginning in 1996 and 1997, coffee production started to migrate north to the more temperate states, concentrating in Esperito Santo, São Paulo, and Minas Gerais. As Brazil's coffee industry was enjoying huge profits from high coffee prices, co-ops started pouring money into new production. Billions of young seedlings were planted. This new investment would change the landscape in coffee for years to come.

News of big profits soon traveled to the Far East, and a new player began to emerge in the coffee arena. Vietnam was ripe to enter, with its cheap labor and near-perfect climate. The world would make room for yet another coffee supplier but, more important, a supplier with little domestic consumption. During the year 2000, Vietnamese robusta production topped 11 million bags, just 1 million bags shy of an average yield from the former powerhouse Colombia. Of the 11 million bags produced that year, over 10 million were available for export.

Combining with the new Vietnamese production in 2000 and 2001 was Brazil's expanded and more densely planted hectares. The flood of coffee supplies was now in motion, and world consumption was helpless in shoring it up. As Brazil's tree population started to mature, coffee output suddenly began to rise. In 2000, Brazilian output reached 34 million bags. In 2001, 35 million bags were harvested, and in 2002, an absolute giant was picked, 51 million bags! While 2003 was an "off year," only producing about 32 million bags of coffee, 2004's harvest is projected to produce about 42 million bags— at the time of this writing.

Traders of coffee should be aware that this longer-term trend in coffee production could plague prices for years to come. Retention schemes, government buybacks, and other attempts at bringing prices higher all pretty much have failed to date. The trees are already planted, and as long as they are producing beans, the farmers are going to pick them.

While coffee prices are not immune to experiencing 10- to 15-cent or more rallies at given intervals, prices have remained near historically low levels since 2000 until the time of this writing. This is a scenario that could continue to plague coffee prices through the decade. Traders of coffee, however, should continue to monitor Brazilian production before deciding on any long-term positions. Disruptions in supply from Colombia or Vietnam also can have an impact on prices.

The fundamentals in this chapter should give you a starting point for researching commodities and the type of information that you will want to seek. The commodities explored in this chapter certainly are not a complete list, and you will want to research and compare findings of your own on these and other commodities and futures markets. You will notice that fundamentals of financial markets such as bonds, currencies, and stock index futures are not covered here.

This is *not* because we believe that knowing the fundamentals of these markets cannot help a trader. This is because the fundamentals of these markets are so extensive and so subject to individual opinion and interpretation that it would have taken a whole chapter to cover each one. However, individual research into these markets certainly can help to give perspective to a purely technical approach.

The next two chapters are devoted to a branch of fundamental analysis known as *seasonals*. We feel that it is important to incorporate seasonal analysis into an overall fundamental outlook for a market. These chapters will show you how.

# 12 CHAPTER

# Seasonal Analysis and Option Selling

Seasonal tendencies of commodities markets, or *seasonals* as they are known to traders, are like option selling in a way. They are one of the most interesting yet misunderstood areas of trading. This makes them vulnerable to misuse and, of course, bad word-of-mouth from the misusers.

As in option selling, traders who see seasonal charts for the first time may think that they have just discovered the Holy Grail of trading, the inside secret, the *real* force driving the market.

The seasonal chart looks so simple. Buy on this day; sell on this day. It's worked 14 of the last 15 years. There were a few authors several years ago who made a lot of money selling books on seasonal trades. There were entire books that just gave lists of dates to buy and dates to sell. All you had to do was follow it. It's magic!

Unfortunately, seasonal analysis is much more complex than buying on one day and selling on another, as many traders have discovered painfully. These statistics are interesting to look at, but they are only reflecting a cyclic occurrence in the market. To be truly able to understand seasonals and trade them effectively, you have to understand what these occurrences or *fundamentals* are and be able to track and measure them to determine if they are indeed occurring this year, to what degree, and on what time schedule. You must know the key reason that typically causes this seasonal tendency to take place and then be able to determine if those same fundamentals are in place *this* year.

Trying to trade on a certain date and get out on a certain date because a book says so is putting your faith solely in statistics and averages. What many traders unfortunately have found out is that the market doesn't care about statistics and averages. Therefore, many traders who have tried this timing method and lost money conclude that seasonals in general are no good. This is a shame for them but good for you! You'll have less competition and more people to take the other side of your trades. You are going to learn how you can combine real seasonal tendencies with option selling into a very potent profit strategy.

## WHY TRADERS LOSE WITH SEASONALS

Before we begin exploring how to make money with seasonals, we first must examine why traders lose trading seasonals. The first reason is that they assume that because the market increased (or decreased) in value between a given two dates on the calendar for *x* of the last 15 years, they will make money if they buy (or sell) on the same date this year and sell (or buy) on the day that pattern says to do so.

These dates often have corresponding profits that show how much would have been made had the trader done the trades in years past. If a trader looks closely, these often show that a few years had big gains, whereas many years had minimal or almost negligent gains. Then you also can see the losing years. Look at how big the losses were in losing years as opposed to the gains. Often you will see a few years with big profits but equally big losses in others and several years in between with small or very small profits. Therefore, a trader could be taking a large risk for minimal gains. This is why the term *average profit* can be very misleading.

The other fact that traders fail to realize is that the winning years often can have large moves against the seasonal average that a trader would have had to "ride out" to capture the profit, whether it was large or small. If the profit from the trade was $300 in year *x* but it had a $2,500 drawdown in the meantime, do you still think you would be in the trade? Even if you were, is that the type of trading you want to do—riding out a $2,500 loser for a $300 gain? Probably not. At least not if you want your trading account to last for long.

To put it bluntly, trying to trade seasonals by picking an absolute day to get in and out every year is not only pointless, but it also could be hazardous to your wallet. The initial mistake traders make is trying to trade this way in the first place. The second mistake they make is trying to do it with futures contracts.

Trading futures contracts requires almost perfect timing to begin with. If you try to time your seasonal trade by calendar dates, even if the seasonal move occurs, what if it is a week or two off this year? What if you go long, and the market decides to take a big dip before making a run higher, assuming that a move takes place at all? You could be stopped out long before the market even goes into a seasonal rally.

There is a strategy, however, that can keep you in the market, even if prices do correct while you are in your position. In fact, you can profit from this strategy even if the seasonal move doesn't take place at all. The strategy, of course, is called *option selling.*

## THE RIGHT WAY TO APPROACH SEASONALS

Selling options instead of trading futures on seasonals can be stunningly effective. However, knowing how and why the seasonal works and the likelihood of it repeating this year are key in a successful seasonal option sale. Do your market analysis right, and the proper option selling months and strikes will become obvious.

Looking at a book of seasonal tendencies is a great place to start in your search for good option sales. Browse through the charts and look for markets that have a strong tendency to make a clear, sustained move up or down at a certain time or times of the year. Look particularly for markets that often go from extreme highs directly to extreme lows (or vice versa) without a lot of "riffraff" in between. Markets that have a tendency to go from yearly highs to yearly lows without a lot of ups and downs in the middle can be excellent candidates for option sales.

Try not to pay too much attention to the smaller ups and downs, or blips, on the seasonal average charts. Focus on the major moves and the long-term tendencies.

## STEP 1: LEARNING TO READ THE SEASONAL CHART

Figure 12.1 is an example of a seasonal chart. The solid line represents a 15-year average of price performance for that particular contract month. The dotted line represents a 5-year average of price performance. The numbers on the side of the chart are not prices: 0 represents the lowest average price of the year, whereas 100 represents the highest average price of the year.

The key word here is *average.* This chart tells us that, on average, natural gas prices tend to increase beginning sometime in early February and continue right up through late May, when they tend to decrease sharply into summer. Does this mean that you buy natural gas every February 1 and sell it every May 28? Absolutely not. This is only the beginning. Seasonal averages are simply raw material for your trade. This provides you with candidates that you will weed through to find a few finalists that have the highest probabilities of success.

The fact that these are averaged from 15 years of price data can be very confusing to the novice trader. A large, random move that happened to occur over the course of a few years often can skew the average and make it look like a small move occurs every year, especially if you are looking at a 5-year average.

This is why you want to look for the markets that tend to move from one extreme to another and not try to catch the short-term swings that show up on a seasonal chart. Look at the big picture.

The second note about averages is the time frame in which the move takes place. Again, the seasonal chart reflects the *average* time frame. This means that a price move in a general direction could have begun several weeks before or several weeks after what is being reflected on the seasonal charts. This is another reason why trading futures

**F I G U R E    12.1**

November Natural Gas 5- and 15-Year Seasonal Overlaid

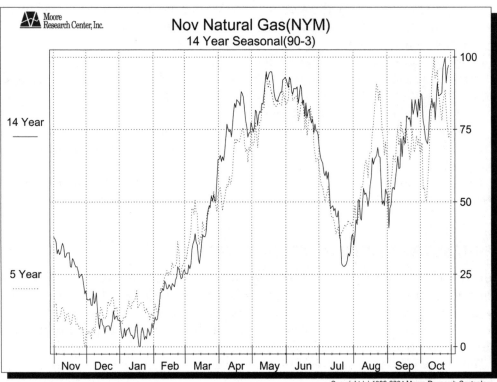

Copyright (c) 1989-2004 Moore Research Center,Inc.

contracts on seasonals is so tough. If you trade off the 5- or 15-year average, you may get in too early for a move that occurs this year and end up stopped out, or you may enter the position too late and miss a move that already occurred.

We recommend looking at the actual price charts from the last 15 years in addition to the seasonal charts before deciding to trade a seasonal average. The closer the actual price charts follow the seasonal, the better trading opportunity you may have. Several years of wide variance above and below the seasonal average with a strong variation in time frames may combine to form an impressive-looking average, but it can be treacherous to trade.

In contrast, markets that demonstrate close historical adherence to the seasonal average can be good trading opportunities. For instance, Figure 12.2 shows a 15-year seasonal average for June crude oil.

The energy complex can offer some excellent seasonal opportunities for option selling. The cyclic nature of energy markets is one reason why the historical price charts

## FIGURE  12.2

June Crude Oil 15-Year Seasonal

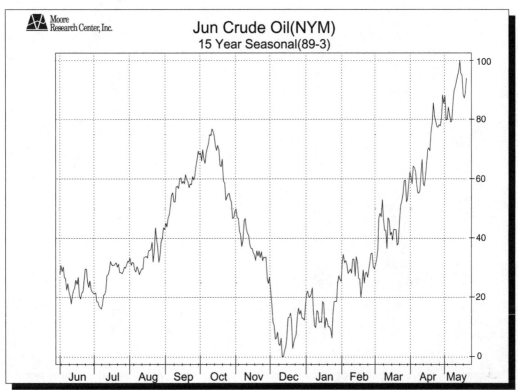

Copyright (c) 1989-2004 Moore Research Center,Inc.

that follow match up relatively close to the seasonal average. Figure 12.3 demonstrates that June crude oil has exhibited a fairly close adherence to seasonal averages in many of the previous 15 years.

The seasonal average versus actual performance for March copper, however, tells a different story (see Figure 12.4).

The seasonal chart for March copper appears to show a fairly steady ascent from lowest to highest price from June through September and then back to the lowest price by December. Yet when one looks at historical performance in Figure 12.5, there is a wide range of price performance that varies considerably from the average. This is an example of prices combining to produce a somewhat misleading seasonal chart.

Often a quick way to determine if you have a consistent seasonal pattern is to compare the 5-year seasonal average with a 15-year seasonal average. If they are fairly uniform, it could be an indication that the seasonal move is consistent. September coffee is a good example of this (see Figure 12.6).

**F I G U R E   12.3**

June Crude Oil 15-Year Price History

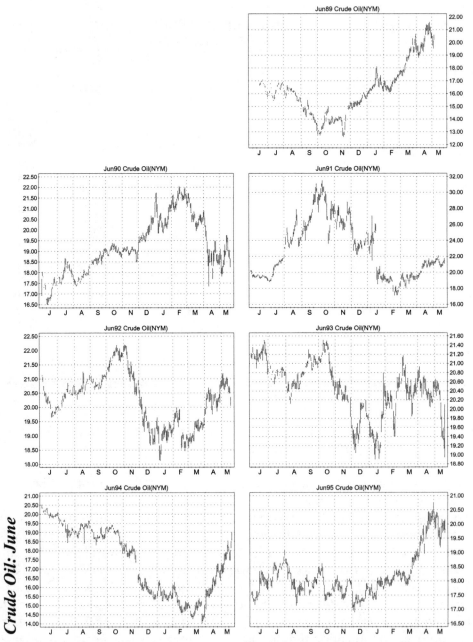

Over the last 15 years, how many years would you have made money selling puts far beneath the crude market in December?

## June Crude Oil 15-Year Price History (*Continued*)

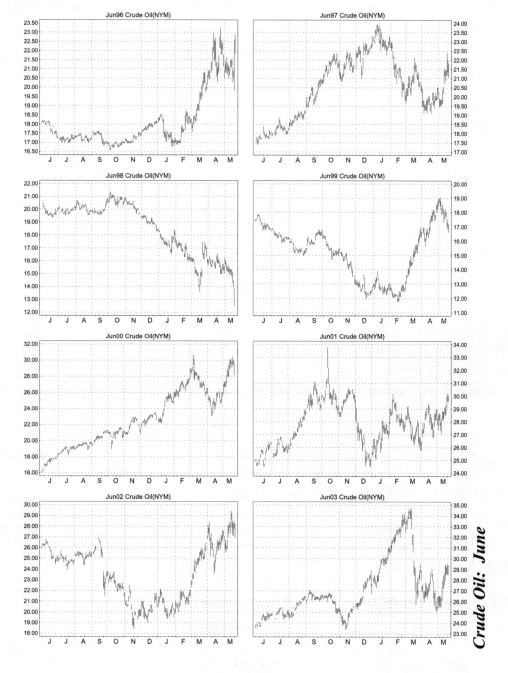

*Crude Oil: June*

**F I G U R E   12.4**

March Copper 15-Year Seasonal

Copyright (c) 1989-2004 Moore Research Center,Inc.

If there is a wide variation between the 5- and 15-year seasonal average charts, it could mean that the moves that occurred in the past may have been random occurrences that combined to make a good-looking seasonal average but were not really seasonal moves at all. It also could mean that a new fundamental has been developing in more recent years that is forging a new seasonal tendency. February gold is an example of a market where 5- and 15-year seasonal averages do not correspond that closely (see Figure 12.7).

## STEP 2: LEARN THE REASONS BEHIND A SEASONAL TENDENCY

Once you have identified a seasonal move that seems to occur fairly consistently at certain times of the year, it is time to find out why. Seasonal moves do not occur magically. There is something that causes them to happen year after year.

# FIGURE 12.5

## March Copper 15-Year Price History

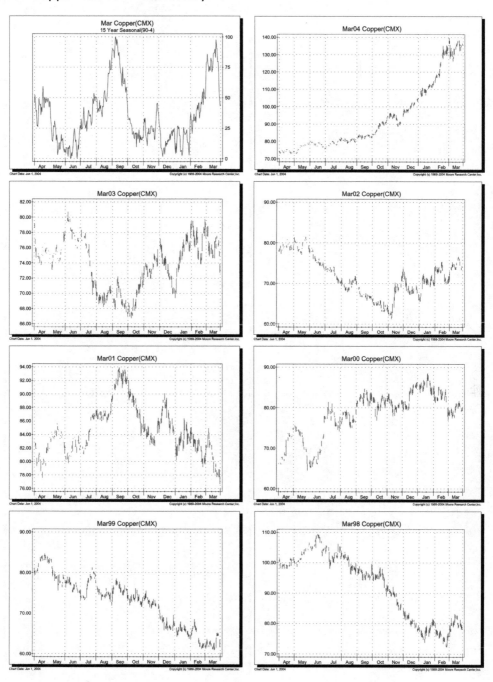

**F I G U R E   12.5**

March Copper 15-Year Price History (*Continued*)

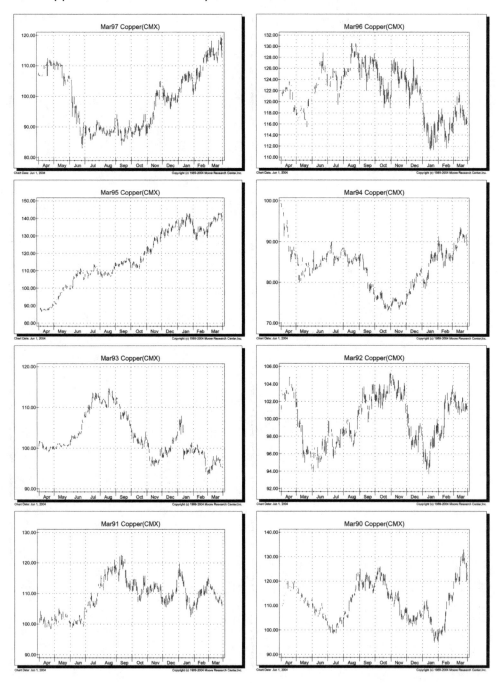

**F I G U R E   12.6**

September Coffee 5-Year over 15-Year Seasonal Average

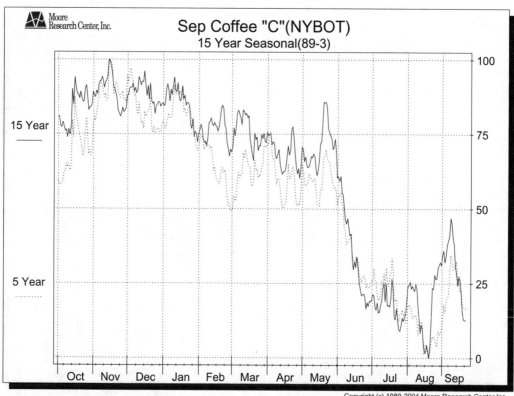

September coffee 5-year seasonal averages match up well with a 15-year seasonal average.
This could indicate a more consistent seasonal price pattern.

We all remember the scene from *The Wizard of Oz* where Toto pulls back the curtain
to reveal a man at the controls of the intimidating and magical wizard. In the end, it
turns out that the wizard was just a man.

When studying seasonals, one of the key roles you must play is that of Toto. You
have to pull back the curtain and look behind the scenes to see what is really causing this
"magical" move to occur. Almost always, there is a key fundamental at the controls.

This tends to be especially true in physical commodities such as grains, softs (such
as coffee, sugar, and cocoa), meats, and energy. These are consumable commodities that
often have production and/or distribution cycles that occur at the same time of the year
every year. There are some years in which outside factors will mute a corresponding
price move in the commodity, but in "normal" years, price may tend to favor movement
in one direction during these time periods.

**F I G U R E    12.7**

February Gold 5-Year over 15-Year Seasonal Average

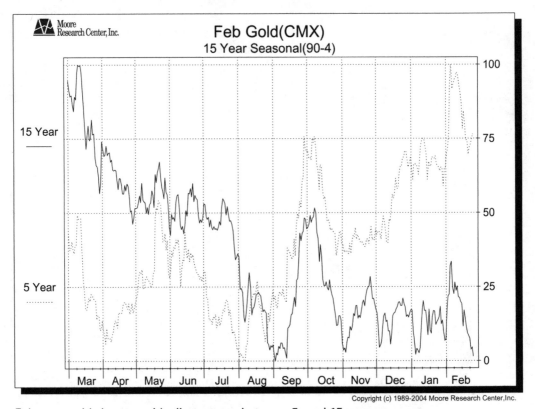

February gold shows a wide discrepancy between 5- and 15-year averages.

Finding out these key fundamentals and learning how, when, and where they occur will give you a key edge in trading seasonal tendencies. Instead of simply looking at a seasonal chart and betting that prices will move higher because the averages say they will, you can follow the fundamentals that historically have driven the seasonal tendency.

For example, if it is a move in relation to a harvest, you can track the progress of the harvest. Is it on schedule this year? What size of harvest is expected? What is the condition of the crop thus far? If everything points to the expectation that this will be a normal harvest year, you may be logical in expecting that prices may react as they have in years past to the upcoming harvest. If there appears to be a special situation this year that could disrupt, enhance, or affect harvest in another way, you may want to dig deeper before deciding on positioning. Experience can play a key role because it is difficult for a novice to determine what may disrupt a key fundamental and what might not.

## STEP 3: LOOK AT THIS YEAR'S PRICE CHART

After you have identified a consistent seasonal pattern and have confirmed that the key fundamental(s) that causes it appear to be taking place on *schedule* this year, it is time to look at the actual price chart. The first thing to consider is if this year's price action has coincided with the general seasonal pattern thus far. If coffee prices are supposed to fall to an annual low in September before rallying, and you look at the price chart in September and the market has just been on a two-month extended rally, you may want to reconsider a seasonal long play.

Other fundamentals may have combined to drive prices away from seasonal averages, making conditions unfavorable to a seasonal move.

Another thing to consider is that the seasonal move came early this year and that you may have missed it already. Or perhaps it is well within seasonal norms, but the seasonal average chart has the move taking place 30 days later. This is why it is important to look at daily price charts and compare their pattern with the seasonal pattern. If it appears that the basic patterns of the chart are the same but that this year's chart is matching up about 30 days early or 30 days late, it may be a good bet that the move you want to catch could take place 30 days earlier or later as well. The following example illustrates this concept.

July soybean seasonal averages point to a seasonal move higher beginning in February (see Figure 12.8). In 2003, the move did not occur in earnest until about a month after the seasonal average said it should (see Figure 12.9). The good news: Distant put sellers that positioned 30 days early most likely would still have had options expire worthless.

## STEP 4: REVIEW RELATIVE PRICE LEVELS

You also will want to be aware of the absolute price of the commodity when considering the likelihood of a seasonal move. If prices generally have traded in a range between $4 and $8 for the last eight years and this year price is at $12, will that affect your seasonal tendency? It very well could. This is why it is so important to know the fundamentals behind the move. If your seasonal average indicates that you should buy, and the price is this high, it could mean that prices are too high to move much higher even though seasonal tendencies favor it. If your seasonal average indicates that you should sell, this could mean that a more precipitous decline will occur this year.

Help often comes from examining price charts from previous years to determine how prices reacted to the seasonal tendency in years where price levels were comparable with today's prices.

**F I G U R E   12.8**

July Soybean 15-Year Seasonal Average

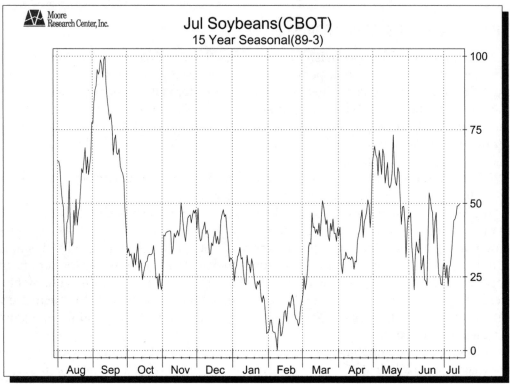

Copyright (c) 1989-2004 Moore Research Center,Inc.

## OPTION SELLING AND SEASONALS

You've gone through the three preceding steps and have identified a market where you feel a seasonal move up or down is likely to occur. Now what? How do you know exactly when to position?

The truth is that you don't. Technical traders can use their favorite indicator for clues when to go long or short during the seasonal time frame. But miss by few days in futures trading, and you're out of the trade. Even if all your research points to a seasonal move, there is still no guarantee that a move will take place. And there is always the possibility, of course, that a *counterseasonal move* could occur. In other words, prices could move in the exact opposite direction from which the seasonal averages indicate they have in the past.

Nonetheless, if you've done your homework and feel that you've got a good seasonal tendency from which to trade, you've already taken a great stride in tipping the odds in your favor. Now it's time to really overweigh the scales.

**FIGURE   12.9**

July 2003 Soybean Price Chart

SN03 - Soybeans-Day Pit, Jul 03, Daily

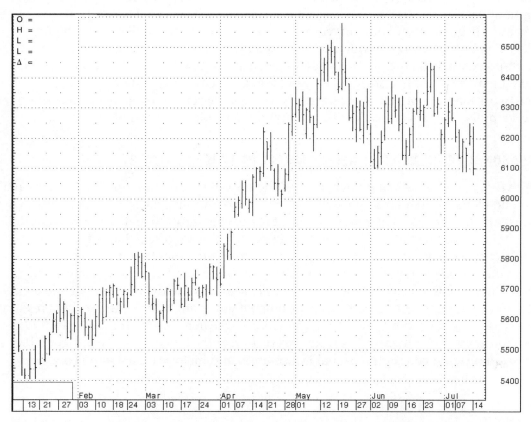

If your seasonal tendency indicates that a strong and sustained price increase is likely to occur over the next three months, instead of trying to time it perfectly with futures, simply sell put options far below the market. If your seasonal chart indicates that a long, gradual price decline is likely over the next eight weeks, instead of shorting the futures, sell the calls high above the market.

In other words, take the high road. Don't try to make a killing. Settle for a solid profit. Sell the options instead, and if the move takes place, great. You make your money. However, if it does not take place, fine, you still make your money. Even if the market moves moderately against you, you make money. If your timing is off and the move comes early or late, you still make money.

Remember the rules from previous chapters: Sell far out of the money. Sell options with low deltas.

By doing this, you force the market to make a true counterseasonal move for you to lose. Not just a short-term correction or delay, it has to make a *major move against* the fundamentals that traditionally have caused the market to move in the opposite direction. You force soybeans to make a sustained move higher when supplies are most plentiful, right at harvest. You make heating oil launch a sustained trend lower right when distributors begin accumulating inventory for winter needs, when demand is highest.

Combining seasonal tendencies with selling distant options can be an exceptionally high-powered technique for accumulating consistent trading profits. Become good at it, and it may be the only trading you need to do in a year. The great part about combining the two is that even if your seasonal analysis is dead wrong, the tool of option selling can be so forgiving that you could still end up with a profit at the end of the trade.

## SEASONAL TENDENCIES OF SELECT MARKETS: WHERE TO START

We've discussed seasonal tendencies and the importance of knowing the fundamentals behind them. In Chapter 13 we will review some of our favorite seasonal patterns, what causes them, and how you may be able to take advantage of them in an option portfolio.

The seasonal tendencies we will discuss are some favorites that we've found to be fairly consistent and match up with corresponding fundamentals during the year. However, there is no guarantee that they will move in the desired direction each year. In addition, this is not to imply that these are the only seasonal opportunities available because there are many interesting patterns to examine if you want to look. An excellent resource for seasonal data is our good friends at Moore Research Center, Inc. You can find contact information for them in the resources section at the end of this book. A good broker also can provide you with seasonal information and historical data at no cost.

# 13
CHAPTER

# The Best Markets for Seasonal Option Sales

In Chapter 12 we discussed how to use seasonal tendencies and make the most of seasonal charts. We have devoted this chapter to exploring some of the more attractive and consistent patterns that we have come across in our years of following seasonals. This is by no means a complete list of tradable seasonal patterns, but it should give you a good basis from which to begin your analysis of seasonal price movements.

You will notice that the focus of this discussion is on the fundamentals that cause the seasonal moves rather than exact dates to buy and sell. It is on these factors that seasonal traders should place their emphasis.

## ENERGY

With the weather patterns in North America, seasonal ebb and flow of supply and demand for energy used for heating, cooling, and transportation can be very pronounced. The energy market can offer some excellent opportunities for seasonal traders, although the market cycles may not be what you would think. For instance, a winter rise in heating oil prices is often touted in radio ads that sound like advertisements for car dealership "blowout" specials: "Demand is highest as people need heating oil and natural gas to heat their homes during winter," they reason.

While it may be true that actual use may be highest in winter on the retail level, distributors begin accumulating inventory for winter needs long before the first green leaf has turned orange in Vermont. Thus demand tends to increase as this takes place, often producing rising prices. Traders who purchase heating oil contracts in the fall may have already missed a seasonal move.

While the entire energy complex shows some impressive and relatively consistent seasonal patterns, option sellers may want to favor crude oil and natural gas contracts. This is so because volume and open interest in heating oil and unleaded gasoline can be thin, especially if you are selling options in back-month contracts. Crude oil and natural gas offer substantially more liquidity. Therefore, for the purposes of this chapter, we will focus on crude oil and natural gas contracts. However, if a trader can find enough liquidity in heating oil or unleaded gasoline options, there are some very enticing seasonal tendencies for these contracts as well.

Crude oil and all the petroleum contracts follow distinct seasonal cycles of accumulation and distribution. These patterns of supply and demand tend to hold true regardless of the actual price of crude oil. This is what makes them such an effective tool in trading.

Crude oil is used by refineries to make gasoline and heating oil. Refineries can gear up their facilities to produce more gasoline or more heating oil depending on what the market is demanding at any given time.

## Selling Crude or Heating Oil Puts in July

During the winter months, demand for heating oil by the public will be at its highest. Therefore, distributors will have to make sure that their supplies are adequate before winter arrives. And refineries will have to produce enough heating oil to meet the distributor demand during this time frame. Refineries need crude oil to make heating oil. Thus, when refineries begin ramping up production of heating oil to meet the autumn demand from distributors, demand for crude begins to rise and thus, often, so do prices. This cycle begins as early as July. Of course, heating oil prices tend to rise as well during this time frame, which makes selling puts in the contract a viable strategy. Options, however, are much more liquid in crude oil. Therefore, selling crude oil puts in July would be the preferable trade for investors seeking to enter a more sizable position (see Figure 13.1).

During late autumn, when distributors determine that supplies will be adequate to meet winter demand, heating oil production begins to taper off, and thus so does demand for crude oil. This is when prices often will tend to fall off as well. Crude oil prices will tend to reach a low some time between November and January, depending on how timely refineries have been in meeting seasonal demand. If refineries are ahead of schedule and distributors have been able to accumulate enough stocks early, prices will tend to bottom out earlier. If refineries are behind schedule, prices will tend to bottom out later.

Weather can play a key role as well. It is primarily the northeastern United States, with many older homes and buildings, that relies on heating oil for winter heating

**F I G U R E    13.1**

October Heating Oil 15-Year Seasonal Average

needs. Particularly cold weather early in the season results not only in early consumption of heating oil, requiring excess production to replace supply, but also can foretell a colder than usual winter season requiring more heating oil production. Therefore, a particularly cold and/or early start to winter often means that crude oil prices will bottom out later rather than earlier.

Yet, just when heating oil supplies have begun to peak and crude oil demand drops off to a low for the year, the market already begins to anticipate the next annual cycle of demand.

## Sell Puts on Crude Oil in December

Crude oil tends to fall to its lowest price levels of the year in the November–January time frame. Thus selling puts in March, April, or May crude oil during this time period often can be an excellent trading approach if the fundamentals appear to be following normal seasonal patterns (see Figure 13.2).

While demand for gasoline remains relatively stable for nine months of the year, the North American and European summer generally produces a spike in demand for gasoline. Not only are roads easier to navigate without snow and ice, making driving easier, but school is out. Summer is the time of the traditional American and European vacation, which almost always entails a road trip. In other words, summer is travel time in the Northern Hemisphere, which means more driving and requires more gasoline. There is no debate that gasoline demand in North America and Europe is highest during the summer months. Do you think that it is a coincidence that you are usually paying the highest prices of the year at the pump during the summer?

To meet this demand, distributors begin stockpiling gasoline supplies during the early spring. This means that refineries will have to retool facilities to focus on gasoline production to meet this demand. This "restructuring" phase generally takes place

## FIGURE   13.2

May Crude Oil 15-Year Seasonal Average

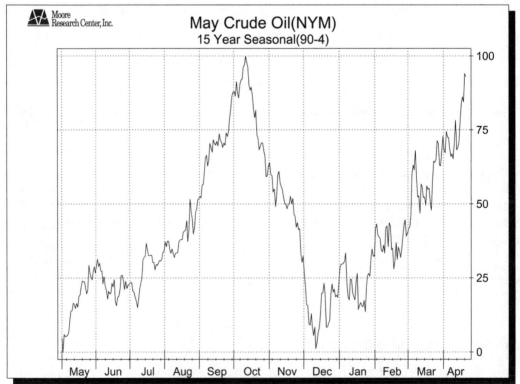

around February and often can mean refineries shutting down for a few days to a few weeks in order to gear their facilities for maximum gasoline production. This in itself often can jump-start a rally in product prices because stocks often show a draw during this period. However, as gasoline production kicks into full gear, demand for crude begins to rise rapidly again, and thus prices often tend to follow. Again, gasoline prices generally are rising as well during this time as distributors are accumulating inventory, driving up demand.

Some time in the April–June time period, when distributors begin to determine that supply will be adequate to meet summer needs, gasoline inventory building will begin to slow, and production of unleaded gasoline will be curtailed, resulting in reduced demand for crude oil. Thus crude oil prices often peak during the height of the accumulation phase, in late spring, and then recede slowly to reflect the reduced demand of distributors.

The energy market often suffers another low during midsummer as demand for crude oil wanes. However, it is during this time that refineries once again switch over to heating oil production, beginning the cycle all over again.

This is the normal seasonal cycle of the energy market. There is no magic here. Just solid supply/demand fundamentals. Of course, other factors also affect the daily price of crude oil, such as weekly builds or draws in stocks or violence in the Middle East. But seasonal cycles are the "big picture" fundamentals. It will help tremendously to focus on these in your trading. As an option seller, you have the luxury of being able to focus on the big picture and not on the day-to-day news and technical timing to which most futures traders are limited.

## Counterseasonal Moves

Just because crude oil prices have a good track record of following seasonal demand cycles, do not be fooled into thinking that they might not move or even might move opposite to what they normally do. This is called a *counterseasonal move,* and although it is not the norm, it does take place occasionally. There are many factors that could counteract seasonal demand cycles in all commodities. For instance, crude oil prices in particular are very sensitive to worldwide geopolitical events. Although this is certainly not the only thing that may cause a counterseasonal move, it would be key factor to consider.

The lead-up to the war in Iraq in 2003 is such an example. Rather than receding in the fall as energy prices often do, crude oil prices began a sharp rally that accelerated right up until the U.S. and British invasion was launched in March. Refineries stockpiled massive amounts of crude during these months for fear that a major crude oil supply disruption was possible. After the attack was launched, prices receded sharply at a time when the seasonal rally normally is just getting going (see Figure 13.3).

This is what is meant by monitoring fundamentals to determine if normal seasonal supply and demand patterns are occurring on schedule. You must be aware of outside

**F I G U R E    13.3**

May 2003 Crude Oil Price Chart

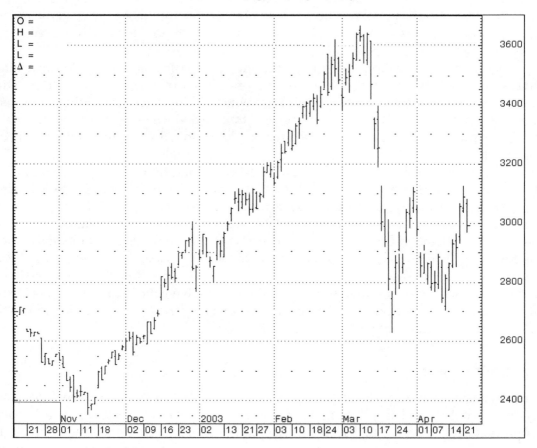

CLK03 -Crude Light-Pit, May 03, Daily

fundamental developments that could disrupt normal supply/demand cycles. You won't always be able to determine if something may or may not affect the cycle dramatically, but an impending war is probably a good reason for pause. Supply/demand cycles can be very strong and can override a lot of other fundamentals, even the ones currently grabbing headlines. Common sense and experience will be your guides.

## How to Position

Should you just start selling crude puts in November and June? Again, let common sense be your guide. For example, if it is December and crude oil is at the highest price levels of the year, the seasonal approach may not be the best play this year. Determining how close the market has followed the seasonal average to this point is very important. If the market has not moved somewhat in conjunction with the seasonal average in the last three or four months, there is a good chance that it will not start following the average after you enter your trade.

If December arrives, however, and crude oil is showing some weakness or has just experienced a sharp correction, selling puts can be an excellent play. Traditional technical indicators can be helpful in timing your entry, but timing is not as important as in futures trading. Sell as far underneath the market as you can while still collecting acceptable premiums. Remember, although your analysis indicates increasing prices soon, you don't need a rally to profit. Your only stipulation is that prices don't fall dramatically.

The same can be said for the seasonal weakness in the summer. This also can be a good opportunity to sell puts. If prices are not seasonally receding, forget the trade and move on. Price declines that occur in summer often are not as extreme as the ones taking place during winter. Nonetheless, it can be an excellent trading opportunity.

We do not recommend selling calls at the levels at which crude oil tends to peak. Although this probably would produce profits most of the time, the crude oil market remains subject to world political events. More often than not, a surprise geopolitical incident is likely to cause a spike in oil prices rather than an abrupt price decline. Many things can happen that can disrupt or threaten to disrupt the oil supply. A few things can happen overnight that would result in a large and immediate surplus of oil. In other words, surprise news events usually are bullish to oil prices.

A notable exception to this was September 11. The U.S. airline industry was grounded. Nobody wanted to fly, and few people felt like traveling by car. Demand for jet fuel and gasoline plummeted, resulting in a corresponding plummet in crude oil demand. Although heating oil accumulation continued through this period, the drop in demand for other oil products was more than enough to offset the increased seasonal demand (see Figure 13.4).

After the initial invasion of Iraq in 2003, prices returned to a more traditional seasonal pattern in 2004. Sellers of crude oil puts in December would have benefited from fast deterioration and little volatility for their short puts.

## Natural Gas

Natural gas tends to follow almost identical seasonal tendencies as those found for petroleum, albeit for somewhat different reasons. As with heating oil, retail demand for natural gas is highest in the winter months for heating needs. Natural gas is used as the primary heating fuel for newer homes, especially in northern and western regions of the United States. Distributors in these regions, then, must anticipate this demand surge and begin accumulating inventory in the months leading up to heating season. These are the months that wholesale demand accelerates, and price tends to follow.

**F I G U R E    13.4**

May 2004 Crude Oil Price Chart

CLK04 -Crude Light-Pit, May 04, Daily

Almost exactly like heating oil and crude oil, accumulation begins to slow some time in late autumn, when distributors determine that supply should be adequate to meet winter needs. This often will be accompanied by a drop in prices (see Figure 13.5).

The second and possibly more powerful seasonal tendency for natural gas tends to begin in the heart of winter. It is ironic that when retail natural gas demand is peaking in the December–February time frame, futures prices often are near yearly lows. This can change very quickly, however.

Demand for natural gas peaks again during the summer months because it is used as a primary fuel to generate electricity to power air conditioners in southern and western regions of the United States. With this retail demand spike expected to begin in June, southern natural gas distributors begin taking advantage of the lower prices and generally begin accumulating inventory some time in the January–February time frame.

**F I G U R E   13.5**

November Natural Gas 15-Year Seasonal Average

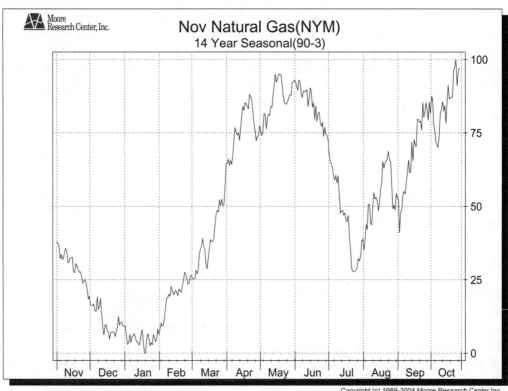

This accumulation phase can become very pronounced in March and April. Thus a price increase corresponding with the rising demand is often the result.

Much as in the fall, once distributors determine that summer supply will be adequate, prices often begin to decline as well into midsummer, when a secondary low often can be established, beginning the cycle over again. While this low is often established at higher price levels than the winter low, it can be a trading opportunity as well.

Put sales far beneath winter and summer lows, then, often can be a great trade in natural gas.

A key figure natural gas traders watch during these times of the year is the weekly injections into storage, which is released by the Department of Energy. This shows what kind of supply is being built to meet summer or winter needs.

An added benefit of trading natural gas is that unlike crude oil, which the United States relies heavily on imports to fill its demand needs, most natural gas used in the

United States is produced in North America. This makes the commodity less vulnerable to geopolitical events overseas than crude oil and its products.

As with crude oil, traders may want to focus on the long side of natural gas seasonals rather than on the short side. There has been a key fundamental shift taking place in this commodity through the first half of this decade that could have dramatic effects in the second half. New demand for the fuel generated from a boom in new housing in the United States over the last few years has outpaced sources of new supply. The public and the media began to realize this shifting long-term fundamental in 2003 when storage figures were abnormally low. This was when everybody from CNN to Alan Greenspan was discussing the impending natural gas "crisis." A mild summer helped the industry rebuild stocks before fall arrived. However, the trend of new demand outpacing new supply sources is expected to continue for several years, which could move natural gas into new "normal" trading ranges and possibly enhance seasonal price structuring, at least from the long side.

You can use technicals, common sense, and a good broker in timing your seasonal option sales in natural gas.

## SOYBEANS

Agricultural commodities tend to have distinctive seasonal tendencies that often can be used very effectively in conjunction with an option selling campaign. Whereas seasonals in energy are based more on demand cycles, seasonals in agricultural commodities often are more the result of supply cycles.

Crops that are grown in the soil obviously will be dependent on the seasons for their growth cycles. Therefore, it follows that supplies would be highest at harvest time and lowest in the months just preceding harvests.

Soybeans have a very dynamic harvest cycle now that South America has eclipsed the United States in total production of soybeans. Until the early 1980s, the world's supply of exportable soybeans was produced primarily in the United States. Thus, following one harvest cycle was all that was needed.

However, with the advent of increasing South American production to today's levels, major soybean harvests now take place twice a year, or every six months. Soybeans are harvested in the United States in the September–November time frame, whereas autumn harvests take place in Brazil and Argentina in the March–June time period.

This results in a large discrepancy in seasonal tendencies between "old crop" and "new crop" soybeans.

### Call Sales in May

The old pattern for November soybeans (considered new crop beans) generally saw soybean prices reaching an apex in May as old crop U.S. supplies generally were dwindling and new crop planting jitters often were peaking. The advent of the Brazilian harvest beginning in June, along with the psychological comfort of the U.S. crop being "in the ground," often would begin to bring prices back down through the summer months. This frequently was the case, but with a few notable exceptions. June–August is also the time for weather problems in the United States. Severe weather causing real or perceived crop damage can send bean prices skyrocketing counterseasonally during summer months. Nonetheless, the pattern typically followed a seasonal norm until the late 1990s (see Figure 13.6).

The years between 1998 and 2003 saw what could be the beginning of a new seasonal dynamic unfolding in soybeans. The 5-year average during these years shows a price pattern almost opposite the 15-year pattern. This may be due to an uncommon amount of weather during these years or the emergence of China as an economic force,

**F I G U R E    13.6**

November Soybeans 5- and 15-Year Seasonal Averages Overlaid

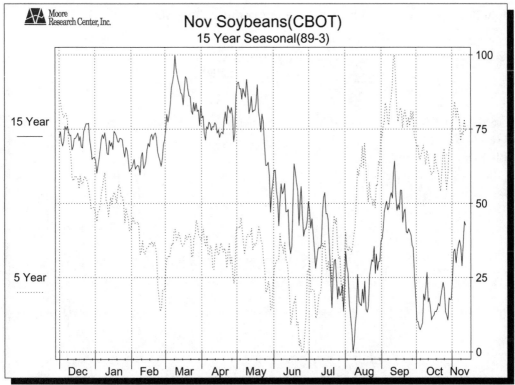

Copyright (c) 1989-2004 Moore Research Center,Inc.

Discrepancy between 5- and 15-year seasonal averages for new crop soybeans. Is this an aberration or new fundamentals altering seasonal tendencies?

electing to purchase more Brazilian beans during the summer months. As a result, price patterns for new crop beans have become a bit skewed in the last several years. Historically, however, selling calls in soybeans during the month of May has produced relatively good results. Poor growing weather in the United States is one factor that can produce counterseasonal moves.

## Put Sales in February

Old crop soybeans, however, have continued to exhibit a generally reliable price pattern and therefore can provide some good opportunities for option sellers. Old crop soybeans, which include soybeans harvested in the last harvest, also include July soybeans (see Figure 13.7).

South American soybeans generally are being planted when U.S. soybeans are being harvested in October and November. Farmer sales of soybeans often are heaviest

### FIGURE 13.7

July Soybeans 5- and 15-Year Seasonal Averages Overlaid

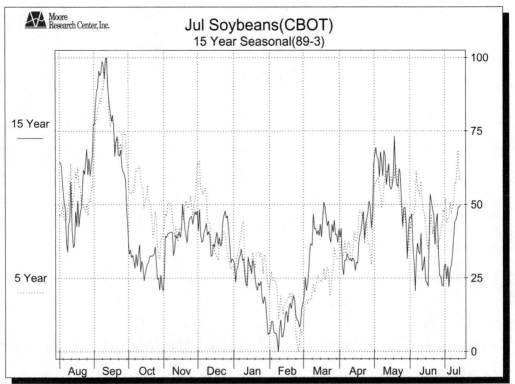

Copyright (c) 1989-2004 Moore Research Center,Inc.

during the winter months as U.S. farmers cash in soybeans from the autumn harvest and use the proceeds to restock supplies and equipment for the upcoming crop year. This selling often reaches a peak in the January–March time frame. At the same time, by February or March, the Brazilian crop generally is all but out of weather danger and is considered "made." The market then begins to price this new supply of soybeans as it reaches the market. These two factors occur generally around the same time period and can tend to drag prices lower in the months of December through February, often reaching annual lows during February. This phenomenon is known in trading lore as the *February break* and has gained a lot of notoriety, especially over the last few crop years.

Usually by March, the available supply of U.S. soybeans begins to decline, and the market generally has already priced in the South American crop. Prices often begin a steady ascent lasting well into summer.

As with other seasonal tendencies, trying to time the low of a February break with futures contracts can be like trying to time your jump out of a falling elevator. Selling options, however, does not require the picking of a low.

If other fundamentals and outside news events have been taken into account, selling puts far beneath the soybean market in February can be as good a seasonal play as any. A broker or news service with access to U.S. export and Brazilian crop estimates can be extremely helpful in this regard.

Again, remember that these are seasonal *averages* and that the February break could occur as early as January or as late as March, if it occurs at all.

## GRAIN

Corn harvest cycles are roughly the same as soybeans in the United States. Corn farmers, however, do not have to contend with a large worldwide competitor as far as exports go. While China used to export corn, by mid-2004, China had exported most of its huge surplus stocks and generally was focused on trying to grow enough corn to avoid having to import large quantities. Brazil is not a large corn producer, but Argentina has been stepping up as a more considerable producer of corn since the late 1990s.

Corn seasonal price tendencies, then, are much more reflective of U.S. harvest cycles. There are several price tendencies to study in corn. However, one of the more consistent is the one we will mention here (see Figure 13.8).

Corn is planted in April and May (spring in the United States) and harvested in September and October (fall in the United States). Corn takes slightly longer to develop than soybeans, and therefore, the planting of corn usually is started ahead of soybean planting. While rumors often will swirl ahead of planting about dry soil or too much rain, once planting is completed and the crop is "in the ground," anxiety tends to dissipate, and prices tend to decline in anticipation of a new crop on the way. Therefore, selling corn calls in May can be a good way to generate revenue through premium collection. You don't bet on a price decline, you only bet against a substantial rally.

**F I G U R E    13.8**

September Corn 15-Year Seasonal

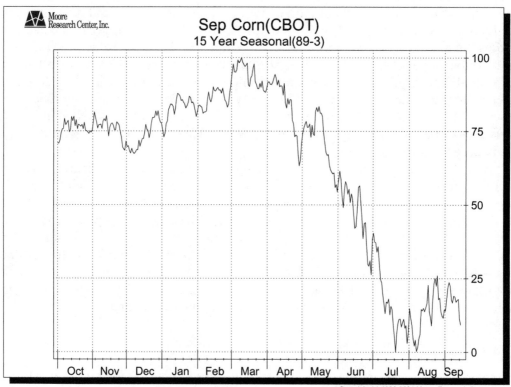

Copyright (c) 1989-2004 Moore Research Center,Inc.

Call sellers seeking higher premiums can begin selling calls as early as March if no abnormal fundamental developments are readily apparent. Again, the further out of the money the better. Options sold in March will have to be held longer, meaning that there is more time for price to move against your position before time decay can begin balancing out adverse moves. However, you also may be able to sell strikes further out of the money than you will be in May. Corn prices can and do rally in the spring. You want to be positioned to ride out rallies in order to take advantage of the bigger picture.

One of the main risk factors in selling corn calls in the March–May time frame is a weather scare. Crop-threatening weather can cause brief but substantial rallies during the summer. Real damage to the crop as a result of weather can result in a longer-term counterseasonal move.

Real weather damage to crops, however, is not as common as one may think. Furthermore, weather problems don't happen overnight. They happen over a period of weeks or months. Set your risk controls and stick by them, and you should not have to fear large losses caused by adverse weather.

## FROZEN ORANGE JUICE

Oranges for juice production generally are produced in the United States and Brazil. While U.S. oranges are grown in Florida and California, oranges for juicing come primarily from Florida.

Because oranges grow on trees, there is no planting season for oranges. However, there is a growing season and harvest for oranges. Since most of the orange juice in the frozen concentrate orange juice (FCOJ) contract comes from Florida oranges, seasonal tendencies for this contract rely heavily on the fundamentals for Florida oranges (see Figure 13.9).

**F I G U R E   13.9**

March Orange Juice 15-Year Seasonal

Orange juice for the March contract comes from oranges harvested in December and January. Harvest season for Florida oranges begins in December. Orange juice has a strong seasonal tendency to make a top in November before experiencing a rapid price decline in December. We wrote an article on this phenomenon several years ago that we feel is relevant in explaining this seasonal tendency for this book. The article appears below.

## ORANGE JUICE FUTURES: APPROACHING HARVEST IS OFTEN A TRADING OPPORTUNITY IN FCOJ

James Cordier and Michael Gross, *Liberty Trading Group*
November 1, 2002

The coming freeze season for Florida oranges often encourages the market to build in a risk premium. By December, however, the market has often done so. But the production season coincides with the freeze season. What does this mean? This means that speculators bid up prices of frozen orange juice futures in November in anticipation of "freeze season" in Florida. Harvest usually begins in December. Therefore, barring a killer frost, the market goes from a frost premium in price to a situation where orange supply is the highest it will be at any time during the year. Thus orange juice prices often go from their highest points of the year to their lowest in a matter of a month. This phenomenon is unique to the orange juice market but often can present a very lucrative opportunity for call option sellers.

### IS FREEZE SEASON STILL FREEZE SEASON FOR FLORIDA ORANGES?

Being in Florida, I am probably quoted more on the orange juice market than on any other commodity. Orange juice also happens to be one of the least written about commodities on the board. This is why I believe that orange juice happens to be a great market to trade fundamentally. There simply is not a great amount of information available to the general trading public about orange juice—at least not as much as there is for a market like soybeans, where we get daily updates on crop conditions, soil moisture, and export news.

There has been a basic fundamental change in orange production in Florida over the last 15 years. Much like the coffee market (which also prices in a "freeze premium" in the month of May), producing areas gradually have moved out of the high-risk freeze areas in recent years. In the late 1980s and early 1990s, Florida's orange crop was ravaged by a series of freezes. Instead of replanting trees in those same freeze-prone areas, producers began planting trees much further south in the state.

Today, Florida orange-producing areas are significantly further south than 10 to 15 years ago and thus are far less susceptible to the damaging freezes that we saw in the late 1980s. The seasonal price rally in orange juice has continued to persist mainly due, in our estimation, to the small speculator.

However, with this year being an off year in the production cycle, Florida's orange crop is forecast at 197 million boxes, 14 percent below last year's 229 million boxes. This will make the market extra sensitive to November cold snaps. Nonetheless, we see no abnormal circumstances with this year's crop and believe that conditions are right for the market to follow the historical preharvest price pattern.

We are fortunate as option sellers because spec-led freeze rallies drive up call option premiums to overinflated levels and can make for an excellent option sale. We are not suggesting that a crop-damaging freeze is not possible, only that it is much more unlikely than it was 10 to 15 years ago. Even in the unlikely event that a cold snap occurs, we feel that if option sales are executed at higher strike prices, traders should be able to ride out all but the most severe freeze. At the time of this writing, it is 80°F outside my window.

Look to be a seller of orange juice calls over the next two to four weeks on rallies. We feel that the orange juice market is basing for a seasonal swing higher, and aggressive traders can position on a 3- to 4-cent rally. However, we will exercise caution and wait until the traditional seasonal top in middle to late November before recommending positioning. We will be working closely with clients in the timing of this trade.

In summation of the article, prices tend to rise in October and November as a freeze premium builds into the market. Once harvest begins in December, prices have a tendency to plummet. While the possibility of a freeze occurring prior to harvest still exists, freezes are less likely now than they were in the 1990s and earlier because the bulk of orange production in Florida has moved further into the southern regions of the state. These areas have higher average annual temperatures and therefore are less likely to freeze.

Selling calls on a November rally in frozen orange juice can be a high-probability and sometimes fast profit opportunity. March calls at high strikes often offer the best bargains.

Again, these are averages, and there is no rule that says that orange juice prices can't go screaming higher in December. A broad look at the overall market and solid risk management obviously remain vital components.

## COFFEE

Coffee is produced in many nations across the globe with tropical climates. Brazil, however, is by far the world's largest coffee producer and coffee exporter, which makes the market very sensitive to the status of the Brazilian coffee crop each year (see Figure 13.10).

**FIGURE  13.10**

September Coffee 15-Year Seasonal

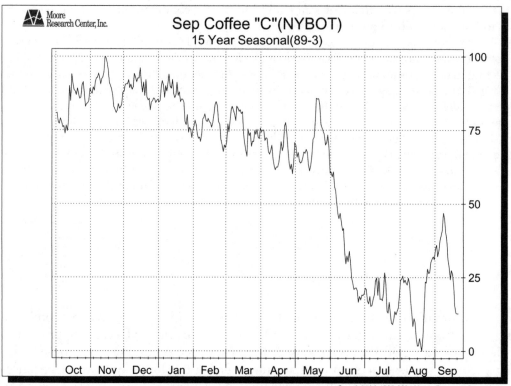

Copyright (c) 1989-2004 Moore Research Center,Inc.

As with oranges, coffee is not replanted each year like corn or soybeans, but rather grows on trees (that actually look more like bushes). Therefore, there is no planting season for coffee, but harvest time often will result in seasonal moves for coffee.

Brazil begins to harvest coffee in May of each year. The seasonal average price pattern for coffee suggests more of a traditional move to "harvest lows" because the supply generally will be highest at the time immediately following harvest. The market often anticipates the increased supply once harvest begins, and coffee prices can experience a steady decline beginning in or around the month of May.

Prices sometimes can experience a rally as harvest approaches as speculators position for the Brazilian "freeze season." The primary risks of a freeze in Brazil come in July and August, the heart of the Brazilian winter.

However, freeze season may not be the risk factor it once was to prices. This excerpt from one of our recent coffee articles explains.

While "freeze season" may get a lot of hype in the press, the chances of a freeze causing significant damage to the Brazilian coffee crop have dropped substantially in just the last six to seven years. After crop-damaging freezes in the 1980s and early 1990s, Brazilian producers began a trend of planting replacement trees further north, toward the equator, moving production to a more moderate winter climate and out of more frost-prone zones. While the chances of a crop-damaging freeze never can be eliminated completely, it is our opinion that this is such a significant fundamental change that the heavy spec buying often seen in May could become a nonfactor within the next four to five years.

Even before this change in growing areas, a sustained summer price rally in coffee has been an extremely rare exception to the norm. Normal seasonal averages generally see coffee experience a short rally in May as bullish speculators buy the market. This often will be followed by a sustained regression in prices as new Brazilian supply gets dumped on the market just when the Northern Hemisphere heads into the lower-consumption summer months.

Coffee, then, is similar to orange juice in its seasonal tendency to build a freeze premium into prices ahead of harvest and then to experience a sharp price decline once harvest actually begins. Also similar to oranges is its susceptibility to freeze damage, which may have been vastly reduced, although not eliminated, in recent years.

Nonetheless, selling coffee calls ahead of the Brazilian harvest in May can be an excellent seasonal trading opportunity in times of normal fundamental market conditions.

## CATTLE

Weather and the changing of the seasons also have a direct effect not only on beef production but also on demand for beef. Since about 90 percent of all beef produced in the United States is consumed in the United States, cattle prices at the Chicago Mercantile Exchange are affected by factors affecting the U.S. herd and by factors affecting the North American appetite for beef.

While a common myth is that beef demand is highest in summer because of "barbeque season," quite the opposite is true. While there is a slight increase in beef demand in late spring and early summer, demand for beef tends to wane during the hot summer months because families favor quick meals and are eating on the run, with summer activities (e.g., swimming, soccer, softball) taking precedence. In addition, lighter and/or cooler foods often are preferred in summer as opposed to sitting down to a pot roast.

Thus, as retail demand falls slightly, beef prices tend to go flat during the summer months.

Feeder cattle prices, however, have a tendency to move in an almost opposite direction to beef demand during the summer months. This is often the time of year when the supply of young feeder calves is at its lowest. Yet feed lot operators begin competing aggressively for young animals to place on feed in August and September to take advantage of new crop corn supplies at potentially lower prices. As a result of both these factors, prices of feeder cattle for late summer and fall contracts tend to bottom out in the April–May time period and then rally through the summer months (see Figure 13.11).

It generally takes four to five months after a young feeder calf is placed on feed before it reaches its optimal meat production weight. Thus the cattle placed on feed in August, October, and November often are the cattle delivered against the live cattle contracts in February and April. This results not only in the lower numbers of animals

### FIGURE 13.11

September Feeder Cattle 15-Year Seasonal

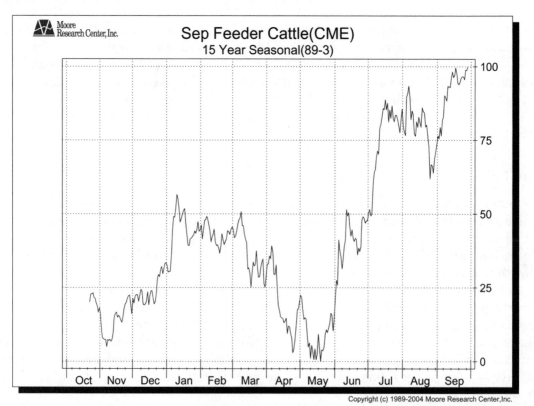

Selling feeder cattle puts during the April–May time period often can be a good summer play.

for slaughter (because there are fewer feeder cattle in the fall) but also in lower weights. This is so because it is harder to put weight on an animal during the cold months of December and January than it is during the summer months.

Winter is also a higher-demand period for beef in North America as families return to a more traditional "sit down" dinner where beef is often the main course. These factors combine to produce what is often a gradual but sometimes dramatic price increase from late fall to early spring in live cattle contracts (see Figure 13.12).

## SEASONALS AND FINANCIALS

We do not put as much stock in financial seasonals as we do in physical commodity seasonals. For one thing, the fundamentals supporting such moves do not appear as

**F I G U R E   13.12**

April Live Cattle 15-Year Seasonal

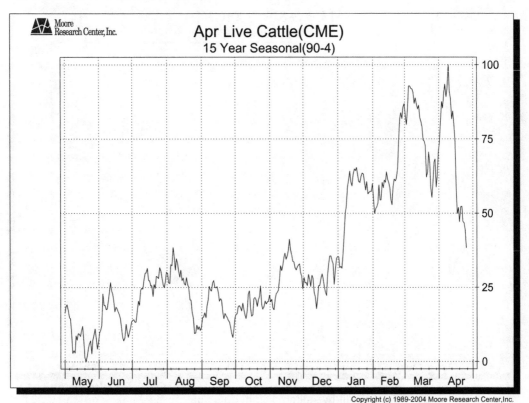

Copyright (c) 1989-2004 Moore Research Center,Inc.

Selling live cattle puts in December often can be an excellent way to generate revenue.

solid. Second, in our opinion, many seasonal tendencies in financials do not seem to be as consistent as those in the hard commodities. There are, however, a few tendencies you may wish to explore.

Many investors have heard that the stock market makes a low in October. While some may dismiss this as myth, the seasonal averages of the March Standard & Poor's (S&P) contract seem to support this viewpoint (see Figure 13.13).

Currencies also exhibit a curious tendency to have a seasonal preference. The yen, for instance, often may exhibit a bias of weakness against the U.S. dollar in autumn because that is when Japanese multinationals repatriate yen for the half-fiscal-year accounting (see Figure 13.14).

While there are many financial seasonals for traders to consider, it is very difficult to get a handle on all the fundamentals that go into the price makeup of a financial con-

**FIGURE   13.13**

March S&P 5- and 15-Year Seasonal Averages Overlaid

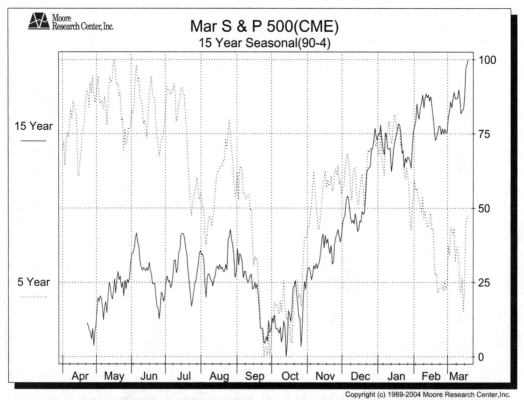

Copyright (c) 1989-2004 Moore Research Center, Inc.

Index option traders may benefit by selling distant puts against the January or March S&P contract.

## FIGURE 13.14

March Japanese Yen 15-Year Seasonal

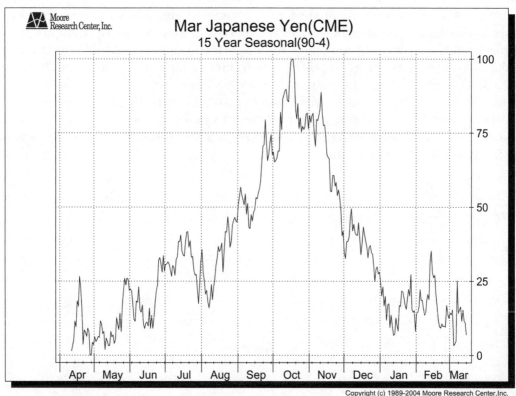

Some tie seasonal moves in the stock market or currencies to the beginning and end of the fiscal year.

tract and gauge if they are coming together on time to make a seasonal move. Financial contracts are also highly sensitive to geopolitical or economic news. Sometimes even minor events can move the market in large intervals.

We also have found that financial seasonals as a whole are not quite as consistent as some of the commodities, having many wide aberrations from the averages.

Nonetheless, they are fascinating markets to trade, and you may want to further research financial seasonals on your own to find potential option selling opportunities.

## SUMMARY

While several seasonal tendencies were covered in this chapter, these are certainly not all that are available. The ones discussed here constitute a limited list of those which have proved the most consistent in our option selling program over the years. You may want to explore seasonals further to discover other tendencies of certain markets that may prove useful to you.

While seasonals certainly are not guaranteed and are only an average of a broad compilation of data, they can be very effective tools to a successful option seller. While futures traders may have to time their trades perfectly, option sellers do not and often can have the great advantage of positioning in favor of the "big picture" without having to be as concerned about timing their entry perfectly.

An option seller can profit from using seasonal charts, even if a seasonal move does not occur. Usually, the market will have to make a sustained counterseasonal move for the option seller to lose. Seasonals can be a great way for option sellers to further increase the odds in their favor.

PART IV

# GETTING STARTED

# 14
## CHAPTER

# Mistakes New Option Sellers Make

Like most other investments or any other endeavor, there is a learning curve that new option sellers must experience on their way to becoming successful. No matter how many books you read or how many back-tested models you study, there is no replacement for tried and true experience. And with experience comes mistakes. Through our careers, we've seen many investors, especially investors new to option selling, make many of the same mistakes when first starting out. While these mistakes can be tremendous learning experiences, it might be easier to learn from the mistakes of others first, without having to sacrifice hard, cold cash.

The purpose of this chapter is to review the most common mistakes made by traders new to option selling. While these days we generally try to preempt these mistakes by new clients, there are those who insist on doing it their way, right or wrong. While experience ultimately will remain your best teacher, the observations on the following pages may make the educational phase of your new investment approach a much more pleasant and hopefully profitable experience.

## MISTAKE 1: TRADING ON YOUR OWN WITH A DISCOUNT BROKER

While this statement may sound self-serving, it is based not only on personal observations but also on what has been written in many other books, courses, and trade journals alike. A discount broker is an order clerk whose job is to answer the phone and take your order. That is it. Discount brokers provide a service to highly experienced traders who do their own research, their own analysis, their own portfolio planning, and their own trade placement.

However, if you are new to trading options, especially selling options, would it not serve you better to work with an advisor who is highly experienced in the field? Even if you design your own trades, selling options is a sophisticated investment approach. In addition to helping you with everything from bid/ask spreads to calling you when something breaks in the market that could affect your position, a good full-service broker can advise you on market news, order placement, stops, and risk control and provide a calm voice of reason in adverse market conditions. If the broker is really good, she can even advise you on new positions that will *make you money*.

As a new option seller, think of yourself as a flight student at the controls of a 747. From your training, you may be able to fly the plane fairly smoothly, maybe even land it by yourself. What happens, however, when you're trying to land in a thunderstorm and all of the sudden the plane starts to shake and a strange alarm goes off that you have never heard before? Would you prefer to have an experienced pilot, specializing in the plane you are flying, to talk you through the landing or even take the controls? Or would you prefer to have a passenger sitting beside you saying, "What are you going to do now?"

Of course, a good full-service broker is going to cost you a little more than a discount order clerk. Costs can be analyzed on an annual or per-quarter basis to determine if your broker is worth the fees. However, a good broker can save you thousands in the long term. While nobody knows what the market will do tomorrow, a good broker will help you to "land the plane." A better broker will keep you out of the thunderstorm altogether.

There is, however, a big difference between a full-service broker and a *good* full-service broker. One can land your plane for you; the other can help you crash it into the ground, maybe faster than you could. You may have to interview several before you find one who is competent enough and whom you feel is right for you.

Squeezing the last penny out of your commission rate may be great if you are a professional trader doing dozens or even hundreds of trades a day and need only a voice or screen to take your orders for you. However, if you are fairly new or even moderately experienced in option selling and/or futures, you may want to consider working with a professional advisor. As in many aspects of life, trying to play it on the cheap could end up costing you big.

## MISTAKE 2: OVERPOSITIONING

The second most common mistake we see new option sellers making is overpositioning. Because of the high odds of success on any individual trade, many new option sellers experience euphoria at having their first few options expire and think that they have discovered the Holy Grail of investing. This often can lead to a "can't lose" mentality.

Combined with the low margins of selling futures options, the potential to sell more options than an account should be holding safely becomes a realistic temptation. Don't do it. Almost invariably the position you choose to "load up" on will be the one that sinks.

Even if you experience early success at option selling, which we can honestly say many of you probably will, you cannot lose respect for the market. Unlike futures traders or option buyers, whose path to success lies in taking a series of small losses while waiting for one big winner, your approach will be the opposite. Your approach will be to take a series of many moderate winners and to avoid one big loser. Given the current rate of success of most futures traders and option buyers, your chances are pretty good. However, overpositioning your account increases the chances that one loss could affect your overall portfolio substantially. We generally recommend that clients not margin more than 50 percent of their total funds at any given time, and we recommend having that portion diversified over at least three to five commodities at any given time for accounts under $100,000. Any more of the former or less of the latter could mean that you are overpositioned.

## MISTAKE 3: TRADING AN UNDERCAPITALIZED ACCOUNT

A pilot friend once said that in training new flight students, planes were taken to higher altitudes, giving students more room for recovery if they made a mistake. The same is true for your option selling account. The more capital you have, the more room you have for recovery in the event of a bad trade and the more flexibility you have in your diversification and risk-management techniques.

Trading an undercapitalized account often means trading scared. It can lead to everything that one should avoid in option selling, including overpositioning, over- or underrisking, and emotional trading.

We generally recommend starting a futures option writing portfolio with at least $25,000. The problem with many futures traders is that they remain in a *gambler* mind-set instead of an *investment* mind-set. Many traders are attracted to futures because they believe that they can take a small amount of money and turn it into a large amount of money in a very short period of time. We already know the track record of most of these traders.

Option selling is not going to do this for you. However, option selling, if done correctly, can take a set amount of money and get a *very* good return on it. This is what is meant by an *investor's* mind-set. What do we mean by *very good return*? If you intend to trade your account in a conservative to moderate manner, according to the techniques used in this book, you realistically could target a 20 to 50 percent annual return on your capital. Do we guarantee that you can do this? Of course not. But many traders ask for a ballpark expectation. Based on our experience, we believe that this can be a realistic objective.

You must, however, be sufficiently capitalized.

## MISTAKE 4: NOT HAVING A TRADING PLAN AND/OR EXIT STRATEGY ESTABLISHED BEFORE TRADE ENTRY

While many traders dismiss the role that psychology plays in the trading process, it has been noted by most top traders and authors that failure to control emotions is probably the number one reason traders lose money. Markets look entirely different to you when you are analyzing trades from a distance than when you are following them with your money on the line. No matter how controlled you think you are, your emotions probably are affecting your thought process without you even knowing it.

Think of it as a Dr. Jekyll–Mr. Hyde type of situation. Before you enter the trade, you are Dr. Jekyll, the calm, rational thinker who forms and implements a controlled plan. Once you enter the trade, you become Mr. Hyde, instinctive, irrational, and reacting and overreacting to every piece of stimuli passing in front of your eyes. There is a little of this in all of us, even the most polished professional trader.

This is why most traders develop a plan or a system. Systems do not have to be complicated. They are simply a set of rules you develop before you enter the trade so that you have a roadmap to follow once you make the "change" from objective analyzer to emotional reactor. Remember plan the trade, and trade the plan? This is another way of saying it.

Systems can range from a couple of simple entry and exit guidelines written on a piece of paper to a multidimensional computer program. Frankly, you probably could do just as well with either in your option selling account.

The most important part of a system is the exit strategy. You must know when, where, and how you will exit the trade and what circumstance will cause you to do so. Never change your plan once you are in a trade.

One of the primary ways that traders lose more than they should is by violating this rule. On the day they enter the trade, they are Dr. Jekyll on the phone, confident, cool, in control. Then, several days or weeks later, after the market has shifted, the same person is on the phone, but it sounds nothing like the rational fellow that spoke earlier. Mr. Hyde is now in charge. His voice is high, maybe a little faster, and he is excited and afraid. He asks his broker nervous questions, such as, "What do you think?" "What are they saying?" and "What should I do?"

Nietzsche once said, "A man without a plan is not a man." While we are not going to question the knowledge of Nietzsche's philosophy, a more fitting quote for modern-day investors might be, "A person without a plan is not a successful trader."

Know your exit strategy *before* you enter. Let Dr. Jekyll do the thinking part. All Mr. Hyde has to do is carry it out.

We work closely with our investors in designing and setting a trading plan not only for their portfolios but for each individual trade. However, if you are doing this on your own, you'll want to make setting an exit strategy your top priority.

Selling options already puts you in an elite group of futures traders who actually stand a chance to make some good money in the market. Setting a pretrade exit strategy will put you above most of even this specialized group.

## MISTAKE 5: TRYING TO PICK TOPS AND BOTTOMS

Although you will have an added margin for error in selling options, trying to pick tops or bottoms remains one of the highest-risk approaches to trading. Not only is it higher risk, but it also is probably unwise.

If you are trying to pick a top or a bottom, you are betting on a reversal in trend. This means that you are trading against the current trend and most likely against the current fundamentals. Markets can make fast and sometimes significant short-term moves in contrast to existing fundamentals. However, a market rarely will establish a long-term trend without some form of base fundamentals driving it. Picking a top or a bottom is trading against the trend, which automatically reduces the odds of your option expiring worthless. Remember the statistics in the earlier chapters? A market doesn't have to have a trend for you to sell options in it. However, if there is a trend, it is best to be selling your options in favor of it.

We had a client for several years who we'll call Sam. Sam would buy and sell futures contracts because he felt the market was "too high" or "too low." Consequently, his strategy often was to buy or sell against the trend. Sam employed a custom version of scale trading in which he would continue to add to his position as the market moved against it. His thought process was that as long as he had enough capital, he simply could continue to average down until, eventually, the market would reverse from its extreme levels. Although Sam had substantial capital in his account, this strategy often required him to meet margin calls to continue to hold his positions. He was a stubborn man, though, and he did well for a while. Although he had some big wins and big losses, he was running at about even after a couple of years.

About halfway through his third year, Sam was betting big that crude oil prices were "too high" above $26. He continued to short futures, and prices continued to go up. As you can guess, Sam's story ends badly. Crude oil continued to increase in price and soon exceeded $41 a barrel. Eventually, Sam got a margin call that he could not (or did not want to) meet. In other words, he ran out of money and was forced to liquidate all his positions at substantial losses. His account was nearly depleted.

Although we tried on several occasions to convert Sam to an option selling approach, he was not interested. However, although an option selling approach may have extended his trading career, we believe that his strategy of positioning suffered from a substantial flaw that eventually would have done him in regardless of the vehicle he was using.

Selling a market because it is "too high" or buying because it is "too low" generally does not make good trading sense. Who determines what is too high or too low? The market does. If it is trading at a certain price level, that is what the commodity is worth that day. It's not too high or too low. It's just right. This is why fundamental trading with futures contracts is so difficult. You may think that a market has bullish fundamentals, so you have to buy it at the price at which it is currently trading. On the day you buy the contract, the price is not too low. It is fairly priced.

With option selling, you can pick a price far below (or above) the current fair price and say, "That price *would* be too low. I do not think the market will go there." Since the market is not there on the day you sell your option, your strike price *is* too low, and therefore, your trade is at least logical.

Nonetheless, if you are selling this option in front of a trend, you could be stepping in front of a locomotive.

Fundamentals rarely change from bullish to bearish or vice versa overnight. Chances are that the fundamentals will change from bullish to mixed to bearish. It is during that mixed time of transition that a trend may start to falter. This is when all the existing fundamentals have been priced, and now the market is searching for direction. However, fundamentals often will start to change before the trend changes. If you think that you have identified a change in fundamentals in a trending market, you certainly do not want to write it off altogether. But don't think of selling options until the market has shown strong indications that the trend has changed or at least ended.

Funds often continue to drive a trend even in the face of shifting fundamentals. If you sense that the fundamental picture is changing, wait until the trend either reverses and establishes a new trend in the opposite direction or at least breaks the current trend and begins trading sideways or falls into a range. This could take weeks or even months. But again, option selling as presented here is a long-term investment approach, not a trading affair.

Weekly and monthly charts can be tremendously helpful in identifying longer-term price trends and potential changes in trend.

## MISTAKE 6: FORMING AN EMOTIONAL ATTACHMENT OR AVERSION TO A PARTICULAR MARKET

Although this may fall under the category of trading on emotion, it is common enough that it deserves a mention of its own. It is not uncommon for traders, especially new traders, to become emotionally attached or averse to a market. These are two extremes of what is basically the same mistake: forming an emotional association with a particular market—positive or negative. We've seen it cause losses as often as we've seen it produce missed opportunities. Both are equally damaging to your portfolio, and you should guard against this all-too-common mistake.

This phenomenon usually develops after a trader experiences a very positive or very negative experience or string of experiences in a particular market. The trader then comes to the conclusion that a particular market is "good" or "bad." The trader who wholeheartedly jumps into a trade because she made money in it before is making the same mistake as the trader who refuses to enter a trade based on a bad experience in that particular market in the past.

As rational people, we know that there is no such thing as "good" or "bad" markets. If you bought a contract for cotton and cotton went down, you lost money and therefore might be hesitant to trade cotton in the future. However, the trader who sold cotton and made a profit may think that cotton is a great market to trade. The cotton market, however, is like the ocean. It could care less about your well-being, but it has no desire to cause you harm either. You could bask comfortably in its warm tropical waters or drown in its cold icy depths. It is up to you what you do with it. However, it is not going to change to accommodate you. The market is the same way.

Let's look at a common example. Trader Mary sells puts in the Euro, and they expire worthless, netting her a profit. Mary feels good about the trade and therefore feels good about the Euro in general and may start to take a particular interest in trading it again. If the fundamentals remain favorable to Mary's positions, she may be able to continue to sell options profitably in the Euro for a long period of time.

The danger comes when fundamentals or the trend for the Euro begins to change. Mary may have formed such a strong emotional attachment to trading the Euro that she overlooks the subtle signs that a basic fundamental shift is starting to take place. Mary continues to sell puts because it has always been a good trade in the past. She feels very comfortable selling Euro puts. The Euro is a "good" market. Mary's emotional attachment has turned to complacency, and she allows it to override her objectivity when analyzing the market. She may even allow herself to overweigh her portfolio in Euros. When prices finally turn, Mary could pay the price for her emotional attachment.

If the attachment is strong enough, Mary may continue to position in the same trade, refusing to accept that the market conditions have changed. We have seen traders take considerable losses this way.

A variation of this mistake is a trader's urge to take "revenge" on a market in which he lost money. In this case, if a trader lost money trading soybeans, he has the opinion that "Soybeans took my money, and I am going to get it back from them."

Of course, this is irrational thinking as well. But it is another example of Mr. Hyde rearing his ugly head to trash the organized laboratory of your portfolio. The trader feels that he has to "get his money back" because it is being held hostage by the market in which he lost it. Therefore, he may want to try to reposition in the same trade or take the opposite position in order to capitalize on the very move that took his money in the first place. The trader refuses to accept that he had to take a loss and feels that if he can get it back in the same market, it will somehow erase the loss altogether because it was all part of the same trade. Never mind that much better opportunities may be available in other markets and that the trader may be passing up countless opportunities to make his losses back many times over.

If you find yourself feeling this way, it is best to take a few days or even a few weeks off from trading and let yourself come down from this experience. You will be in a much better state of mind to begin approaching the market rationally when you come back.

Even if your actions are not this extreme, traders often form long-term biases in particular markets based on past experiences. Try not to let past experience cloud your judgment when analyzing new trades.

An example of this can be taken from the mad cow example we discussed in Chapter 13. A friend of ours was short put options when the mad cow news broke in late 2003. While he had been able to exit his position at reasonable losses, it nonetheless left a bad taste in his mouth for trading cattle. He had developed an emotional aversion, even though it had no basis in reality.

By February 2004, it appeared that an exceptional opportunity was available in the live and feeder cattle markets. The main reason that cattle prices fell (other than immediate investor knee-jerk reaction) was not because the market believed that people would stop eating beef. It fell because importers of U.S. beef closed their borders to the product. Since exports made up about 10 percent of total U.S. beef production, it was felt that supplies would rise and, therefore, prices would be lower.

Cattle fundamentals before the mad cow disease scare, however, were extremely bullish. Demand was at a record high, and supply was not keeping pace. The calf crop was near a 50-year low. The U.S. border had been closed to Canadian beef, which met up to 10 percent of U.S. demand, due to an earlier mad cow disease outbreak in that country.

These fundamentals were still in place, even after the export pace was slowed. Within a period of about nine weeks, cattle prices had come back to pre–mad cow disease levels. Demand for beef had not waned after the mad cow disease scare, but the borders were still closed.

The public, however, had seen the reaction of the market after one mad cow disease incident. This brought out the small-spec fortune seekers who dreamed of retirement by buying cattle puts and hoping for another mad cow outbreak.

Put option prices skyrocketed as more of this money poured into the market. Whereas before the mad cow scare, option prices could be sold maybe $7 to $8 out of the money for decent premium, the same premium now could be had at strikes more than $20 out of the money. What is more interesting is that these options were up to $10 below the lows achieved during the 2003 mad cow disease outbreak.

The key fundamental here is that price had to adjust lower from mad cow because the borders of the main U.S. imports had been closed. Now they were already closed. They couldn't be closed again! Even in the unlikely situation that another mad cow discovery would occur, if the borders were already closed, why would the market fall to the levels of late December, let alone $10 beneath them? Buying options on a market because something might happen is outright gambling. Betting on a price level that is highly unlikely to be achieved *even in the event that the certain something takes place* is downright foolish.

It looked like a slam dunk to sell these puts so far beneath the market. Yet our friend was downright opposed to doing any type of trading in cattle. His emotions had produced an aversion to trading cattle. In his mind, he had taken a loss in cattle, and therefore, trading cattle was "bad."

He had let his emotions keep him out of what would have been a very profitable opportunity. If he would have sold the cattle puts at these levels, he would have been rewarded with options that eroded fairly quickly and smoothly, in addition to being positioned in a seemingly low-risk trade. And although it was a fundamentally sound trade, it also had something else going for it. It faded the public, which is almost always a good idea.

Don't let your emotions get in the way of such opportunities for you. Accept that no market is good or bad. Only your position is good or bad. Keep an open mind, and approach each trade as a brand new opportunity, independent of past profits or losses.

If you can avoid these mistakes, you'll be able to skip over some of the pitfalls that new option sellers make and give yourself a much higher chance of profiting consistently.

Chapter 15 will explain how to tell if you have a good broker and give advice on finding one.

# 15 CHAPTER

# Finding a Good Broker or Money Manager

Robert Kiyosaki, in his highly successful book, *Rich Dad, Poor Dad*, suggests that there are several strategies and philosophies that separate the rich in our society from the poor and middle class. Kiyosaki points out that one of these key differences is that the rich tend to seek out experts to advise and manage much of their financial affairs, whereas the poor and middle class seem to subscribe more to a "do it yourself" mentality. He argues that in an attempt to save money up front by handling legal, accounting, and investing matters on their own, the poor and middle class end up losing money in the long run.

If you were being sued, would you read a book on law and attempt to defend yourself? Would you go through all the ads in the Yellow Pages to find the "cheapest" lawyer you could find? Or would you seek out the best litigation attorney you could find and launch a vigorous defense to dismiss the case and countersue for court costs?

If you needed heart surgery, would you seek out a "discount" doctor—perhaps a first- or second-year intern who agreed to cut you a "really good" deal? Or would you research and interview to find the most experienced, skilled surgeon you could find?

Most people would want to hire the best in either of these situations. Yet, when it comes to money matters, many look to hire the broker with the "cheapest" commission. They do this because they do not see the need or use for a qualified broker, or they have had a bad experience with a broker in the past. Nowhere is this more true than in futures trading. Everybody has a story about the broker who "didn't get me out" or "told me to buy on the high." Others tell of outlandish commission charges leveled by an incompetent broker.

It is true that these brokers exist. Yet it is unfortunate that many of the people who have been turned off to brokers because of a bad experience will never experience the pleasure of working with a true professional. The actions of a few can tarnish the image of the hard-working professionals whose complete focus is on improving their clients' performance.

Some traders don't see the need for a qualified broker until they run into trouble. We cannot count the times that we have had distraught traders call and explain the precarious trading situation that they had gotten themselves into and ask how to get out of it.

"I sold these options" he'll explain, "and then I bought one of these to offset it, but then XYZ happened. What should I do?"

"Why don't you ask your broker?"

"He doesn't give advice," he'll respond. "It says on your Web site that that is what you do."

"Yes, I do. To my clients."

We have spoken to other brokers who dedicate their lives to studying the markets and improving their clients' bottom line. They are amazed at the public's expectation that their services simply can be obtained for free. Several times a month our firm receives e-mails from readers of our articles that state simply, "Please send me your best trades with strikes and risk zones. Thank you." There are several variations to this request, but this is the main theme. Yet, if they read an article by an accountant about saving on their taxes, would they write a letter to the accountant and ask for free tax advice?

This expectation, however, may not be all the public's fault. Some brokers who telemarket their services will hand out recommendations left and right to anybody who will listen. Sooner or later they may get one or two right. Beware of the trader passing out trades like popcorn. To paraphrase a quote from Mr. Kiyosaki's book, *Rich Dad, Poor Dad,* "Free advice is often the most expensive advice."

"You get what you pay for" is another piece of timeless wisdom. This does not suggest that the higher the commission, the better the broker. It does suggest that, on the whole, if you want competent advice and guidance, you probably are not going to get it on the cheap. This holds true in almost any profession.

It is true that there always will be a certain portion of traders who possess enough knowledge and skill themselves that they only need an order taker or an online trading platform to place their trades. We also forget that to many, regardless of what they say, making money is not their primary reason for trading. They trade as a hobby or pastime and seek the challenge, excitement, or fun of trading. Going it alone is part of the challenge. There is nothing wrong with this.

However, if your sole purpose is to increase the size of your investment, and you want to do it using the sophisticated strategy of option selling, a broker who knows what he is doing can be the difference between success and failure. A good broker should pay for himself many times over through the course of a year or years.

Throughout this book we have told you about the various benefits and advantages of working with a good broker. We promised earlier to define what a good broker actually is and what a good broker actually does to help your bottom line. This chapter will describe this along with how you can find a good broker to help you sell options profitably.

Before we delve into the subject of what makes a good broker, let's first examine what types of brokers and advisors are available.

*Discount broker.* A discount broker is generally a firm that employs a group of "brokers" whose job is primarily to be an operator or order taker. Their only function is to take orders. Many firms provide online research and even quotes for their clients. They are very popular with the day-trading set, as well as with professional traders who watch the markets as a full-time pursuit. Discount brokers serve a valuable function and are very useful to these types of individuals. However, if your career or business is not full-time trading, you may be better served elsewhere.

*Full-service broker.* Full-service brokers can play several roles. They can act as a professional "caddy" to your trading, providing you with up-to-the-minute research reports and custom charts, calling you with market updates or developments in your account, watching your account for you, assisting you with placing the right orders, personally working your order for a specified price, and generally being there to support you in any way they can. An inexperienced broker can still serve you well in this regard, as long as she is focused on personal attention to your account. The other role that a full-service broker can play is that of a trading consultant. It seems like common sense that a professional who is close to the market every day would have to pick up a few "tricks of the trade" along the way. However, just because a person is a broker does not mean that he is a good trader, nor does it mean that he is competent enough to give trading advice. It is in this regard that gaps in competence levels are widest. Yet a broker in the business for two months can give advice just as easily as a broker in the business for 20 years. And there is no guarantee that either one of them will provide you with good trading advice. This is why doing your homework is important when you are selecting a broker.

*Commodity trading advisor.* A commodity trading advisor (CTA) is quite different from a commodities broker. A broker gets paid to execute your trade for you. A CTA gets paid to manage your account. In other words, you hire a CTA to trade your account for you. CTAs generally charge an annual management fee (usually a small percentage of total equity in your account), in addition to an incentive fee. The incentive fee is a percentage of profits generated in your account.

If you hire a CTA, you are turning over the trading in your account to a professional trader. CTAs are required to provide a monthly performance record to prospective clients to show the results of their trading in the past. CTAs are also required to provide you with what is known as a *disclosure document* that describes in detail their fees, account sizes, the trading plan that will be used to invest your funds, and many pages describing risks.

Like brokers, CTAs come in a wide range of experience and competence. While a CTA does have to be licensed, there is little involved in getting one. A CTA does not have to pass any test determining his trading savvy. Many CTAs are simply individual traders who are registered to be able to trade other people's money. While some CTAs have little more knowledge or trading experience than the average individual investor, there are many skilled professionals in this field who manage many millions of dollars.

## WHAT YOU SHOULD KNOW ABOUT BROKERS

While the tide is beginning to turn back toward working with a full-service broker, many books that we have read on trading in general are antibroker. In other words, they encourage you to do everything on your own because brokers are basically commission-hungry salespeople, eager to take as much of your money as they can before they help you lose the rest in the market.

Having worked as brokers in this business for a combined 28 years, we feel that we may be able to shine a little light on to this perception.

Sadly, in some cases, the preceding perception of brokers is correct. In some cases brokers are converted salespeople from another field who got a license and now, instead of selling advertising or cookware, are selling brokerage services. Although this does not mean that they are bad people, it does mean that their ability to help you make money is limited. If you are looking for a discount broker, this may not make much of a difference. It takes little talent to pick up a phone and place an order. If you are looking for a market professional to guide you through the golden minefield of the futures markets, it could be critical. Fortunately, there are many skilled professionals in the field. However, you'll have to look a little to find them.

The word *broker* can encompass so many different job responsibilities that the range of individuals and how they view their jobs is endless. A choice that is recommended to many brokers starting out in the field is to decide whether they want to be traders or equity raisers. Since most brokers (or "account executives") are not good traders, they focus on raising equity. The test to become a futures broker is mainly on rules and terms and how the market works. There is nothing about trading or how to be a good trader. Therefore, if a broker wants to be a good trader, in most cases he has to learn on his own. There are some larger firms that offer some training to help brokers trade better. In most cases, however, a broker is doing his best with limited company or outside research or his own very limited knowledge to help you invest your money.

Why should a broker have to be a good trader? He doesn't. There are great brokers who are not good traders. But if he is going to give you recommendations, shouldn't he be at least a marginally better trader than you?

## THREE TYPES OF BROKERS TO WATCH OUT FOR

### The Salesperson

Any professional from a dentist to an attorney has to market his or her services. However, the manner in which these services are marketed often tells much about the person or company that is being represented.

There is no way to know for sure if you are talking to a good or bad broker by the way her services are marketed. However, there are some general guidelines that can tip you off to the fact that you may want to keep looking. The broker who calls you out of the blue, with no prior contact, and begins a pitch on a "great trading opportunity" that you have to get in on "right now" is probably *not* the market professional that is going to be a long-term partner in your investment program. How does she know if it's a great investment for you? Does she know your financial situation? Does she know your risk tolerance?

Salesperson brokers have one goal—to open accounts. They are often people who have little interest in futures or commodities except that it is the latest thing they are selling. They can be smooth talkers, but they seldom last long in the business. To be a true commodities broker is a demanding job, and one has to love his work to excel in it. People with little interest in the market that become brokers to try and "make a lot of money fast" are often disappointed.

As we've stated, a good broker does not necessarily have to be a great trader. But he should have some interest in the market and be able to talk about it intelligently. If you have somebody who continues to pitch you on a single trade or commission rate but stumbles repeatedly when you ask anything about the market or trading, you probably have a salesperson.

### The Rookie

Futures brokers have one of the highest turnover rates of any profession, especially within the first two years of their careers. Therefore, a large number of new brokers enter the field every year. Being new does not necessarily make them good or bad. But they are going to have to learn the business by making mistakes. Do you want them to learn on *your* account?

Of course, some rookies eventually will turn into good brokers someday. However, you need somebody who can help you now, and this is probably not the person, especially if you are going to rely on her for trading advice and guidance.

## The Grifter

Almost all brokers, as well as the firms that employ them, are paid on a commission basis. This automatically creates a conflict of interest. With this arrangement, the broker can become susceptible to allowing his primary interest be the number of trades that can be generated from your account rather than the performance of your account. There are brokers and even unscrupulous brokerage firms who intentionally recommend that their clients get in and out of trades early and often for the sole purpose of generating commissions rapidly. This is known as *churning,* and it is not only a strict violation of Commodity Futures Trading Commission regulations, it is also illegal.

In the movie *Boiler Room,* Ben Affleck plays the "pit boss" in a brokerage such as this. If you saw the movie and think that it was an exaggeration, it is not. The "brokers" in these types of firms cold call hundreds of people in a day and use high-pressure tactics to get unsuspecting investors to send them funds. If you feel that you are being pressured into investing in futures or have a telesalesperson that sounds extremely excited on the phone and is insisting that you have to send money right now, you may be talking to one of these people. They are often not very knowledgeable about the market in general and sometimes are hesitant to answer questions about the background of their firm or themselves. But they usually are very forceful and aggressive in telling you about the "golden opportunity" that they have uncovered in the market, which, coincidentally, probably will be gone in a few short days (just enough time for you to send them a check).

If you have doubts about the person, ask for his and/or the firm's National Futures Association (NFA) identification number. The NFA does a good job of weeding most of these types of people out of our industry, but there are always a few who slip through the cracks. The NFA is like the Better Business Bureau for brokers. The NFA Web site at www.nfa.futures.org gives the background and complaint history of all its brokers and member firms. All practicing brokers and firms are required to be members. If the individual in question is not a member, or if the report on the broker or the firm pulls up a long list of complaints, it's best to steer clear.

If you can avoid these types of brokers, it will allow you to focus on merit and skill when choosing from the remaining group of brokers. What you are looking for is a true market professional—a pro.

However, if you want a quality, professional broker, chances are that you are going to have to find him because he's probably not going to find you. This is not to say that there are not good brokers who telemarket their services. For years, this was the primary way for brokers to find clients. If you have ever purchased or ordered anything even remotely associated with trading, chances are that your name and phone number are on a list somewhere. Many brokerage houses purchase these lists for calling or mailing purposes. However, with the advent of the Internet, Web sites, and various new trade publications, brokerages can advertise much of their services relatively inexpensively. It is also through these media that some brokers can begin to establish names for themselves through market commentary or self-published articles on the markets.

Just because a broker may have written a few articles on the markets does not mean that she is a great broker or trader. However, it does show that her head is in the right place and that she has some awareness of and interest in the markets and may have something to offer you.

These days, most established, experienced brokers do not have to cold call phone lists to get new clients. If you get an unsolicited cold call from a broker you have never contacted, it does not mean that he is a bad broker or is doing something unethical, but it could mean he or his firm is new or inexperienced, and this is how they have to acquire new clients.

Since there are no clear-cut rules on how to determine if a broker has the right stuff, you will rely much on gut feel and common sense. However, the following list may be helpful in knowing what to avoid when searching for the right broker.

Red flags that the broker on the other end of the phone may be inexperienced or not have your best interest at heart:

1. The broker is vague or elusive when you ask him for background information about himself or his firm.

2. The broker stumbles or changes the subject repeatedly when asked about markets or trading knowledge.

3. The broker is *overly* enthusiastic about what she is talking to you about.

4. The broker is pitching you on a "rare opportunity" or tells you that you have to get into the market right now or you will "miss out."

5. The broker's company advertising is high-profile radio or TV ads touting huge profits with little risk or "secret" trading strategies that have produced huge profits in years past.

6. The broker's company has advertising or literature that shows people with large luxury cars, fancy homes, or yachts (chances are that these items belong to the owner of the company).

7. If you feel like you are being pressured or get the feeling that you are talking to a used car salesperson. If you've never heard of this broker or his company before and he is pitching you on a trade within five minutes of introducing himself, this is not a good sign. A broker's first conversation with you should

give you the feeling that you are getting to know each other and beginning a new professional relationship.

8. If the broker is asking for excessive commissions. Full-service brokerage firm commissions and services vary in cost, and it is difficult to say how much is too much. Most full-service brokerages these days charge somewhere between $35 and $100 per round turn commissions. However, if you are paying over $100 per round turn, you are probably paying too much. If the broker is asking for *a lot* more than this, treat her like a robber breaking into your house because that is exactly what she is trying to do. Tell her not to call back, and then hang up the phone. We've heard horror stories of firms charging $200 to $300 per round turn. There is nobody who can justify that kind of commission. The top stars in the industry will charge you less than that. How can a smooth-talking salesperson justify that kind of commission? She cannot, and chances are that she or her firm cares about little else.

## WHAT TO LOOK FOR IN A GOOD OPTION SELLING BROKER

### Experience

Futures brokers have one of the highest turnover rates of any profession. Many brokers who start in the business wash out within the first two years. The ones who make it beyond this point must at least have learned how to do something right. To succeed over the long term, a broker has to love what he does and be at least competent in it. Hopefully, what he loves to do is help his clients trade the markets effectively! Look for a broker who has been around the block. There will always be some young up and comers that may be honest and helpful on the phone, but you don't want them to learn with your account. If you are serious about your trading, especially in the advanced technique of option selling, look for somebody with at least 5 to 10 years of experience.

### Credentials

Just because somebody has been in the business for a while does not guarantee that she is a good broker. Find out her background and accomplishments in the industry. Where has she worked before? Does she have any other certifications? Does she have any complaints on file with the NFA? Has she published any articles in publications you may have heard of? Does she publish a newsletter? Does she give any market opinions to the media? Look for things that show that the broker or money manager may have a respected name in the industry. The more involved she is in her industry, the more likely it is that she respects her business and her clients.

## Honesty

This should go without saying and is up to your judgment. However, as a guideline, beware of brokers who talk about big gains and little risk. Disregard a broker who tells you that you have to get in right now or you'll "miss out." It is likely that this broker has a sales quota to meet or a contest to win, and if you don't send your money today, *he's* going to miss out. There are always new opportunities tomorrow. If you feel a lot of pressure to open an account, chances are that you are dealing with a salesperson broker.

## Knowledge of Option Selling

As we've said before, some brokers are inexperienced or undereducated in selling options and may be little more versed in it than you are. This is fine if you are dealing with a discount broker simply to place orders for you. However, if you are hiring a full-service broker and paying for it, you are more or less hiring an advisor. For this reason, you want to hire the best advice you can find. You may have to interview a few before you find one who is friendly to and experienced in option writing. Be thorough. Some brokers will say anything to get you to open an account. "Option selling? Ah, yeah, sure, I do that all the time!"

Have some good questions for her, and listen to how she answers them. If she stutters and backtracks or puts you on hold several times to get answers to your questions, you probably have, at best, a neophyte.

## Focused on You, Not on Himself

Regardless of whether he realizes it or not, a broker's purpose is to help you to succeed. In talking to him, you should sense that you've found an ally to help you through the course of your option selling investment. If you instead get the feeling that the person on the other end of the phone is standing on top of his desk hawking snake oil, his focus probably isn't on you. Good brokers know that they're good. In talking to them, you should feel like you're talking to a cool, relaxed professional.

Some brokers also become CTAs, which means that they can be your broker *or* manage your account for you. This does not mean that she is good at being either one. However, it does show that she at least has some experience in actually making trading decisions and will have a track record of how she has performed as a CTA. Retail brokers cannot provide a track record, even if they are making winning trade recommendations to their clients. CTAs do not, however, have to be brokers. In fact, most are not.

Like any business, the futures industry has good and bad people in it. The good news is that the dishonest or disinterested usually don't last long as brokers. Brokers who open investors accounts to "turn and burn" them in order to make a quick buck usually will get burned themselves before long. The true professionals in the industry have learned that the only path to long-term success is to put you, the client, first and to build long-term, lasting relationships built on trust.

By hiring a broker or advisor, you are more or less hiring somebody to go to battle for you in the tough, winner-take-all world of futures options. Especially with the sophisticated vehicle of option selling, you'll need one with competence, honesty, and skill. You'll probably have to wade through a pool of salespeople and rookies before you find a broker who has the right combination of all three. But there are some talented people out there who really can make a difference in your trading.

Your job now is to go find one.

# 16

CHAPTER

# Option Selling as an Investment

At this point in the book, if you are beginning to consider an option writing portfolio or are getting some ideas for ways to enhance or improve your current portfolio, you may have some questions on some of the key points of option selling or how some of the aspects of the approach may affect your particular situation.

Many of our prospective clients tend to have these same questions, and we have listed them in this chapter along with our answers. The question-and-answer format has proved most helpful to many prospective option sellers, especially in the finer details of the strategy that may not have been discussed thoroughly enough in other chapters.

Hopefully, you will find this chapter useful in tying up some of the loose ends in answering some of the more obvious questions you may have in beginning an option writing portfolio. Most of these questions are taken from actual conversations between us and traders who are considering an option selling approach. Some of the answers may reflect our personal bias in trading techniques. However, our biases are carved out of many years of ups and downs in the futures markets.

**Q: What is your overall view of futures trading in general?**

A: Interest in investing in commodity futures trading has been exploding. New records are being set at the Chicago Merchantile Exchange in volume in several contracts. Managed futures in particular are growing at a torrid pace. People seem to realize now that commodities are the staples of life and that investing in them or financial futures products can be a key diversification tool in a portfolio. The problem is that most people don't understand leverage and that futures contracts are a highly leveraged invest-ment. Trading the conventional way is a high-risk, high-return proposition. Many traders approach the market as a gamble. It has been our experience that if you approach this highly leveraged form of investing in a conservative manner, you often can achieve a very attractive return on your money. This is where selling options on these contracts comes into play.

**Q: How do you recommend a new account go about positioning in the market?**

A: We would first recommend limiting your amount of trades. Our most successful accounts don't trade very often. When we feel there is an opportunity, we generally rec-ommend taking the most conservative position possible and then enter it in numbers. In other words, instead of trading every day or every week in 10 different markets, only trade when you believe there is a stellar opportunity to sell premium, and then don't be afraid to build a healthy position there. Our most successful accounts over the years have only traded on average about once or twice a month. It is this same philosophy that we employ in our commodity trading advisor (CTA) capacity.

**Q: I've read several books and literature on options, option spreads and straddles, and so on. It seems that there are some strategies out there that offer some big profit potentials with little risk. I've looked at delta-neutral strategies, free trades, and so on. Do you recommend any of these strategies?**

A: Yes, if an opportunity presents itself. If you read Chapters 6 and 7 on spreads and recommended spread strategies, you know that spreads often can benefit your broker more than they can benefit you. However, there are a few that can work well. Strangling the market can be a profitable approach in certain situations. We also recommend the ratio credit spread.

**Q: Why do you suggest naked option selling in some situations?**

A: One of the strengths of naked option selling is its sheer simplicity. If you're bullish on a market, you sell puts. If you're bearish, you sell calls. We've seen traders have great success through the years in simply picking general market direction in a few select markets. If they're wrong, they can still make money. If they're really wrong, they get out if and when the option premium hits their predetermined risk parameter. We see no need to make it more complicated than that.

The downside, of course, is that the market potentially can exceed your risk param-eter. For this reason, some investors are more comfortable in covered or spread posi-tions, even though it may mean reduced profits on the options sold. It is really a matter of personal preference and risk tolerance. We suggest a mix of spread and naked strate-gies across several markets until you can determine which approaches are more con-gruent with your personality.

**Q: What criteria do you use when selecting markets to trade and strike prices to sell?**

A: We use a combination of fundamental and seasonal analysis, and we are looking at general price direction over a two- to six-month period. We are selecting far-out-of-the-money options with two to five months time value remaining. We try to select price levels that could only be achieved through a radical change in fundamentals. The object is to select the options with the highest probability of expiring worthless, even if we have to wait a few months for them to do so.

**Q: Fundamentals. Isn't that long-term trading? What about technicals?**

A: Technicals can move the market temporarily, but eventually, prices will have to reflect the fundamentals. Of course, we use technical indicators in timing our option sales, but they will not dictate what markets we trade. Many traders and even brokers use technical analysis as their sole means of trading simply because they don't know the fundamentals or don't want to take the time to learn them. Learning the fundamentals of a market and how they can affect price can be time-consuming and difficult. However, in our opinion, trading solely on a technical basis is like trying to hit a baseball with one eye closed: Your perspective is going to be off. If you're investing capital into a commodity trading idea, you should at least try to become familiar with the base fundamentals of the market you're trading or be working with somebody who understands these factors. An approach using a combination of fundamentals and technicals should help to give you the full picture of what is going on in a market.

**Q: How about volatility? I've read that volatility is the most important factor to pay attention to when trading options.**

A: Most option books tout volatility as the most important factor when deciding which options to trade. We are certainly aware of the volatility and would prefer to sell options at the higher end of their volatility ranges. However, isn't study of the factors likely to affect the price of the underlying more important than the volatility of the option? Would you want to sell a put option in a market with extremely bearish long-term fundamentals simply because the put options were exhibiting high historical volatility? We've had more success by incorporating some projections for longer-term market direction (or at least projecting where the market won't go) rather than focusing solely on volatility.

**Q: What about the risk? Doesn't selling options entail unlimited risk?**

A: Yes, theoretically it does. It carries the same risk as a futures contract, but no more. Some traders will dismiss option writing as "too risky." (We find it amusing to note that many of these traders, however, will trade futures contracts without hesitation.) Without knowledge, anything is risky. Experienced option writers (who, incidentally, generally are commercial or professional traders who are gladly selling options to small speculators) know that although selling an option bears the same theoretical risk as a futures contract, the value of the option will almost always move more slowly than the futures contract. Same risk but slower speed. Nonetheless, having an excellent risk-management plan is the key to consistent profits.

**Q: I know that if the option expires out of the money, I will keep all premiums collected as profit if I am the option seller. But what can happen in the meantime if the market is moving against my position? Will my option value increase? Will my margin?**

A: Yes. Both can increase. This is one reason that you'll want to use only a certain percentage of your account funds and keep the rest as backup capital. Remember that while you will have a fixed risk parameter in place, you can still buy the option back to close the position at any time. Your risk-management plan should revolve around keeping losses small. Certain spreads can limit or reduce margin increases and/or losses on an option position.

**Q: How much would the value increase? How much would the margin increase?**

A: It all depends on the option, the volatility, and how much time is left on it. Keep in mind that if you are selling far-out-of-the-money options, the values generally will increase very slowly, even if the market is moving against you. Remember also, when selling options, that the market can move for or against you, but time value is always working for you. The value of your short option almost always will move for or against you at a slower pace than the futures contract.

**Q: What percentage of my account funds should I keep as backup capital?**

A: As a general rule of thumb, we would recommend margining no more than 50 percent of your account at any given time unless you are open and willing to meet a margin call should you get one. Ultraconservative accounts may want to margin less than that; aggressive accounts can margin more than that. We've watched investors margin up to 70 to 80 percent of an option selling portfolio and achieve eye-popping returns. However, we've also seen them get margin calls and subject themselves to larger losses. If they're good positions, you can still make money by holding them. You just have to add more deposit money in the meantime. The trouble comes when the investors overposition and then can't or don't want to meet a margin call when it comes, even if their positions are good! Then they have to take potentially profitable positions off at a loss, after paying commissions on those losing positions. This can happen even if the options only exhibit minimal fluctuations. The good news is that managing your margin is pretty easy if you don't get too greedy.

**Q: What is the risk-management technique that you suggest?**

A: As with any trading method, you must learn to take some losses. The difference with option selling is that, statistically, most of your trades should be winners. Thus it becomes even more important not to let one big loser eat away all your profits or, worse yet, cause a significant drawdown in your portfolio. We recommend that beginners start out by using the "covered" technique that we described in Chapter 9. In other words, they should use a portion of the premiums collected to buy some closer-to-the-money options, providing at least partial coverage. We also suggest exploring strangling strategies to novice and experienced investors, as the strangle can offer a risk-balancing feature and can protect traders from moves against either side, to a certain point.

For naked option sellers, we have found over the years that the *200 percent rule* is a good way to limit losses while at the same time giving option values room to fluctuate. By the 200 percent rule we mean that if the option doubles in value from the point at which you sold it, you exit the position. It is true that many of these options also will expire worthless eventually. However, you cannot take the chance that the option that you are holding will be the one that makes an extended move against you. When you begin to learn the personality of a particular market, you may be able to adjust the 200 percent rule to allow more or less leeway in certain markets. Until then, it is a good stop-out point to help keep you on track and away from big losers.

Any of the techniques described in Chapter 9 can be effective in managing risk. Again, much depends on the individual investor.

**Q: With regard to the 200 percent rule, how often does this happen—an option doubling in value after I've sold it?**

A: How often have you bought a far-out-of-the-money futures option and had it double in value *for* you? Much will depend on your option selling savvy and technique. However, with time value working in your favor, the majority of your options sold should be expiring worthless.

**Q: How many options should I try to sell in a month?**

A: We would not focus on the number of trades you feel you have to accomplish. Rather, focus on trading only when an opportunity presents itself. Our experience with successful accounts is that they usually have about six to eight major positions a year, which works out to about 12 to 14 different trades. These generally are "investors" not looking for "action" but rather for high percentages and returns. If you are looking for excitement, you'll be best served going to a discount firm and opening a day trading account.

## Q: What would you consider a position?

A: We define a *position* as a series of strike prices and/or contract months all in one market. For instance, if you were bullish on crude oil in the winter of 2003–2004, you may have sold May $28 and $30 puts along with June $26 puts. All these options together could be considered your position. You may take weeks or months to establish this position, staggering or layering options on at what you feel are opportune times. This concept of layering is central to the approach we recommend to investors.

## Q: Explain layering?

A: Layering is a concept we recommend to "smooth out" the equity curve for investors. It was designed for investors seeking a steady, income-producing trading plan. Layering is the practice of selling different options in different markets with expiration dates about four to six weeks apart. If this is done correctly, the trader should have a set of options expiring approximately once a month. As some options expire and others deteriorate, the trader then uses the premiums collected to sell more options three to five months out, set up the same way, increasing position sizes if he desires. Of course, not every option sold will be profitable, but this is the structure for which you may want to strive in an effort to produce more evenly distributed returns. One note about layering: Your first 60 to 90 days of trading may seem slow because you are more or less "filling a pipeline." After your first set of options expires, however, things should begin to get a little more interesting.

## Q: What type of premiums do you recommend an option seller target to collect on individual options?

A: Much of that depends on the investor and her risk tolerance and return objectives. Most of the options that our clients prefer will collect between $300 and $700 in premium. We generally won't recommend selling an option if it has less than a $300 premium. You want to strike a balance between time remaining on the option and distance the strike is out of the money. There is no hard and fast rule for this. This part is more experience and personal preference.

## Q: I've had brokers tell me that I can offset or hedge the risk of my short option if I buy or sell a futures contract at the point the option goes in the money? Is this a viable strategy?

A: This strategy looks good on paper but often opens up the proverbial "can of worms" for the investor using it. What if the market moves your option into the money, then back out, and then back in again? Are you going to keep buying it and selling the futures contract(s) again? Or are you going to risk an adverse futures move that will cause losses far outstripping any gain you may receive by having your option expiring worthless? And this doesn't even include the additional transaction costs you are going to incur by buying and selling the futures contract(s). If you enter a futures contract, where are you going to set your stop for that? How will you time your entry? Now you have two trades to worry about instead of one. You're watching the market tick by precious tick, trying to time entry and exits, worried about placing stops, and trying to guess where the market will go tomorrow. Aren't those all the things we're trying to avoid by selling options in the first place? Offsetting with futures may work in some situations, but our experience has been that it's best to set a firm exit point when you enter a trade and abide by it. Again, simplicity is your best avenue to success.

**Q: I've found a broker who sells options, but he tells me to sell options with only 30 days until expiration or less because that is when they lose their value the quickest. Is this true, and do you recommend this approach?**

A: Yes it is true. Although there are exceptions, for the most part, we do not recommend this approach unless you are into active, fast-moving trading. It may work better in stocks, with traders willing to take possession of the stock if the option goes in the money. However, if you are selling options purely to collect premium, especially in futures, the options you sell could carry a higher risk of going in the money.

It is true that the closer options get to expiration, the faster they begin to lose value. This time decay accelerates in the last 30 days in the life of an option. However, when an option reaches its last 30 days of life, chances are that it has already lost most of its time value. Therefore, the only options available to sell generally will be options very close to the money. Selling options this close to where the market is trading can mean that even the slightest market "hiccup" can put your option in the money and you taking the same losses you would in a futures contract. Once again, you're back to day trading and trying to pick short-term market direction—exactly what we're trying to avoid.

Another reason that brokers may like to recommend selling short-term options is that they can trade in and out quickly, often producing many more commissions than a long-term approach could net them. Of course, all brokers are not like this, but you should be on the look out for ulterior motives. Some brokers will "outbid" others on commission rate, only to make up the difference in increased transactions.

Sell as far out of the money as you can at strikes that appear highly unlikely to ever be attained.

**Q: How can I expect to collect any premium if I am selling far out of the money? Aren't these options cheap because they are so far away?**

A: Only if you are looking at options that expire in the short term. The further out in time you go, the further out-of-the-money options you can sell. We are not aware of any official studies on this; however, our experience has been that you should look to trade time value for distance out of the money. While they both help make up the value of the option, there is a 100 percent chance that time decay will happen, yet it is always an uncertainty what the market will do. Therefore, sell the time value and force the market to make a large move against you for you to lose. Good research can help to sway the odds of positioning away from where the market will go in the longer term. It can do little to predict what prices will do tomorrow.

The only caveat to selling time value is that if you sell too far out, you leave too much time for fundamentals to change in the market. Again, it is about striking a balance. You don't want to wait 12 months to make a few hundred dollars either.

### Q: If option selling is such an effective strategy, why doesn't everybody just sell options?

A: Most people are attracted to futures trading initially for the potential for huge gains. They want to take some "play" money and, well, "play." Since futures trading often looks scary because the potential exists to lose more than one has in the account, buying options starts to look pretty good. Limited risk and unlimited profit potential sound about right for what they are looking for. Brokers clamoring for their business know this and often will drive this point home, especially to traders trying futures for the first time. Most of these traders buy options, lose their money, close their account, and conclude that futures trading is "bad" and then tell everyone who will listen what a terrible investment futures are and how anybody who invests will lose.

A few, however, will stick around, curious as to who made all that money that they lost and how they did it. These few, along with sophisticated investors who have already discovered the approach on their own, will combine with the professionals to make up the option selling crowd.

Misunderstood risk, misunderstood margin, and the general hesitance of the industry to promote the strategy are some top reasons why most traders aren't selling options. Compared with striking it rich in crude oil or buying at the low of what "research" shows will be the move of the year, selling options looks pretty slow and boring. What do you think is easier for a salesperson to pitch to a new trader, ready to hit it big in commodities?

You'll find very few investors whose first foray into futures trading will be in option selling. The investors selling options are usually intermediate to highly experienced investors who have been down that road years ago. They don't look at their option selling portfolio as "play" money. They view it as a serious investment. Gambling is for Vegas.

We've heard many traders refer to their first experience in futures as "paying for their education." If you are new to futures, perhaps now you can skip or at least minimize this often costly first step.

**Q: I see Standard & Poor's (S&P) puts that I can sell for close to $500 that are available at strike prices that I don't ever think the market will reach again. What would be my margin on an option such as that?**

A: There is no way to really tell until you can give an exact option and strike price and have a SPAN margin run for it. Most decent clearing firms have SPAN software available and can provide brokers with the margins within minutes. Most of the time, if you have SPAN for one option in a particular month, you can estimate the margins for other nearby strikes in that same month. You also can purchase the SPAN software from the CME. But that really shouldn't be necessary unless you are a professional trader. Most of the options that our clients sold last year had out-of-pocket margin requirements of 100 to 200 percent of the value of the premium collected. However, larger and more volatile contracts such as the S&P and energy sometimes can have larger margin requirements as a percentage of premium collected, meaning less return on capital invested.

**Q: I just sold an option for a premium of $500. I had to put up a margin requirement of $600 to hold the position. Therefore, I have $1,100 total tied up in escrow. Do I have to wait until this option expires to use this capital?**

A: No. If and when the value of the option begins to deteriorate, not only does the premium gained become available in your account, but the margin requirement generally will drop as well. For example, if this option fell to a value of $300, that would mean that $200 ($500 − $300 = $200) of the value of that option would move into your general funds available for you to use in another trade. However, the margin requirement may have dropped to, say, $250 as well. This would be an additional $250 back into your general funds for you to use to leverage new positions. This gradual deterioration effect continues until the option expires, and the option's value is zero (assuming that it expires worthless), at which time the full $1,100 will be out of escrow and back into your available balance. Of course, by this time you already may have moved these funds into other trades. This means that you don't have to wait for old options to expire to add new positions. Just remember that it can work both ways.

**Q: What would you say is the number one reason that traders *lose* money selling options?**

A: Overpositioning. Hands down. Traders start out selling options, have a little success, and get so excited that they're making money trading commodities that they go way overboard with it. Bulging with overconfidence, they load up their accounts and way over margin themselves. This can either set them up for a big loss or put them in a position in which they can get forced out of a trade on a very small move against them. Of course, this assumes that traders have some idea of the fundamentals and technicals of the markets with which they are dealing. If a trader has no idea or is not working with somebody who has an idea of the base factors affecting price, he may lose before he has the chance to overposition. Even so, if he's selling options, he probably could go on trading successfully for a while before the market eventually calls him out.

**Q: I don't have the time to watch all this and study charts, fundamentals, and strike prices all night long. Can I still do this and be effective?**

A: Of course. This is why investors choose to go with managed accounts or hire an account advisor to do the legwork for them. There are investors who are just concerned about a good return and don't have time to watch the market, and there are traders who like to be a little more hands on. What type you are will determine what type of industry professional can serve you best.

Hopefully, this chapter has answered some of the questions that you may have had lingering in your mind. Chapter 17 will offer a review and conclusion to the material covered in all the preceding chapters.

# 17 CHAPTER

# Pulling It All Together

Hopefully, by reading this book you have gained some helpful insights into option trading and the futures industry in general. While there are certainly other books and publications that you can read that will give you layers on layers of theories, data, and statistics, it is our opinion that everything you need to know to begin selling options effectively is contained within the covers of this book.

As you've noticed, a few central themes have been repeated throughout these chapters. They are as follows:

1. Selling options, if done correctly, can offer some wide and distinct advantages over buying options or trading futures.

2. "Know your market" is every bit as important, if not more so, than "Know your option." Technical trading sometimes can help traders with short-term direction and timing, but selling options for annual returns means projecting where prices won't go in the long term. This is why knowing the fundamentals, as well as the technicals, is important.

3. While option selling can be a very consistent approach, one losing position that is allowed to run can cancel out weeks or months of option profits. For this reason, a solid risk-management strategy is essential and should be decided at the time of entry into a position.

While these are the core concepts you have read about, there are key points from this book that will be reviewed in the following pages. Hopefully, this chapter can serve as a summary if and when you decide to review the key concepts of the book at a later time.

In Chapter 1 we discussed the benefits of option selling. We learned that most options held through expiration expire worthless. Profit taking becomes much simpler and easier when selling options. Time always benefits the option seller, giving him an advantage over the option buyer, who always has time working against him. Option sellers also benefit from the fact that they do not have to determine where prices are going to go. They only have to determine where prices *won't* go, and they have a large margin of error if they are wrong. The timing of entry into short option trades is also very forgiving. The seller of options does not have to have near-perfect timing like the futures trader does.

In Chapter 2 we discussed the growing popularity of futures as an investment vehicle and the fact that most small speculators who enter the market end up losing money. We learned how option selling can lift you above this crowd. Commercial traders are defined as people in the industry of a particular commodity, such as a large sugar producer. Commercials use futures to hedge their product against future price moves. Large speculators generally are fund managers who can manage millions or even billions of dollars in equity and often can move markets with their entry and exits of positions. Both these types of traders have advantages over the small speculator.

In Chapter 3 we learned that an option is the right to buy or sell a stock or commodity at a specified price. This right can be bought or, in our case, sold. We learned why investors buy options and the drawbacks to this approach, specifically that the market generally must make a large move in a short period of time for an option buyer to profit. The value of an option is made up of *time value*, *intrinsic value*, and *volatility*.

If the value of the underlying contract moves beyond the strike price of an option (above a call or below a put), the option is said to be *in the money*. If the value of the underlying contract is at the strike price of the option, the option is said to be *at the money*. If the value of the underlying contract has not yet reached the strike price of the option, the option is said to be *out of the money*. Volatility should be considered when selling options, but some traders become too caught up in measuring volatility without thoroughly examining the fundamentals of the underlying market, which ultimately can be more important. The delta of an option is a measure of its volatility. We learned that a seller of options can have the same risk as a futures trader but that the position moves much more slowly than a futures position, giving a trader more time to exit. Sellers of options can exit their positions by buying them back at the current market price at any time during the life of the option (provided they entered the market with sufficient liquidity). While an option will expire worthless as long as it does not go in the money, the value of the option, as well as its margin requirement, can increase in the meantime if the market is moving closer to the strike.

Chapter 4 taught us how margins work on short options. *Buying on margin* in equities trading has a completely different meaning from *margin requirements* in futures trading or option selling. Margin is the deposit that you, the trader, provide out of your trading account in order to hold an option position. In futures option selling, this margin is determined by a system called SPAN, which takes volatility, distance from the money, and other factors into consideration before placing an appropriate "risk deposit" on short option sales. There is not a set formula for SPAN, but you should be able to get a SPAN margin for just about any option from your broker. Serious self-directed traders also can order SPAN software from the Chicago Mercantile Exchange and calculate SPAN margins yourself. The benefits of futures options over stock options include lower margin requirements, higher premiums for distant strikes, and better liquidity in most instances.

Chapter 5 covered the basic strategy of selling naked options on futures. We suggested limiting your search for sellable options to markets with very clear long-term fundamentals, bullish or bearish, and then selling far-out-of-the-money options with low deltas in the opposite direction of the fundamentals. We recommended selling options with three to five months of time value in order to allow you to sell strikes further out of the money and still collect good premium. Do not rule out a market simply because it has already made a significant move. These markets are often moving in the direction they are for a good reason and can provide good opportunities for option sales (in favor of the trend). Open interest often can be a tipoff to what side of the market the small speculator is betting. Heavy open interest in calls and substantially less open interest in the puts of the same market often indicate that the public is bullish on the market. This can be a good opportunity to sell call options because the public is often wrong. The "sweet spot" of deterioration of an option is generally the last 90 days of its life. Selling ahead of this time period will enable you to collect the maximum premiums before the fastest period of deterioration occurs. Staggering or layering options throughout different contract months not only provides diversification but also allows an investor to experience option expirations nearly every month (conceding, of course, that she will have to cover a few of them).

Chapter 6 explored how spread trading is often misused by risk-adverse traders who focus too much on limiting risk as opposed to managing risk. We learned how spreads often can run up commission costs and benefit the broker much more than the trader. Many spreads are impractical for use by individual investors and can have costs that often outweigh the benefits or safety they may provide. It is important to focus more on potential *for* profit than on potential profit. Potential profit sometimes can look very great, but the chances of achieving it are often slim. Focusing on potential profit is like trying to win the giant stuffed bear at the carnival by throwing a ball into the can. The potential prize is large, but the chance of winning it is small. Many spreads are so cumbersome and difficult to implement that they are not recommended for individual investors. These include multiple-option spreads such as *butterflies* and *condors*. Beware of spreads recommended by brokers that have many options involved because these often can be a way for an unscrupulous broker to generate multiple commissions while providing you with little benefit.

Chapter 7 explained that spreads are not inherently bad or good because each has a particular set of circumstances in which it may work. However, we suggested a few of our favorites that have produced the best results over the years and, in our opinion, keep the odds favoring you, the investor. Spreads can be entered all at one time, or the trader can try to time his entry by entering one side at a time. The latter is known as *legging in* and is considered a more aggressive approach. Spread strategies that we recommend are the short-option strangle, the ratio credit spread, and writing the covered call, which we feel is more practical in stocks than in commodities. We recommend that any spread be established at a credit or net short options. This means that if all options in the spread expire worthless, the trader will still net a profit after commissions.

Chapter 8 advised that you should seek out options with open interest of at least 1,000 contracts to ensure sufficient liquidity before positioning. A *bid* is what the closest priced buyer is willing to pay for an option. An *ask* is the price at which the closest priced seller is willing to sell an option. Option prices cannot lock limit up or down like futures contracts. Therefore, you usually can get out of option positions whenever you want, although it may not be at a price you want to pay. Being assigned on an option, otherwise known as having an option exercised, is a fear of many new option sellers, but in reality it rarely happens and shouldn't happen unless that is your intention. It generally will only benefit an option buyer to exercise her option if it is deep in the money at or near expiration. This can be avoided easily by buying your option back before it goes in the money. Even if an option is exercised, it is generally not the worst thing. In this event, you would be assigned a futures position that could be closed out immediately, most likely resulting in a loss similar to what you would have experienced in buying back your option.

Chapter 9 explains the key topic of risk control when selling options. Risk management begins before you enter a position by selecting far-out-of-the-money options with low deltas for your selling. Diversifying your portfolio and deciding on your risk parameters before you enter the trade are also key factors in managing risk. There are many different ways to manage or offset risks in option selling. We do not believe in offsetting losing positions with new positions because they can create two problems out of one. Instead, we recommend two simple risk-management techniques. These are basing your exit point on the value of the option or basing your exit point on a specific price level of the underlying commodity. Placing stops on options can be an inefficient risk-control method in your portfolio. Rolling options can be an effective strategy in a market that you believe is still favorable to your views, but your short option values have reached risk parameters.

In Chapter 10 we learned the difference between fundamental and technical analysis and why incorporating both of them into your trading is important. Technicals may be helpful in timing trades and projecting short-term direction, but fundamentals ultimately will determine the direction of prices. Furthermore, fundamentals also can be very helpful in selecting price levels the market will not attain. After using fundamentals to determine which markets she will enter, a trader can then use technical analysis to assist in the timing of her entry.

Chapter 11 reviewed some of the key fundamentals of a select group of commodities and futures markets. While some commodities are produced and consumed globally, others may be produced and/or consumed regionally, giving them fewer fundamentals to follow and therefore making them easier markets in which to form a fundamental opinion. It is important to focus on long-term fundamentals that may affect prices up to three to six months down the road. Key sources of fundamental information include the U.S. Department of Agriculture (USDA), the American Petroleum Institute (API), the Department of Energy (DOE), major news services, and of course, your broker.

In Chapter 12 we examined how seasonal analysis can assist a trader in making successful option selling trades. Seasonals often are misunderstood and misused by novice traders. A seasonal average is just that, an average. Markets can make wide variations from the average. A trader should focus on the overall move during a certain time of year and realize that although the market may have a bias to move higher or lower at certain times of the year, trying to match your trade to exact days based on a seasonal chart is unwise. Traders should realize that behind every seasonal tendency there is usually a set of fundamentals that causes the seasonal move to occur. Traders should know these fundamentals and be following them closely. Traders also should take the relative price of the commodity into account when considering seasonal tendencies. It is wise to look not only at the averages but also at the actual price performance of the last 15 years to determine how close they have been to the average.

Chapter 13 contains some of our recommended seasonal patterns to consider for option selling. These include selling energy puts in December and July, selling soybean puts in February, selling corn calls in May, selling orange juice calls in September, and selling coffee calls in May.

Chapter 14 listed some of the most common mistakes that new option traders make. These were ordered as follows:

1. Trading on your own with a discount broker
2. Overpositioning
3. Trading an undercapitalized account
4. Not establishing a trading plan or exit strategy before entering your trade
5. Trying to pick market tops and bottoms
6. Forming an emotional attachment or aversion to a particular market

Avoiding these mistakes will not guarantee that you will be profitable. However, it will help you to avoid some of the most common pitfalls and may increase your likelihood of success.

Chapter 15 discussed how and why to find a good broker or money manager. Believe it or not, who you work with could be your biggest determinate of success or failure in selling option premium. Many of the most successful people in history have attained their success by surrounding themselves with the most talented, competent advisors they could find. The hard part is finding them. A discount broker is basically an order clerk and offers cheap commissions. A full-service broker can offer you a wide range of services and help. A commodity trading advisor (CTA) is a professional trader who trades your account on your behalf. All brokers are legally required to be registered with the National Futures Association (NFA). Background information on all registered brokers and firms is available to the public on the NFA's Web site at www.nfa.futures.org. To find a good option broker, look for career experience, credentials, honesty, experience with and knowledge of option selling, and a focus on you, not on himself or a particular trade.

In Chapter 16 we answered some of the most popular questions that investors new to option selling have been known to ask. Among subjects addressed were recommended position sizes, diversifying, and criteria used for selecting trades. Conservative traders should margin no more than 50 percent of their portfolio at any given time. Traders may want to consider the 200 percent rule when first starting out—if an option doubles in value, get out. We recommend targeting premiums of between $300 and $700. Selling options close to the money with less than 30 days left produces quick expirations, but trades can move almost as fast as trading actual futures contracts.

The information that you have read in the preceding pages is the product of our years of trading futures and options. Through these years, we have come to the conclusion that selling options is the best way for the small speculator to compete successfully and consistently with the pros. Like all futures trading or investment strategies, it has its risks. It has drawbacks. It has detractors. Regardless, it has been our experience that investors choosing to sell options as their primary (or only) futures trading strategy have fared *substantially* better than the average futures trader. It is not a strategy for the action-seeker. It is a strategy for the serious *investor*.

Hopefully, the knowledge in these pages will help you to become a successful option seller. At the very least, it may help you to decide if option writing is a strategy that fits right with your personality and individual investment style.

Despite the gimmicks, hyped up "courses," and salespeople disguised as industry professionals, there are many good people in the futures industry that can help you to be successful. We've listed some suggested Web sites and resources in the back of this book that may help you get started.

You've now completed *The Complete Guide to Option Selling*. You've learned the what, where, when, who, and how of option selling. Now it is time to ask yourself the question that will decide *your* trading future:

Is option selling for you?

*Note:* You'll want to interview several brokers and/or money managers before deciding on one that is right for you before you embark on an option selling portfolio. If you already have a broker, you may want to reinterview him or her to determine his or her experience and views toward option selling. You may want to consider our firm, Liberty Trading Group, for these purposes as well. You can find our contact information in the back of this book. There are many competent brokers and money managers around, however, and we encourage you to talk to other members of our professional community before making your final decision.

# REFERENCES

## Bibliography

Caplan, David L., *The New Options Advantage*. New York: McGraw-Hill, 1991.

Elder, Alexander, *Trading for a Living*. New York: Wiley, 1993.

Kiyosaki, Robert T. with Sharon L. Lechter, *Rich Dad, Poor Dad*. New York: Warner Books, 2000.

Schwager, Jack D., *Market Wizards*. New York: New York Institute of Finance, 1989.

Summa, John, "Option Sellers vs. Buyers. Who Wins?" *Futures*, March 2003, pp. 52–55.

## Resources

**Liberty Trading Group**
401 East Jackson Street
Suite 2340
Tampa, FL 33602
James Cordier, Michael Gross
Phone: 800-346-1949; 813-472-5760 (outside US)
E-mail: office@libertytradinggroup.com; Coffee1@aol.com
Web site: www.libertytradinggroup.com; www.optionsellers.com

*Comment:* Futures brokerage specializing in option writing. Self-directed and managed accounts.

**Bloomberg Financial News Service**
www.bloomberg.com
Subscriptions available

**Chicago Board of Trade**
141 West Jackson Blvd.
Chicago, IL 60604-2994
312-435-3558
www.cbot.com

*Comment:* The exchanges have some of the best resources and educational material available on trading futures and options.

**Chicago Mercantile Exchange**
30 South Wacker Drive
Chicago, IL 60606-7499
312-466-4410
www.cme.com

**Consensus, Inc.**
*National Futures and Financial Weekly*
P.O. Box 520526
Independence, MO 64052-0526
816-373-3700
www.consensus-inc.com

*Comment:* Commodities newspaper with good viewpoints of market fundamentals.

**CQG, Inc.**
201 Centennial Street
Suite 150
Glenwood Springs, CO 81601
800-525-7082
www.cqg.com

*Comment:* Professional-quality quotes, charts, and news service.

**Dow Jones Financial News Service**
www.dowjonesnews.com
Subscriptions available

*Futures Magazine*
P.O. Box 2122
Skokie, IL 60076-7822
888-804-6612; 847-763-9565 (outside US)
www.futuresmag.com

*Comment:* Articles and insights on trading the commodities and futures markets.

**www.marketmavens.com**

*Comment:* Financial Web site with various commentaries on commodities and futures markets.

**Moore Research Center, Inc.**
85180 Lorane Highway
Eugene, OR 97405
800-927-7259; 541-484-7256
www.mrci.com

*Comment:* The experts on seasonal analysis.

**National Futures Association**
200 West Madison Street
Suite 1600
Chicago, IL 60606-3447
312-781-1410
800-621-3570
www.nfa.futures.org

*Comment:* Background information on futures brokers and CTAs.

**New York Board of Trade**
One North End Avenue
New York, NY 10282-1101
212-748-4000
www.nybot.com

**New York Mercantile Exchange**
World Financial Center
One North End Avenue
New York, NY 10282-1101
212-299-2000
www.nymex.com

**www.optionetics.com**
*Comment:* Web site on options trading strategy and a good source of information to get volatility rankings on commodity options.

**Reuters Financial News Service**
www.reuters.com/finance.jhtml
Subscriptions available

*Trader's Source Magazine*
219 Parkade
Cedar Falls, IA 50613
319-277-1271
www.traderssource.net
*Comment:* Articles and insights on trading the commodities and futures markets.

# INDEX

Note: page numbers in **bold** indicate figures

# ABOUT THE AUTHORS

## JAMES CORDIER

James Cordier is president of Liberty Trading Group, a registered commodity trading advisor and brokerage firm in St. Petersburg, Florida. With 21 years of trading experience, he manages option portfolios for investors in North America, Europe, and the Pacific Rim.

James and his firm specialize in option writing and recommend a strategy of selling out-of-the-money options on futures contracts. Over the years, Liberty Trading Group has tailored this approach to meet the needs of the individual investor.

James's study of the commodities market began at age 14, when a silver coin collection sparked his interest in silver futures. He began his career as a broker at Heinold Commodities in Milwaukee in 1984. Several years of working with commercial business enabled him not only to build a solid knowledge base of market fundamentals but also to establish a network of producers and end users that remains in place today.

In 1999, having established a solid reputation and a certain level of acclaim within the industry, James founded Liberty Trading Group.

James's fundamentally based articles have been published by The New York Board of Trade, Yahoo Finance, and *Futures Magazine*. He gives regular commentary on the futures markets to Oster Dow Jones News, Reuters, and Bloomberg News, where he has appeared on Bloomberg television. His market commentary and observations have been published in the *Wall Street Journal, Investor's Business Daily*, and *Barron's* and have also been featured on ABC's *World News Tonight*.

## MICHAEL GROSS

Michael Gross is director of research and a licensed futures broker at Liberty Trading Group in St. Petersburg, Florida.

After graduating from Indiana University of Pennsylvania in 1990 with a degree in business administration, he began a study of the commodities markets. His futures trading career began in 1994 when he started trading contracts in grains, precious metals, and energies.

In 1996, Michael became a registered commodities broker specializing primarily in the grain and energy sectors.

In 1999, he joined Liberty Trading Group where, along with James Cordier, he developed various approaches to selling option premium and managing portfolios. Michael remains an active broker at Liberty Trading Group, where he authors many of the firm's research articles and assists in developing trading strategy.

Michael's published articles on the futures markets and option trading have appeared in *Futures Magazine, MarketMavens.com, Optionetics.com,* and *Consensus*. His market comments have been published by Bloomberg News.